Branna,

I hope that this finds you well and in Christmas spirit. Your determination, skill, and operation were extraordinary in completing of this project. I am eternally humbled and grateful that our Lord chose you. May our politics glorify God and honor the free. Fathers vessel for America!

God Bless,

POLITICS
OF
IMMORTALITY

POLITICS
OF
IMMORTALITY

JAMES E. BENESCH

DW Productions, Inc.
Franklin, Tennessee

Cover and Interior Design by DW Productions. Inc.
P.O. Box 681623, Franklin, TN 37068

Politics of Immortality

1. Economics 2. Founding Fathers 3. Government Debt 4. Causation

ISBN: 978-0-9774424-0-9

Printed in the United States of America

10 09 08 07 06 05 04 03 02 01 1 2 3 4 5

This book, my first fruits,
is dedicated to
my Father in Heaven.

CONTENTS

Foreword

Introduction   1

ONE
Debt Storm   9

TWO
The Birth of America's Death   27

THREE
Amat Victoria Curam   51

FOUR
Common-Sensanomics   69

FIVE
From Net Worth to "Net Worthless"   101

SIX
AmeriCom   127

CONTENTS

SEVEN

Taxaquences   155

EIGHT

Chain Gang   183

NINE

Aliendemic   213

TEN

Greed: Never Enough!   237

ELEVEN

Eleventh Hour   267

Conclusion 301

Notes   305

Appendixes   319

FOREWORD

In all our lives there are defining moments that speak volumes about us. In the following pages you will read about a man who has revealed his heart and mind to his countrymen. In his correct views on America's worsening situation in the world and at home, his pleas fall on deaf ears in the circles of powers that be. Circles that need to take a fresh look at themselves and put aside arrogance and piety. This said, it is time to remind all of our leadership that they were elected and appointed to serve the majority of the citizens of the United States of America and not put other countries first.

These writings are not about any one organization, person, or party, but a warning to Democrats, Republicans and all other party affiliations alike. Instead of pointing fingers at each other and doing nothing, it is time to turn yourselves around and do as you promised the American people.

May God in His infinite wisdom and our Savior Jesus Christ help my son on his mission.

—Edward J. Benesch

Edward J. Benesch, retired Vice President for Local 705 Teamsters, Chicago, Illinois

INTRODUCTION

"Units 7 and 8, this is Base…over."

"Unit 7 here. Go with your traffic…over."

"Unit 8 here…"

"Unit 7, Patrol Supervisor Benesch and Unit 8, Maguire, proceed to the Community Club and see the manager. Says there's a man with a knife, threatening the patrons. Check it out…call covers code 3…over."

"Ah…10-4, Base. En route."

Picking up the coded lingo from my shift supervisor, I turned on my lights and accelerated my vehicle toward the post club, where the soldiers at Fort Pickett hung out when they were off duty. During peacetime, my beat as a military policeman was the confines of this installation near Blackstone, Virginia. Here 70,000 military personnel lived, worked, and ate Army regulations. The only action we saw was some drug traffic, the usual drunks after a little too much weekend partying, and an occasional domestic flare-up. Like any street cop, it was my job to defuse potentially volatile situations and restore law and order. This was no covert operation in the jungles of Honduras. It was just an ordinary summer night on a military post within the borders of the United States, but club night at the post was a jungle of another kind.

McGuire and I hadn't been at the NCO hangout for more than half an hour before we got another call from the dispatcher. "Return to the station for shift change…over."

Shift change! When we hadn't completed the mission? "We've been unable to make contact with the suspect, Sergeant, and our presence seems to be keeping the calm. As patrol supervisor, I strongly recommend that we stay a while longer…over."

"Negative, Units 7 and 8! Contact, Base, lima, lima!"

As soon as I could get to a land line, I put in a call to headquarters. "Sergeant Dirksen, Benesch here."

"Hey, Benesch, you and McGuire need to get back pronto so we can close out the shift. I don't want to stick around all night."

"Sergeant, we're dealing with a credible threat. This guy has a knife and now he's slipped into the crowd. There are several hundred people in the place tonight, and I think we should keep a presence here."

"Look, Benesch, you and McGuire get your *bleep bleeps* back here!"

"Sergeant, what if this guy comes back? We could have a serious problem on our hands."

"No! I'm the shift supervisor…your superior officer, Benesch, so *I'm* giving the orders. Get back here…

now!" I could hear the sound of the phone being slammed into the cradle.

"Yes, Sergeant!" I jerked my thumb toward the patrol vehicles parked outside. "Let's go, McGuire. Dirksen's pulled rank."

Halfway back to the station, another panicked call came in. "Units 7 and 8, proceed immediately to the rear of the community club. A man's been stabbed! And Unit 7, since no medical personnel are available, you're the lead."

I had been training for this evening for quite some time now. As the Intelligence Officer for a special reaction team (SRT), I was also trained as an Emergency Medical Technician and licensed by the State of Virginia. You never knew when an SRT mission would require life-saving skills.

Shifting into reverse, I spun my squad car around, taking a shortcut down a gravel road leading from the baseball field behind the club. I raced back, careening wildly, dust billowing from beneath my tires. On the way I passed four guys running in the opposite direction, one with a blood-spattered shirt. Braking to a stop, I turned on the spotlights, illuminating the chaotic scene.

Bending over the victim of a knifing, I performed a quick triage. "Unit 7 to Base. I've got a white male, early twenties, with a stab wound to the center of his chest. He is unconscious, not breathing, no pulse. I say again, the victim has no pulse. Pupils are fixed and dilated. I'm starting CPR. Fly a Medivac to my location!"

The scenario was surreal. Flashing lights, sirens screaming, people crying and running through the darkness, a friend shouting in his fallen buddy's ear, "Wake up! Don't you die on me…ya hear me? Don't die!" The horror, the sadness, the rowdy crowd watching as a life slipped into eternity….

Dead at twenty-three, he was the first man who ever died in my arms. Despite everything I could do—performing CPR on his already lifeless body—I felt like a total failure. Today, the pain of losing that Army Reserve soldier serving his two weeks is so severe at times, I often find myself crying during the middle of the day. As the memories of that horrific evening come rushing back, I resent the flippant abuse of power and the self-absorbed decision of my shift commander!

After I returned to the Provost Marshal's office, I pulled Dirksen aside. He went right into his spiel, trying to make me feel better about the night's events. "Jim, you did all you could do—good job! Besides, you can't save everyone, can you?"

"The hell you can't!" I lowered my voice ominously. "If you ever pull rank on me again, I'll take you down, Sergeant! You got it? I'll take you down!"

As I walked away, I considered what had just occurred, realizing that once you give up on your leaders, you can no longer follow them. I knew that Dirksen could never again be trusted with the lives he had taken an oath to protect—the same oath that had been pledged by our great-great-grandfathers who sacrificed their fortunes, their honor, their homes and yes, their very lives for the protection of the yet unborn.

Throughout our history many have died defending our sovereign nation. That kind of steadfast sacrifice is foreign to our leadership today. Yes, our nation is becoming increasingly vulnerable to those bent on killing us off and yes, they are derelict in their sworn duty to protect the sovereignty of this free nation and its legal citizenry. But when we confront them, they only smile and say, "Trust me." Well, enough is enough! The line has been drawn and their party is over.

If we do not stand and confront our leadership's purposeful allowance of blood-letting, our nation will die and we will not be able to revive her. Do you not see the knife that is threatening you around the corner? Will you leave your post because someone is tired of the fight and wants to go home?

And after we halt the killing spree, will you help us rebuild—neighbor by neighbor, family by family, so we can stand again for what made us great? Will you help us reclaim liberty for our children's future and for the future of those from any nation who respect and obey our laws so they, too, can prosper in a safe and peaceful place?

What about the victim of that senseless killing at Fort Pickett? That was more than twenty-two years ago. The incident destroyed the future of an American soldier who was married with two small children. The memory of that night has never left me. Since then I have committed myself to the protection of this treasure we call the United States of America, one family at a time. I have determined never to let anyone else suffer for the self-interest of arrogant, condescending leadership.

It was on the basis of this reality that I find myself in the center of a nation that's being torn apart by self-aggrandizing progressives from both political parties, leaving the working citizens without strength, without power, without security and without a sustainable future. I will no longer tolerate hollow elected officials, who have sworn to keep watch over this country, but have chosen to destroy our currency, confiscate our wealth, sell off our sovereignty, abort our legal citizenry, build an opposing army, neglect our perimeters and bow down to the oligarchies of other nations. Because we now know the truth!

In the treatise to follow, I will take you through the blueprint of the dismantling which has already occurred and that which is presently being perpetrated by both political parties. Further, I will propose a plan to put an end to the insatiable thirst for the lifeblood of our country, our Constitution, our freedom and our immortality, so help me, God!

As a very important source of strength and security, cherish public credit. One method of preserving it is to use it as sparingly as possible; avoiding occasions of expense by cultivating peace, but remembering also that timely disbursements to prepare for danger frequently prevent much greater disbursements to repel it; avoiding likewise the accumulation of debt, not only by shunning occasions of expense, but by vigorous exertions in time of peace to discharge the debts, which unavoidable wars may have occasioned, not ungenerously throwing upon posterity the burthen [burden], which we ourselves ought to bear. [1]

—President George Washington
Farewell Address to the Nation
September 17, 1796

1

DEBT STORM

The rich rule over the poor,
and the borrower is servant to the lender.
—Proverbs 22:7

Blessed are the young,
for they shall inherit the national debt.[2]
—President Herbert Hoover
Address to the Nebraska Republican Convention
January 16, 1936

This flippant remark, proposed by our 31st president to his political colleagues on a blustery winter day, was served up in opposition to the spending policies of the emerging progressive movement. Hoover felt that progressivism[3] was the very threat forewarned by the Framers of the Constitution in what they regarded as the tendency of all human governments. The unveiling of a new era of debt spending showed great promise for the people of the day and set the precedent for today's fiscal irresponsibility. Since then, progressives serving on both sides of the political aisle and from all walks of public life have given in to the insatiable appetite for spending their way into the re-election halls of political idolatry.

America used to be a democratic republic. This form of government is one in which elected officials represent the majority of its citizens. Today, however, our officials are serving only a select few—the elite classes and special interest groups. It's called progressivism.

Most of the citizens of the United States are under the delusion that we are still a democratic republic. Not so. We are in the gap between "almost" and "not yet"—and because we are on shifting sands, we are at great risk for exchanging progressivism for communism where there will be no opportunity for free enterprise or individual rights. America is no longer the "land of the free"; it is a nation under bondage—the bondage of debt.

Using America's inheritance—hard-earned dollars of the nation's working class—and massive debt accumulation policies, government leaders are heaping bone-crushing debt onto the backs of America's youth. In fact, the monumental amount of the rising national debt will keep future generations paying for this one's material abundance until their children's children are deprived of all property and wealth. Then, sometime in the not-too-distant future, a generation of Americans will wake up homeless in what was once the richest nation in the world.

Do you remember what happened in Indonesia at Christmastime, 2004? In many resorts by the sea, visitors and residents alike were not concerned when the sea was sucked off the shores. They took note of the strange occurrence but decided to go about their vacations. Others just shook their heads and went back to work. Boat owners shouted to their employees to run after the boats and bring them back. Only the animals ran for high ground. What the people did not know was that, very soon, their lives would be changed forever.

In the Holy Bible, we read: "My people are destroyed from lack of knowledge."[4] According to oceanographers, when a large volume of sea water is displaced from the ocean bottom by a massive disturbance like an earthquake, the vacuum creates a powerful wave. The size of these waves—sometimes as tall as one hundred feet—is equal to the vacuum created by the fall of the ocean floor. The sea will then return to its rightful place with a vengeance, covering all low-lying areas and completely destroying everything in its path. It can happen so quickly that unless you have the knowledge to discern the signs of imminent disaster, you cannot outrun the devastation such a tidal wave holds for the unsuspecting, the ignorant and the arrogant who ignore the warning. For the people of Indonesia, over 230,000 lives were lost, families were separated, entire ecosystems were displaced and billions of dollars in economic damages were incurred—all within twenty minutes.

The massive tsunami facing our U.S. prosperity

and its security is the national debt. In other words, coming soon is a giant tidal wave of economic devastation that continues to increase with every dollar spent beyond national revenues. The speed and size of this tidal wave of debt is unprecedented; it is ready to unleash its energy, permanently drowning the value of the U.S. dollar and eroding the nation's purchasing power along with its prosperity. How have we allowed it to happen... and what can we do about it?

A New Definition of Debt

In preparing this manuscript, I have had many discussions with the politically elite, educators, government leaders, accountants and lawyers. I have scoured books, surfed the Internet and poured over our treasuries and personal notes to convey the best possible definition for the discussion of this chapter. While I have been exposed to the highly technical, sophisticated and scholarly definitions of the term, I have reached my own conclusion. Debt, quite simply put, is "a means to create wealth where no wealth exists."

When this great nation was forged out of the fires of war, the Framers of the Declaration of Independence and Constitution kept it simple. Applying the rationale of "less is more," they clearly and succinctly established a nation's principles and stated the purpose for the United States of America in a few pages. For some reason, subsequent lawmakers have come to believe the opposite of "less is more." They have created a government that exalts arrogance and pays tribute to egocentrism. In endless pursuit of proving to the world just how advanced they have become, leaders have inundated our Treasury, law libraries and an entire government bureaucracy with reams of unending rhetoric.

I, like our Founders, believe that definitions cannot afford to get lost in embellishment or grandeur. For if the people continue to pander to the pride of the academically elite, the "common-man" theory propagated by our Founding Fathers will be lost in the abyss of the egocentric mind, masking the identity of the enemy found in debt. Then, financial independence will have no means of flourishing as the debt of a nation consumes freedom, liberty and justice for all!

The Nation's Debt—from Billions to Trillions!

Would it help if I spelled it out for you? The debt of a nation is equal to all public and private current revenues, minus all current expenditures, including all future financial commitments—regardless of whether or not surety or collateral has been pledged. In other words, the formula for determining the *Debt of a Nation = Public Current Revenue + Private Current Revenue − Current Expenditures − Past and Future Financial Commitments.*

The nation's debt is not to be confused with the

national, or federal, debt. The nation's debt is not just created by municipalities, county or state governments but includes the federal government, corporations, financial institutions, businesses and individual households. Instead, debt is created by all of the above, and all of the above combined create the debt of a nation. Today, the debt of the United States of America stands at about $57 trillion.[5] That's right—a staggering, heart-stopping $57,000,000,000,000. "Unbelievable!" you say. "Oh no, this guy is crazy! That's impossible! Honey, take this book and get our money back!"

Oh, I see, maybe you have heard these numbers thrown around: $4.2 trillion, $7 trillion or the federal debt beginning in 2007, which totaled $8.7 trillion. Perhaps you heard or read about the actual federal debt on June 24, 2009: $11.36 trillion ($11,365,652,939,856.33).[6] Maybe you saw these figures: $700 billion, $780 billion, $100 billion or the 2010 budget deficit predicted to top $1.8 trillion dollars alone!

The truth is that over the past couple of years, you have probably seen all of these numbers on the news, read them in the newspapers, listened to them on talk radio or heard your representative or even the president of the United States discussing them during congressional and presidential debates. Nevertheless, these numbers are just part of the story and only represent a fraction of America's total debt problem. Whether you believe it or not, the debt of this nation is—at the time of this writing—$57 trillion and rising. Daily, the total debt of the nation is escalating by a dollar amount so large that it doesn't even fit on most calculators.

If you are one of the few people who do believe that the debt of this nation is $57 trillion and rising, then you may also believe that someone else is responsible for the municipal, county, state and federal debt—not you! After all, most U.S. citizens didn't sign up for this kind of debt, right? Wrong! In fact, every American—man, woman and child; illegal aliens *not* included—is responsible for $37,109.48 of the federal government debt,[7] or $185,668.00,[8] which represents all public and private U.S. debt outstanding and payable to someone. For a family of four, the amount owed is a shocking, suck-the-oxygen-out-of-the-room $744,672.00.[9] If, today, every American had to come up with his or her portion of the total debt, it would drive most families into bankruptcy.

The voices of the opposition—comprised of the elites and the progressives—are saying, "Ah, don't worry! That will never happen!" To which, I reply, "Watch out for the wave!" If you had been privy to the discussions I have been a part of, you, too, would dismiss the voice of the opposition in a New York minute. Of course, your debt payment already includes any car note, house mortgage, medical bills, college loans, washer and dryer, and so on. So…take a deep breath…$746,868.00 covers everything. But don't *hold* your breath…because the debt keeps rising and the $746,868.00 bargain is slipping away fast.

Think of it this way: The average mortgage in the U.S. just went up about a half million dollars. I sure am looking forward to socialized health care—oh, excuse me, I mean "government-sponsored health care insurance"—which is being conveyed as a tool to create competition to lower the cost of health care. Yeah, right! This assumption defies economic logic and the very fundamentals of competition.

Look at it this way: If the demand for a particular product or service increases without an increase in supply, the cost for that product or service increases as well. For those who think that the laws of supply and demand are different for mixed or controlled market conditions, guess again. These laws are basic and apply to every market condition and currency type in the world—without exception, that includes government spending.

No Finger-Pointing! U.S. Spells Us!

So, exactly how did the United States of America go so deeply into debt? How did a nation—laced in silver, gold and worldly riches—get so far behind? If we as a nation are so wealthy, how come we are forced to borrow to maintain our lifestyle? You might argue, "But I'm not the one with the villa in Italy or the fancy yacht!"

Before we resort to finger-pointing, let me be specific about what debt looks like and how it continues to grow. If debt is a way of creating wealth where no wealth exists, another way to express it might be: "Debt is a condition of owing something to another—for example, arrearage, arrears, indebtedness, liability or obligations."[10] One might also say that debt is a way of obtaining something today by promising to pay for it tomorrow, at some other time in the future or in installments.

Debt is brought on by credit. Whether it be in the form of a store account, lay away, credit cards, bank installment loan, auto loan, insurance loan, bonds, the fabled Treasury, derivatives or any other instrument, when credit is given and there is no storehouse of cash to pay for goods and services, debt is created.

Now let's take a look at household debt because it is part of the debt of a nation. Today in America, household spending is out of control. If you're honest with yourself, you might relate to this statement. It is my hope that if readers begin to apply responsible fiscal policies at home, they will demand the same from their leaders. In fact, with sound fiscal household policies, Americans can help to avert the economic collapse facing this country.

In every household, as in yours, there is only so much income to go around. This is true no matter where you work or for whom. An individual can work at a bank, at a school, in a mill, in a factory or any other place. A person can collect subsistence from welfare or from a trust fund. A worker can be rich, poor or somewhere in between. Debt doesn't discriminate nor is it selective. Debt is not discrete, it is not prejudiced, and it will strike consumers anywhere and at any time. Even for millionaire CEOs, there is only so much cash with which to work. Although the revenue of a millionaire CEO may be more than yours, there is only so much money coming into the household coffers each week. Don't forget—the more we make, the more we spend. Revenue is relative to a person's lot in life. Just because a person makes a lot of money doesn't necessarily mean that he/she is not in debt. Enter my earlier comment: "If we as a nation are so wealthy, how come we are forced to borrow to maintain our lifestyle?" Maybe it's because, as Granddad used to say, "Some folks have champagne tastes and beer budgets!"

On the other side of income are expenses, and there are plenty of expenses that come along with everyday life—especially when life revolves around a family. Expenses in themselves are not bad—if individuals and family members have all that they need, want and desire in exchange for the household income and, most importantly, when they do not live beyond their means.

That Dirty Word—*Budget*

In every household there is a tool available to assist with spending. The same is true for governments, corporations, etc. This tool is called a budget. A budget helps to outline the sources of income/revenue and to prioritize expenses. A budget is an easy way to track income and expenses on paper prior to actually earning income or paying bills. A budget aids an individual or entity in foreseeing the potential for living beyond his/her means and averting financial disaster caused by over or reckless spending. Budgets are helpful when people want to predict future expenses and plan for major events such as purchasing a home, new car, bass boat or planning that dream vacation.

"Plan your work, then work your plan." This basic business philosophy is the very reason budgets came about. Everyone who uses a budget to plan the family finances is successful in accomplishing his/her goals; furthermore, they have no trouble navigating financial difficulty when faced with the unexpected. Even governments refer to budgets when planning the next calendar year. As mentioned earlier, every household has a different financial profile.

All households in America fall into one of the following three categories: surplus, balanced, or deficit. These budgets are conditions that stem from spending after all expenses are subtracted from all sources of revenue.

1. **Surplus budget** occurs when revenues exceed expenses. Also known as "being in the black," this traditional budgetary concept honors the American Dream and should be the goal for every spending scenario. Surplus budgets set up a financial condition known as "true savings." True savings can only

result from surplus budget conditions when there is no debt. True savings is not the same as savings or savings accounts. Without going into too much detail here, true savings cannot exist without a surplus in the budget; otherwise, you only have "cash on hand." Don't get me wrong—any cash on hand is better than no cash at all. Any money in a savings account is also great, but true savings is the sign of true wealth. If debt is "creating wealth where none exists," then true savings is the opposite of debt. If you get this concept, you will understand that true wealth produces a healthy economy and contributes to a safe and secure nation.

2. **Balanced budget** is better than a budget deficit. Known as "break even," balanced budgets result from revenue resources being equal to expenses. The concept of a balanced budget can be found in the 2008 Republican Platform—something that was missing from their office the day they were elected. Given all of the misfortune that can befall a person, a balanced budget is not a bad place to be. A balanced budget is a true example of middle-of-the-road financial philosophy, but falls short of preparing for the proverbial rainy day.

3. **Budget deficit** is the budget profile of progressives and is the least desirable of the three profiles. Sound

familiar? Many families live with them. It is also the last household in which a person wants to reside as financial distress in a family is the most commonly named reason for divorce in America. Known as being "in the red," "code red" or "red alert," a budget deficit occurs when expenses exceed revenues and there is a cash shortfall between financial obligations and the total amount of household income. Whether the shortfall occurs weekly, every two weeks, monthly or annually, most individuals find themselves caught in this dilemma when they fall upon hard times—job loss, sickness, injury, death of a family member. Some other misfortunes include floods, tornadoes, hurricanes, wild fires, earthquakes or wars.

Budget deficits can cause a person to borrow from retirement funds, which only increases future expenses. Most people who dig into their retirement, however, have no idea of the havoc they are creating when they tap into their own future. "It's my money," you may say. Maybe so, but whatever you do, don't put your retirement into 401k and IRAs which are used by government and corporate conspirators to collateralize layers and layers of debt to pay for their pleasures.

America has been duped into lending big business her fortunes, then has been convinced to borrow it back to pay for cars, homes, educations and shopping sprees. What do we the people receive in return for our generosity?

We are paid a whopping plus or minus ¾ percent interest on passport savings and 2 percent on long-term CDs. Americans have also lost anywhere between 30-60 percent of their retirement nest eggs and now must pay 5-25 percent to borrow our money back from those who have borrowed from us! When faced with budget deficits, there is no end to the length to which desperate individuals, businesses and governments will go.

Do you see that if America maintained a budget surplus, then people wouldn't have to lend their money at ¾ percent interest, only to be required to pay 25 percent to borrow it back? If we don't possess true wealth, we can be exploited by predators who will try to convince us that we must participate in a financial dead end.

Now, let me show you what we can do about this madness.

Benesch Bullets

To the leadership of the United States:

- Declare a national state of fiscal emergency and immediately stop all deficit spending.
- Balance the federal budget no later than 2011. For the next three years—through 2013— America must not spend more than she earns in revenue.
- Initiate a state balanced budget program to

force states to live within their means. States cannot be allowed to rely on other states to bail out their financial mismanagement.

- Sell and auction—to Americans only— unneeded items such as real estate, vehicles and other assets.
- Stop throwing away Senate and House office furniture every couple of years. Government must live within its means and make do with its current accommodations.
- Restructure current debt obligations to reduce interest payments on outstanding debt. Start negotiations to shave percentage—basis— points off outstanding loans with foreign lending nations now, not later.

To my fellow citizens:

- Stop deficit spending.
- Plan your expenses with a budget.
- Balance your household budget no later than 2011. For the next three years—through 2013—expenses must not exceed income.
- Sell or auction unneeded household items, vehicles and other possessions that are just lying around.
- Consider selling overly expensive automobiles, boats and other luxury items.

- Decrease expenses. Begin with comfort items such as extra telephone lines, cable television, satellite radio, and so on. Recently, the Benesch household cut out over $600 per month by just reducing excess and without selling cars or the house—a large sum of money by anyone's count.
- Stop finger-pointing. Remember, debt does not discriminate. Democrats, Republicans and others are all responsible for excessive spending.
- Do not allow your "whims" to drain your retirement so that you become a burden to your family. Independent living after retirement is the best gift we can bestow on our children.

My fellow Americans, if you can't afford to put food on the table, a decent set of wheels under you for your trip to and from the office, or secure shelter over your children's heads, you can't afford to put money away for retirement or your children's college education either. Enough said? Your personal finances are nobody's business, but the government has made it theirs. So let's move on to what everyone is talking about—something that affects us all.

Let's talk about the U.S. government's part in this tidal wave of debt. Their part is called the federal debt— the very thing that is going to lead to Social Security bankruptcy,[11] which will leave my generation without the same benefits afforded my father's generation.

Let's talk about the Medicare and Medicaid systems that will also be bankrupt in the foreseeable future. Along those same lines, I will mention the reality of the proposed healthcare reform that the progressives claim will "save us money in the long run" or what this author believes is another stimulus initiative our nation just can't afford. Let's talk about the cost of war that far too many Americans are always ready to fight. And let's talk about the mountain of "IOUs" piled up so high and in such a disorganized mess that even our U.S. government can't explain them.

Then, leaving no stone unturned, let's dig into the fiscal irresponsibility of a nation's government that is determined to lead America to her economic grave.

I am not among those who fear the people. They, and not the rich, are our dependence for continued freedom. And to preserve their independence, we must not let our rulers load us with perpetual debt. We must make our election between economy and liberty or profusion [unrestrained abundance] and servitude. If we run into such debts, as that we must be taxed in our meat and in our drink, in our necessaries and our comforts, in our labors and our amusements, for our callings and our creeds...[we will] have no time to think, no means of calling the mis-managers to account; but be glad to obtain subsistence by hiring ourselves to rivet their chains on the necks of our fellow-sufferers...This example reads to us the salutary lesson, that private fortunes are destroyed by public as well as by private extravagance. And this is the tendency of all human governments. A departure from principle in one instance becomes a precedent for a second, that second for a third; and so on, till the bulk of society is reduced to be mere automatons of misery, and [will] have no sensibilities left but for sinning and suffering. Then begins, indeed, the bellum omnium in omnia *[war of all against all], which some philosophers...have mistaken for the natural, instead of the abusive state of man. And the fore-horse of this frightful team is public debt. Taxation follows that, and in its train wretchedness and oppression.*[1]

—President Thomas Jefferson
In a letter to Samuel Kercheval
July 12, 1816

THE BIRTH OF AMERICA'S DEATH

Let no debt remain outstanding,
except the continuing debt to love one another.
—Romans 13:8

The real problems are the structural [perpetual] deficits and
the structural [ongoing] debt that we've been accumulating
and all of us are complicit in.[2]

—President Barack Obama
Address to the Fiscal Responsibility Summit
February 23, 2009

During the first year of the newly formed American government, by an act of Congress, the United States Department of the Treasury was formed. At that time, all the debt from America's War of Independence, accumulated by the colonies, was transferred to the U.S. Treasury and became what is known as the "federal debt."

In the interest of keeping it simple, let's define federal debt. Federal debt is a means whereby the U.S.

government *creates wealth where no wealth exists*. It can also be said that the federal debt is the total of all budget deficits, past and present, created by and signed for by the U.S. government. The U.S. means us—our children, our grandchildren and every generation that succeeds us. Remember, no one is exempt, because debt doesn't discriminate; it only creates a tidal wave of devastation.

In 1789, after this fledgling confederation had fought to create a sovereign identity, the federal debt was $75 million and accounted for approximately 40 percent of America's Gross Domestic Product (GDP).[3] Even under these extreme circumstances, Thomas Jefferson, along with other fiscally conservative Founding Fathers, pushed to pay off the war debt quickly. The Framers were vehemently opposed to debt spending and worked feverishly against the philosophy of Treasury Secretary Alexander Hamilton. Jefferson believed that debt led to tyranny, "a form of government in which the ruler[s] is an absolute dictator, not restricted by a constitution or laws or opposition."[4]

Washington and others believed that too much debt could disable America's ability to fight her enemies. In stark contrast, Hamilton believed that some debt was good. He pointed out that by keeping the debt, the country's credibility would grow as the nation prospered and production increased.[5] Hamilton surmised that increased production would mean greater revenues for the government through taxation and that the government would be better able to pay off the debt of America's Revolution.

Both sides applied their reasons to the debt problem and resolved their differences in a compromise. As a result, the nation's capital was built in present-day Washington, D.C.[6] The government issued bonds to pay for construction of the capital, resulting in additional federal debt. Hamilton was correct, however, and under the watchful and fiscally responsible eyes of America's patriots, the new Treasury experienced great success.

This is exactly how and when our current deficit spending habits were first introduced. *Creating wealth where no wealth exists* was viewed as a splendid philosophy. Dismissing the fact that this did not keep to the spirit of patriotism, the early Fathers did know that debt spending always leads to financial ruin, as from generation to generation, leaders stray farther and farther from responsible behavior. America had now set her course for economic greatness and collapse with the single stroke of a pen. The chains of what both Jefferson and the Bible have called "bondage" had begun rattling.

Even though the nation moved forward under Hamilton's philosophy, Jefferson warned (behind closed doors) that America's next revolution would be against those who spent the nation's freedom.

Is War Good for the Economy?

The inevitable War of 1812 brought with it greater budget deficits. But under the leadership of our seventh president, Andrew Jackson—also known as "Old Hickory"—the nation was finally able to pay off this bill in 1835, forty-six years later.

A tough, usually undiplomatic statesman, Jackson is the only U.S. president never to have left a national debt footprint. He viewed debt exactly the same as America's greatest patriot, George Washington, and followed closely in his footsteps. Jackson regarded Washington's Farewell Address to the Nation as the "voice of prophecy foretelling events and warning us of the evil to come." [7]

Jackson's fiscal responsibility and compassion for the working class of this nation gave birth to a conservative Democratic Party. His fiscal policies, however, are ignored in the halls of Congress, led by today's progressive Democrats! Perhaps they—like disobedient, rebellious sons—don't believe their father knew what he was talking about. They clearly underestimate the significance of the role Jackson played in the economic prosperity and survival of the nation. If it were not for his diligence, America would surely have been bankrupt long before now.

After Jackson's administration, budget deficits pushed America back into debt, and by the emergence of the Civil War, the nation had no choice but to increase the debt as the country shed the blood of its patriots. Once again, in the pursuit of freedom, the Civil War brought death and casualty; but for the third time in America's history, she was burdened by the debt millstone and driven to the brink of bankruptcy. At that time the federal debt accounted for 33 percent of the GDP.[8] As in the past, America quickly began to pay her bills, and by 1913, the nation's debt accounted for only 7 percent of the GDP.[9] (Remember this date and the low percentage of debt.) Implementing sound fiscal policies found in balanced and surplus budgets, America was once again poised for economic prosperity.

By now, I hope it has become apparent that war carries with it heavy tolls in economic hardship. As it turns out, war is not the great engine of prosperity that certain economists and elitists have been preaching—you know who I'm talking about—the "War is good for the economy" bunch!

Given to this nation as a gift from President George Washington, his Farewell Address to the Nation posits two prevailing thoughts: First, that credit should be used sparingly because second, war is inevitable. Whether one agrees with the reasons or not, war is the destiny of freedom.

Counting the Cost

Government must always ensure that there is enough

money, credit and men to fight the enemy in order to guarantee that freedom endures. If not, America must consider her enemies too formidable a threat and war, too expensive to fight at the given time, and she must seek peace. Scripture explains it like this: "Suppose one of you wants to build a tower. Will he not first sit down and estimate the cost to see if he has enough money to complete it? For if he lays the foundation and is not able to finish it, everyone who sees it will ridicule him, saying, 'This fellow began to build and was not able to finish.' Or suppose a king is about to go to war against another king. Will he not first sit down and consider whether he is able with ten thousand men to oppose the one coming against him with twenty thousand? If he is not able, he will send a delegation while the other is still a long way off and will ask for terms of peace" (Luke 14:28-32).

Without exception, war interferes with progress and cuts deep into a nation's savings; if there are no savings, war piles on debt. It appears that a lesson still remains to be learned: Nations must save in order to fight the inevitability of war. Aw, what does George Washington know anyway?

Great Depression II?

As you know, the Great Depression followed the end of WWI, but it wasn't the first economic folly of its type in U.S. history. In fact, economic depression has occurred on more than one occasion in the United States. If the economic engines of national wealth are not restored, the United States may dive headlong into Great Depression II.

Prior to the Great Depression, our nation experienced the Long Depression of 1873-1879, which stemmed from too much deficit spending prior to, during and after the Civil War. The Long Depression was followed by years of on-again, off-again recession. Then the Great Depression came on the heels of the 1929 stock market crash and gave rise to the progressive movement, which was born out of Republican President Theodore Roosevelt's inability to force conservative Republicans to adopt his social reforms.

Though many congratulate the progressive philosophy of his cousin Franklin D. Roosevelt's New Deal, most economists of the day believed that once the markets collapsed and settled out, economic growth and prosperity would naturally occur without government intervention. Others believed that WWII restored economic prosperity to America.

I believe both of the latter to be true and feel as though Roosevelt's progressive social programs launched today's national view toward the "right of entitlement." With large debt dollars being pumped into the economy for the military machine, how could America *not* have more jobs and experience better living conditions brought about by deficit spending? And how could any human being resist taking from a government that was all too ready to redistribute wealth from one family to another?

The economic backlash from debt spending prior to and following World War II was offset by the United States immediately converting the war machine to domestic manufacturing. Manufacturing afforded America the ability to pay off most of her war debt and spurred the next ten years of economic prosperity. This economic prosperity allowed for most to achieve the American Dream, although that "dream" was far different from our understanding today. At the time, most post WWII families owned only one car, much smaller homes and one black-and-white television set—if they were lucky! The Americans that some have called "the Greatest Generation" were content with what they had. I believe their generation was made up of great Americans; however, in my humble opinion, it was our Founders who were the greatest generation, with perhaps the WWII era a close second.

By 1950, America once again found herself entangled in war, which ended quickly in armistice. The overzealous leap into war without first counting the cost set into diplomatic policy the arrogance in leadership that exists today. The Korean War created a line of demarcation, leaving the inevitability of war for future generations to fight. Though the war in Korea didn't pile on debt as did wars of the past, probably because of its short duration, it did leave in its wake unfinished business, tense diplomatic relations and the need to spend money for security that would not have had to be spent if the war had ended in clear and concise victory. This war did, however, cause a shift in manufacturing exports to manufacturing for domestic war consumption, which proved to bring deficit spending and recession.

Johnson: The Great Society

The Kennedy and Johnson presidencies fanned the flames of recession and inflation once again. Pushing forward with the Vietnam War, the national debt began to build. In addition, this era brought about the onset of increased federal debt spending in pursuit of the final frontier.

After the assassination of President John F. Kennedy, President Lyndon B. Johnson crafted the Great Society legislation, which only compounded the inherent debt spending found in war. The nation's debt began to explode with the expansion of civil rights and with Medicare and Medicaid. Johnson recklessly spent the nation's inheritance in blind pursuit of ending poverty. The "war on poverty," though a worthy notion, has proven to be difficult given the shift in leadership prowess.

Lacking the fortitude of Washington, Jefferson, Jackson and Lincoln, our leaders appear to have become complacent and pitifully satisfied with just doing something quickly, even if it isn't the right thing. Their shortcomings have done nothing but create more misery. This new leadership ideology panders to every agenda, causing the symptoms of federal debt to worsen.

Johnson escalated the Vietnam War, greatly increasing the struggles of his own nation while tossing death, casualty and poverty onto another. War was once again in full swing, contracting the U.S. economy by placing too much debt burden on society, which always results from not saving for the inevitability of war. Truly a tragic time in our nation's history!

Nixon: Manufacturing Exodus

President Nixon, most commonly known for the Watergate Scandal, is also the U.S. president responsible for initiating troop withdrawal from the Vietnam Theater. He supported a passive war, however, and built up the federal debt by sending money and providing military equipment to support one side of warring nations—in this case, Vietnam. Nixon gave in to the pressure to pull out the troops but was not interested in pulling the U.S. out of the war altogether.

Nixon is also the first U.S. president to visit China. During his time in office, Nixon initiated bipartisan discussions to seek peace through Global Economic stabilization. He felt, as many progressive leaders do today, that by stabilizing foreign nations through sustainable employment, they would not go to war. By sending U.S. manufacturers to communist block nations, Nixon and his comrades believed that they had found a new way to avert the inevitability of war. What many have failed to recognize is that his actions created sanctions against domestic business enterprises and, in so doing, initiated the U.S. "manufacturing exodus."

Nixon and his supporters believed that they could send the environmentally dirty, physically unsafe and lower-paying jobs to other countries and replace them with environmentally clean, physically safe and higher-paying jobs of the service industry. The service jobs sought were in education, the emerging new world of tech, and in big finance. Another worthy notion…I mean a paper cut at a desk is much better than losing a finger at the knife sharpening wheel, isn't it?

This gamble with the U.S. economy was an initiative that replaced the economic lifeblood found in U.S. manufacturing. To subsidize their failures—I mean, to finance the transition from manufacturing to service—the federal Treasury turned the money presses on high and began to print the U.S. right into oblivion. Can someone older than I please explain to me again what was so wonderful about Nixon's opening the door to China? He may have opened the door to the Chinese, but he closed it to Americans.

Carter: Peace without Prosperity

President Jimmy Carter was a great diplomat for peace and most deserving of his Nobel Prize. It's a different story when we consider his "contribution" to the economic picture. From 1977-1980, he only managed to increase the intensity of recession. Not wanting to be outdone by his predecessors, he added to an already struggling economy the burdens of high gas prices and fuel shortages and increased the national debt as no other peacetime president before him. His presidency will be forever scarred by his failure to rescue the hostages from Iran, his giving away the Panama Canal, his incurring some of the highest interest rates in history and by the recession and fuel shortage. I'd like to give him a "peace" of something!

Reaganomics: The Trickle-Down Effect

After Carter's short stay at the White House, the United States entered a new era of debt spending under President Ronald Reagan. The years from 1981-1989 proved to change the way government viewed the economy. Quick to bring the Iran hostage crisis to an end, Reagan implemented what George H.W. Bush called a "Voodoo Economic Policy."[10] Termed "Reaganomics," "supply-side economics," or "trickle-down economics," President Reagan began spending money like a Hollywood movie star.

When Reagan took office, he inherited a $909 billion federal debt and quickly charted new spending waters. He immediately spent the future of America, taking the national debt across the trillion-dollar mark. He believed that by depositing taxpayer dollars into banks for lending and businesses for consumption, the economy would free itself of recession. President Reagan managed to almost triple the federal debt, increasing it to $2.6 trillion prior to completing his double term in office.

Reagan's assumption about supply-side economics was correct. It is true that when a government or any other source creates artificial money-flows in an economy, that economy will prosper. Nations must be careful, though, because this philosophical sword is double-edged. Creating money-flows outside of naturally occurring markets leads to inflation, which can bring about the collapse of a nation's currency. In fact, history proves that countries have gone to war without firing a single shot. Known as economic warfare, nations have killed foreign economies by applying this very same supply-side strategy. Stimulus and bailout are artificial monetary policies and, if used by one nation against another, is considered to be economic warfare! Although supply-side economics may bring about temporary gain and economic euphoria, this policy is really financial terrorism in the long run. This is how Reagan defeated…or did he defeat…Russia?!

Reagan's presidency is marred by the Savings & Loan debacle which added $1.2 trillion to his debt footprint. Yet his policies are still applauded in the conservative Republican caucus on Capitol Hill.

Bush I: Easy Come, Easy Go

Reagan was followed by his vice-president, George H.W. Bush, who was elected in 1988. Bush I saw the errors in President Reagan's ways and what he had termed "Voodoo Economic Policy." But he also noted how popular Reagan had become by tapping into America's future prosperity and exponentially increasing federal debt. Bush eventually became painfully aware that he was absolutely correct about his concerns regarding "Reaganomics"; however, he sought to take advantage of this new policy that seemed to be giving way to a new American attitude toward debt.

America had begun its romance with easy money created through debt spending—not realizing that out-of-control inflation, the derivatives markets and a whole host of other financial measures would soon be looking to rob them of their equity, savings and retirement. Bush is well known for his campaign promise: "Read my lips—no new taxes."

Bush even believed that, given the chance, he could outspend Reagan and so he did. In just four years, he pushed the federal debt to almost $4 trillion. He moved from his platform of opposing "voodoo economics" to becoming its "high priest"!

Clinton: Surplus Budget!

President Bill Clinton took office in 1993, and during his next eight years in office, Clinton spent far too much money. In comparison with the "Reaganomics" years, however, he spent about half as much as his predecessors. Even though Clinton believed in the Nixon philosophy of peace through global economic stabilization, he saw the handwriting on the wall with regard to federal debt. So he implemented strict budget policy by eventually balancing the federal budget and then creating surplus budgets. But he also signed North American Free Trade Agreement (NAFTA) into law, pushed for Central American Free Trade Agreement (CAFTA) and loosened restrictions on banking. As I said before, much like Nixon.

Clinton greatly transformed the financial world in an attempt to make home ownership a right for every American without regard to his/her future ability to pay for that right. His policies helped the economy in the short term, but the credit burdens placed on the economy helped launch America into its current fiscal crisis, teeing up for the current banking and sub-prime lending crisis. Then along came Bush II....

Bush 43: "Going Down in History"

The forty-third president, George W. Bush, continued

the legacy of President Clinton and his father by signing CAFTA into law and taking financial deregulation to a place where President Clinton only dreamed of going. President Bush also fired up the "trickle-down economics" machine, driving the nation's federal debt to double digits.

Bush printed money at an unprecedented rate and thrust America into not one, but two wars. Having spent more money in his two terms than all the presidents in the previous two centuries, Bush II is sure to, as he said himself, "go down in the history books." *Way* down!

"Obamanomics"—Practice Makes Perfect?

Elected for his Hollywood charisma and because of America's disdain for the previous administration, it appears that yet another U.S. president has either failed to learn the lessons of years gone by—that credit must be used sparingly and that the debtor is slave to the lender—or is deliberately creating a slave nation. In the 2010 budget, "A New Era of Responsibility," President Obama cites that he has his finger on the pulse of the people. His budget, however, is unprecedented in U.S. political history as he and his administration are embarking on a single-year budget deficit greater than those of 2004, 2005, 2006 and 2007 combined.

The current White House has pulled an old trick out of the bag—that of deception—by redefining the term *budget*. This administration defines a budget as "more than simply numbers on a page. It is a measure of how well we are living up to our obligations to ourselves and one another."[11] He's full of it! In Chapter 1, I provided the true definition of budgets, so don't be fooled. President Obama seems to be looking to outdo both Roosevelt and Johnson when it comes to social programs while successfully outspending George W. Bush, then trying to cover up his fiscal irresponsibility with some fancy footwork.

By early 2009, Obama had already spent an additional $787 billion for the "American Reinvestment and Recovery Act" (ARRA)—an exorbitant amount of money above and beyond the trillions being thrown around on the Hill, much like I throw around five spots at the County Fair. This debt was not planned for, nor has it been accounted for in any fiscal year's budget. It is just money that is being desperately spent for votes… oh, excuse me!…I meant to say, in an attempt to breathe life into a Thanksgiving turkey. He and his unpatriotic accomplices have also removed the word *American* from the ARRA in an unachievable pursuit of world acceptance.

Let's take a look at health care reform being sold to the public as a way to reduce overall health care costs. First, when has the government ever spent less on a project than first promised? And second, when did government health care programs begin providing the safety net guaranteed the public? That being said, Obama first proposed that

America's new health care initiative would increase the nation's budget obligations and national debt by $1.4 trillion over the next ten years. During the first several months of his administration, responding to the pundits' criticism, the new president backed off his first estimate of the cost to $1 trillion, then to $800 billion.

It seems as if the current administration does get one thing—that growing federal debt is crushing this nation. In fact, according to my calculations, the actual health care initiative will not only cause health care cost inflation, it will also increase the national debt footprint an additional $7.2-$8.6 trillion. On top of that, given the average life expectancy, the eventual mandatory care of illegal aliens, interest on the increased debt and population growth over the next thirty years, Obamacare could increase the national debt by $50 trillion. That's right—fifty times more than the original claim!

Information provided by government agencies and population growth predictions—combined with evidence provided by historical health care costs, Medicare, Medicaid, welfare and Social Security spending during the past sixty years—supports my theory. That should be just enough to trigger the debt tidal wave.

To further complicate matters, Obama is poised to spend an additional 1.8 trillion deficit dollars in 2010. Experts predict that during his next four years, America's federal debt will increase from $10.7 trillion to over $14 trillion. At the rate Obama and his administration are spending billions and trillions of dollars, he should easily beat the predictions.

If you're not angry enough, let's throw in the situation with China. Their leaders warned Obama not to recklessly increase U.S. debt which will deflate the dollar, adversely affecting returns on China's loans to America. China has already begun shaking its fist! It appears that the U.S. federal debt could not only lead the nation to war, but also hinder America's ability to fight one.

Hope for America

Some have appraised the Hope Diamond's value at $250 million—a grand price for a stone that began to form beneath the earth where coal is extracted. Scientists have determined that when continuous heat and pressure are applied over a long period of time, this natural resource becomes the rarest and most sought-after jewel.

Deficit reduction is an absolute necessity and savings, a must. Waste, fraud and abuse have to be squashed. Unpaid debt can no longer afford to be ignored, dismissed or delayed. For America, an extended period of continual pressure, in the form of disciplined spending, and heat, in the form of sacrifice, will be necessary to restore the nation's status as a gem. Let me explain how:

Benesch Bullets

To the leadership of the United States:

- Beginning in 2014, the nation should begin paying off $250 billion of the federal debt per year, or $1 trillion every four years. At that rate, the current federal debt of $12.371 trillion (as of February 10, 2010) will not be paid off until 2063, or forty-nine years from the date of this printing!
- Leave no debt outstanding. As President Obama himself said, "It is the perpetual debt that is the problem." Progressive policies create budget deficits without a plan or intent to repay the loans created by deficits. At home, at work and in government, the nation must balance all budgets!
- Prioritize spending by deciding what is most important. America must also eliminate programs that she cannot "cash and carry."
- Initiate a 10 percent federal savings program to begin on the fourth year after balanced budget practices begin—2014. The federal government must begin to save for natural disasters, war and the unexpected.
- Correct the definition of *budget*. Misleading the public is not honorable and demonstrates a

lack of integrity.

To my fellow citizens:

- Pay all debts in full and forgive debts owed to you every seven years.[12] Paying debt in this manner renews the credit system and prevents perpetual debt from accumulating and causing economic downturns such as the one which began in December 2007.
- The entire nation—including corporations and governments—must begin saving 10 percent of all income/revenue in addition to creating balanced and surplus budgets. Remember, Washington warned that war is inevitable and so are economic downturns. This nation must save for the "rainy" day, which is always waiting to rob America of her dignity.

The debt of the nation—especially the federal debt—is too serious to ignore. If America were to stop deficit spending today, balance the budget, and then begin paying off the debt per my recommendations, the federal debt would still remain long after I am dead and linger unpaid until 2063. As I have said, Americans are passing the debt of our excesses on to our children and grandchildren. Can we continue to do that with a clear conscience? Like a gemstone, America must be willing to endure the pain, pressure and heat of strong, long-term, responsible spending policies. Unlike a diamond, it will take far less time to right the nation's fiscal policies and repair America's world monetary image, but we must begin this process today!

God Forbid we should ever be 20 years without such a rebellion. The people cannot be all, & always well informed. The part which is wrong will be discontented in proportion to the importance of the facts they misconceive. If they remain quiet under such misconceptions it is a lethargy, the forerunner of death to the public liberty…what country before ever existed a century & a half without a rebellion? & what country can preserve its liberties if their rulers are not warned from time to time that their people preserve the spirit of resistance? Let them take arms. The remedy is to set them right as to facts… what signify a few lives lost in a century or two? The tree of liberty must be refreshed from time to time with the blood of patriots & tyrants. It is its natural manure….[1]

—President Thomas Jefferson
In a letter to William Smith
Paris, November 13, 1787

3

AMAT VICTORIA CURAM

Blessed are those who are persecuted
because of righteousness.
—Matthew 5:10

The best and only answer to a smear or to an honest
misunderstanding of the facts is to tell the truth. And that's
why I'm here tonight. I want to tell you my side of the case.[2]
——President Richard Milhous Nixon, "Checkers" Speech
September 23, 1952

I intend no disrespect here, but I don't believe most people understand the meaning of *amat victoria curam*, Latin for "victory favors those who take pains." Maybe, as a nation, we have forgotten the pains of sacrifice or have deliberately chosen to spare ourselves the anguish that comes along with doing what is right.

If we continue down the path of fiscal irresponsibility and immoral behavior and do not wean ourselves of debt spending, this nation will fail. No ifs, ands and buts about it. We are not blind to right and wrong, but for some strange reason, we have decided to sit down and shut up. Why? How did our forefathers know when it was time to stand up, speak out and bear arms?

In the aftermath of 9-11, the Commission's report contained a confession from an FBI special agent attached to the CIA-run Counterterrorism Center.[3] In a television interview, the agent stated that the plot that initiated the collapse of the Twin Towers, damage to the southwest wall of the Pentagon and the crash of United Airlines Flight 93 in Pennsylvania pastureland could have been prevented. Government policy, however, prohibited him from disclosing vital information to his own agency.

As I watched, I could see his facial features contort with the pain of recalling that unprecedented event in our history—the first terrorist attack of this sort on American soil. If he could only do it over, things might have turned out much differently.[4] Like the ghosts of my own memories, I can't help wondering if the voices of over 2,900 people killed that September morning haunt this special agent's dreams just as the voice of one 23-year-old soldier still haunts mine.

I believe that we Americans have abandoned our founding principles and the lessons etched in blood by the nation's patriots. Regretfully, I am also convinced that this nation is suffering because too many in leadership have rejected the Creator's Code of right and wrong, good and evil. Furthermore, I believe that the forces of evil have stifled common sense and have woven a global web of lies, deception, discontent, ignorance and arrogance and that a new form of global progressivism is the forehorse of this frightful team!

I believe that people have become obsessed with winning over standing for what is right and embracing evil over attaining eternal life. I believe that most people root for their party candidates as if political campaigns were some sort of sporting event. This is not how it is supposed to be—of that I am quite certain. You know it, too!

But this doesn't give me, you, or anyone else the right to "remain quiet under misconceptions" and give in to "lethargy." So I write to ensure that people know the truth. In the quotation that sets the stage for this chapter, Jefferson concluded that if the people misconceive the truth, their misunderstanding would become the forerunner of death to public liberty. In fact, ignoring the truth is regarded as willful neglect, both unpatriotic and un-American!

A New Movement

On November 5, 2009, at Fort Hood, Texas, thirteen American soldiers were killed and thirty-one others injured by terrorist Nadal M. Hasan, wearing the uniform of a U.S. Army officer. Shortly after the suicide attack, soldiers began grumbling because the terrorist had been promoted to the rank of Major earlier the same year. This, after fellow soldiers reported the actions of Hasan to the FBI, who dismissed the complaint even after concluding that this killer was communicating with Imam Anwar al-Awlaki (Aulaqi)[5]—a suspected senior talent recruiter and motivator for terrorist organization al-Qaeda—but did nothing.[6] When I served in the Army, we had a saying that still appears to be prevalent today: "Mess up, move up!"

After the incident, Secretary of Defense Robert Gates again raised the ire of the military ranks as he "declined to characterize the Fort Hood shootings as a terrorist attack, and that no conclusion should be drawn.... In a nation as diverse as the United States, the last thing we need to do is start pointing fingers at each other."[7] Excuse me, Mr. Secretary, but that is exactly what we need to be doing. A terrorist is a terrorist, no matter the diversity.

For several years now, many in the nation have been progressing toward a national belief that diverse people— those who are different from the mainstream—are more valuable to the progressive agenda. According to a U.S. Department of Homeland Security report, Christians, veterans, Anglo-Americans and others with traditional family values have been singled out as potential "domestic terrorists" because their cultures do not line up with the new movement.[8]

As a result, protecting a select few is now "job

one" for progressive leaders, as they appear to believe that diversity cannot afford to get lost in the midst of a murderer's rampage. To people like Secretary Gates, offending the peculiar would be a greater tragedy than the murder of U.S. soldiers by a terrorist on a military installation here at home!

Prior to Fort Hood's own 9-11, government agents had investigated the lone gunman who committed this horrific act of treason. They knew who this guy was, knew that he was collaborating with the enemy and that his allegiance had shifted. To make matters worse, civilian and military leaders were aware that this jihadist was a walking, talking suicide bomb about to go off and that, if pushed into fighting his Islamic countrymen, he would detonate himself. So, how did his superiors handle this loose cannon? They ignored him, crossed their fingers and hoped that their salutary neglect would lead to a peaceful end.

Wait. I can hear government officials whispering the same words Sergeant Dirksen spoke to me. *Come on, it's getting late. If we dig any deeper into this guy's background, we'll be here all night filling out paperwork...not to mention the fact that we will ruffle some diversity feathers.* After their short and not-so-serious investigation, they dismissed the terrorist threat, walked out of the club and turned their backs on those they were supposed to protect. Once again, our nation had fallen prey to leaders who cloak themselves as America's protectors—much like my shift supervisor, who just wanted to go home early that fateful night at Fort Pickett.

Leaders like Dirksen and Gates lack courage and will. They have assigned themselves to a new agenda, embraced the enemy and turned away from true patriots. Dirksen, Gates and their colleagues protect the enemy, insulate them, allow them to force their ungodly behaviors on Americans, pay them, feed them, clothe them, lend our wealth to them and then cross their fingers, hoping that the enemy doesn't turn on them. And when that happens—when Americans are killed by the enemy within our borders—officials run to their defense, cover up the truth, bury the memories of our heroes and bring the enemy before the court jester, making a mockery of justice. All the while, leaders and elites ensure that there is ample entertainment to distract opposition from confronting the new movement. You haven't heard a peep out of Fort Hood since, have you?

This new movement is caught up in diversity, measured response and a sick sense of informal—social—diplomacy.[9] We are at war, America! And even a hint of suspicion that a jihadist is within the ranks cannot be tolerated. You see, victory is not even on our protectors' minds. Respectfully, Mr. President, I submit that the American people haven't lost their will to fight as you have lost yours. Well, that's how an old soldier sees it anyway.

My hope is that you can now trace the anger harbored by our military men and women who have sworn the same oath that all protectors, including public officials, must honor. The anger within the ranks stems from a movement whose systems and processes do not conform to the mandates of the Republic. The duty of our military is not to blindly follow edicts that deviate from America's most important document; instead, it is to preserve and protect the right to life, liberty and the pursuit of happiness for all individuals. Please don't confuse individual rights with diversity.

It seems as if the Republic is adrift. Something sinister is concealed in an eerie mist of politically correct rhetoric. The image comes under the guise of peace, righteousness and goodwill. It appears to be well-intentioned and bears the gift of what is called "A New America." So what can it be? Is it a person or a thing?

Oh, wait, maybe you're one of those who thinks this obscure image is the Union, Barack Obama or those Greedy Corporations. In fact, it is not any one of these, yet it is all of the above. It is a political movement—one that defies God, America's national sovereignty, its people, their property, liberty and freedoms. This movement proposes a new way of life with a twisted definition of equality—seeking to destroy Christianity, veterans, traditional family values, American patriotism and democracy. The objective is to trade America's heritage for a form of government that replaces Almighty God because the belief is that the movement's creed is all-knowing and all-powerful.

Aiding in this endeavor is the rule of law—the world's version, that is. The law has become a whip, the new taskmaster. Simply put, jurisprudence is evolving into the tool of progressivism. Passing hundreds of new laws annually, progressive leadership is working feverishly to convince America that the world should be a place where people blindly follow the new rule of law that overreaches by expanding taxes, creating new spending, putting special interests over individuals and abusing the majority by impeding freedoms. An aside is that the Constitution, the supreme law of the land, was just four pages long, in contrast to the new health care bill, which is over two thousand pages. They are selling this concept to a nation that desires its laws to be fair, kind, gentle and just, but what they are really doing is sending in more troops.

This new order of government is a political arrangement within both political parties, or what James Madison called a "faction." Madison defined faction as "a number of citizens, whether amounting to a majority or a minority of the whole, who are united and actuated by some common impulse of passion, or of interest, [adverse] to the rights of other citizens, or to the permanent and aggregate interests of the community."[10] This faction has been evolving and weaving itself in and out of the political ecosystem that is supposed to protect and preserve the framework of the Constitution. The faction, in this instance, is the evil predator infecting its American host. It is the very scorn absorbing freedom and liberty as darkness absorbs light.

Crossing Over—"Progressive Globalism"

Lurking in the chasm between republicanism and communism is a form of "government" that threatens every freedom we have ever fought to achieve. We are not a communist country…not yet. But we are no longer a republic either. This philosophy's cover-up can be found in both parties—Republican and Democrat. It is shrouded in such noble ideals as humanitarianism, peace and a sense of community. Progressive globalism uses the susceptability of nations to lace its deceptive doctrine with a deadly poison, wrapping its tentacles around society, entangling every thought, system and process.

Progressive globalism is the bridge to the final stage of society in which the sovereignty of the states has withered away and all the resources are distributed among the people as authoritarian leadership sees fit. In other words, the will of 250 million free people has fallen upon deaf ears as America "progresses" right into the embrace of communist China.

To some, this may sound just fine. One may call it an epiphany, even Paradise. *I don't have to make any more decisions!* For those who share this view, they have just accepted a dictatorship. They have slapped the chains of bondage on their own wrists, and are willing and eager to slap them on their neighbors. Shame on them! Abraham

Lincoln died to set them free.

Progressive globalism will destroy free will and free expression as it transitions society from what used to be into what it will become. It is the road that leads from freedom to bondage, from abundance to poverty and from life to death. It is the very opposite of all that is good and holy!

Progressive globalism looks like positive change. It sounds good, but…every thought will be zoned. Every job will be assigned. Every family will be arranged. Every trip will be approved. Every action will be controlled. All speech will be censored. As this globalist beast is allowed to gain strength, it will devour the very book you're reading.

Politics

In this era of dysfunctional families, mine was the exception. My parents were God-fearing, hardworking and law-abiding citizens who were faithful to each other and to the flag. But on the matter of politics, they didn't see eye to eye. My mother was a Massachusetts Republican, a kind of oxymoron, if you ask me. My father was a Chicago Democrat. I know what you're thinking, especially if you listen to the hard right. But my dad doesn't begin to resemble the picture that side of the aisle has painted of him.

In fact, my parents and I share similar views on life, debt, the economy, abortion, same-sex marriage and a whole host of other issues. Growing up in our house, I noticed that after my mother and dad had aired their views, they retired to their respective corners and continued to spar with each other. "So what if Clinton did what he did in the Oval Office!" my father would shout. "Do you Republicans think 'Tricky Dick' was any better?"

"Well, Richard Nixon would never stoop to anything so disgusting as what Clinton did!" my mother would counter. That's how some of the discussions went—as my sisters and I giggled in the adjoining room where we supposedly were watching cartoons.

Perhaps you can begin to understand now why I have always been somewhat conflicted when it comes to party loyalty. Prior to his retirement at the turn of the century, my father was a prominent labor representative. Since then he has been convicted by the Spirit of God and now refuses to stand by any candidate who supports the execution of those yet unborn, even if that candidate is from his beloved labor party.

I know my father feels as though he betrayed his party because during the 2008 general election, he voted for the presidential candidate who stood for life instead of his party candidate. However—and listen up here: In my opinion, his decision to champion life, based on his belief that God is the only One who can determine one's life span, will help to ensure that my father's spirit will continue to live long after his physical body expires. Did you get that? His immortality—the eternal state of existence after physical death—is much more important than dollar-an-hour pay raises, health care, gay rights or any other issue that is polarizing this nation.

So what is politics anyway? You may think you know the meaning of the word, but even the dictionary definition eludes the deeper and broader interpretation. According to Webster, politics is "the art or science of influencing or guiding governmental policy; the art or science concerned with winning or holding control over a government, etc."[11] Huh? Art *or* science? Even Webster confuses the issue, doesn't he?

Many believe that politics is a separate entity—something set apart, a force that directs and governs the actions of a people. Some even see politics as a diplomatic tool, a virtual chess game of strategies to outwit the opponent. Nothing could be further from the truth. In fact, politics is an unsystematic approach, subject to change without rules or structure. It is a process by which groups of people make decisions that affect their neighborhoods, schools, job security, and local, state and federal governments.

Actually, I would even go a step further and offer the Benesch definition: Politics is *your* belief systems and the manner in which you practice your morals, values and ethics—not the system of rules and regulations imposed by some group of professional politicians on Capitol Hill. If you're one of those people who has always considered politics to be some vague, obscure anomaly—one that only affects you when it's time to vote—guess again.

Coming from a politically divided family, I have observed the good and the evil in both parties, and I no longer trust either one of them. The Democrats claim to have taken up the cause of the poor, the disabled, the downtrodden and the working men and women of America, while the Republicans favor traditional family values, big business and national security. Every one of these issues on both sides is a noble endeavor, but the end does not justify the means.

To do good for the poor is not to impose more tax burdens on the wealthy. It is not to teach our babies sex in kindergarten in the name of education. It is not to allow pedophile priests to preach the love of God for His children. It is not to sanction starvation of other nations in the name of diplomacy or to oppress working men and women for the profit of a few. It is not to steal and call it taxation or to convince people to spend their hard-earned dollars in order to save the economy. It is not to redefine terms in order to fit a political philosophy. It is not to discriminate to achieve equality, nor is it to murder to prevent killing. It is not to erase God from society in the name of separating Him from government. Finally, and most importantly, it is not to kill the Prince of Peace to promote peace on earth.

So, pardon the expression, but "push does come to shove." By the way, we are there! In the absence of America's patriots, our nation's foundation has crumbled around us while today's "protectors," fathers and others sit on the sidelines, cheering on their political parties. We have neglected America's heritage, squandered her wealth and lost the Republic.

Some of you might say, "But, Jim, I'm still breathing, my family is still alive, and some of us still have jobs." Yes, but the tsunami is coming! Our very way of life is threatened and the warning has been sounded. Now we must reassess.

Benesch Bullets

To the leadership of the United States:

- Restore to the Republic its values and principles. Set aside progressive globalism and its foolish ways.
- Stop giving in to the dangerous enticements of communist practices.
- Prosecute war policies as if you yourself were physically confronting the enemy in battle. Do not treat death as a chess game.
- Stop "informal—social—diplomacy" and passive war policies.
- Seek victory in war, or seek peace.

To my fellow believers:

- Put feet to your prayers. Stop crawling into the polls to elect public officials who champion the causes of abortion, same-sex relations and beliefs that are not consistent with the Word of God.
- Stand up and stop doing wrong! Learn to do right. Seek justice and encourage the oppressed. (Read Isa. 1:16-17; 59:1-21.)

To my fellow citizens:

- Restore America's heritage—her founding principles.
- Reject "diverse groups" who only seek to steal American tradition.
- Do not ask Congress for war unless you are personally prepared to kill or be killed by the enemy.
- Seek peace, even when at war. We should not be involved in war for decades at a time.
- Victory requires those who are willing to suffer for a cause that is greater than themselves.

Many readers may find themselves confused at this moment asking, "How could we be anything but a 'democracy'? We still have free elections, haven't we?" Be careful not to confuse changes in leadership with democracy—for even Iran, China and Russia change their tyrannical authoritarian rulers from time to time. America's forefathers knew that.

Progressive globalism is not a peaceful government religion; rather, it is a dangerous predator that consumes all forms of democracy as it transforms nations into communist cultures—dictatorships. The United States is no longer a republic, for it has been lost in misconceptions and willful neglect!

Comforts lead to lethargy. Resist the dangerous enticements of certain comforts found in progressive globalism and use your common sense.

As the safety and prosperity of nations ultimately and essentially depend on the protection and the blessing of Almighty God; and the national acknowledgment of this truth is not only an indispensable duty which the People owe to Him, but a duty whose natural influence is favorable to the promotion of that Morality...without which social Happiness cannot exist nor the Blessings of a Free Government be enjoyed;...the United States of America are, at present, placed in a hazardous and afflictive situation, by the unfriendly Disposition, Conduct and Demands of a foreign power...Finally, I recommend, that on the said day, the Duties of Humiliation and Prayer be accompanied by fervent Thanksgiving to the Bestower of every Good Gift...by His Holy Spirit...that the Health of the Inhabitants of our Land may be preserved, and their Agriculture, Commerce, Fisheries, Arts and Manufactures be blessed and prospered; that the principles of Genuine Piety and Sound Morality may influence the Minds and govern the Lives of every description of our Citizens; and that the Blessings of Peace, Freedom, and Pure Religion may be speedily extended to all the Nations of the Earth. [1]

—President John Adams
Proclamation of Day of Fasting, Humiliation and Prayer
March 23, 1798

4

COMMON-SENSANOMICS

Remember the LORD *your God, for it is he who gives you the ability to produce wealth.*

—Deuteronomy 8:18

Facing the prospect of financial collapse, we took decisive measures to safeguard our economy…but the toll would be far worse if we had not acted…We will restore our economy… We will show the world once again the resilience of America's free enterprise system.[2]

—President George W. Bush
Farewell Address to the Nation
January 15, 2009

"Sin City" has begun opening its massive 16,979,000-square-foot, $8.5-$11 billion city center project that will stand as the new "Capital of Second Chances."[3] The financially troubled world's largest desert developer, Dubai World and MGM Mirage, began this joint venture at the site of the old Boardwalk Hotel and Casino in Las Vegas, Nevada. It is known as the largest privately funded venture of its type in United States history. Since its inception, much of the "private part" has been shifted to the "public part," though. "Public part?" you ask. You know, the part that is placed on the backs of the American taxpayers in the form of bonds. (See Chapter 5.)

As a development professional, I can relate. In America, the average cost per square foot to build a house is approximately $100 to $150, with the average home costing $270,000 for approximately 2,350 square feet, according to government statistics released at the beginning of December, 2009.[4] The largest church or commercial project I have ever participated in cost roughly $300 per square foot...and that's with all of the bells and whistles. So, with the Las Vegas project, I'm talking the "Taj Mahal" here. At $11 billion—and it will take every penny of that, I'm sure—the city center will cost $654.88 per square foot.[5] Oh, I think I've found the problem. No, my Republican friends, it is not the union. Union carpenters average about $26.50 per hour and, of course, time and a half for overtime.[6] But feel free to call me and let me know if you disagree, would you?

Early in December, 2009, Dubai World's $60 billion financial meltdown sent shockwaves across global stock markets as greedy corporate executives once again destabilized world economies.[7] Chairman of the board of one of the world's largest holding companies and developers, headquartered in Dubai, His Excellency Sultan Ahmed Bin Sulayem, and his executives/corporate gatekeepers sucked the life—profit and equity—out of the corporation. After pulling off this shady act, they placed what rightfully belonged to the company into the silver-lined pockets of the world's financial and political elites. You know, a little here to grease this squeaky Congressman and a little there to quiet the storm brewing over at the Capitol. From the beginning, Dubai World and corporate elites have spread tens of millions of dollars across the re-election landscape of America.

These corporate protectors stripped everything from the business, leaving tens of thousands of employees sitting at cubicles with their mouths wide open, like baby birds waiting for Mama Bird to bring their dinner. But these "protectors" aren't the only ones to commit such misdeeds. Many other corporations, banks, local, state and federal government agencies, too numerous to mention, have committed similar acts of malfeasance.

If the American voters continue to pander to selfish ambition, what is going to happen when money is just not available to feed, clothe and house their families? As in the case of Dubai World, when will everything of value be drained from all businesses and all governments? How will government tax revenue become available to pay for stimulus to sustain failed corporations that began as sustainable employment initiatives? Take a deep breath....

If our tax dollars and loans are what keep government projects on track—and I believe this is true—and we continue to lose American jobs at an unprecedented rate, who is going to pick up the tab for unemployment, cash for clunkers, home purchase incentives, road projects, infrastructure? And the list goes on.

Who's watching the gatekeepers who are stealing everything for themselves? How are they accomplishing this outrageous coup? How will the average American pay the mortgage, car note, student loan and other bills when governments and corporations run out of dough? If the nation no longer converts raw materials into finished products and exports those products across the globe, how will people make a living? Enter the economy…the way it is supposed to be, that is.

Keepin' It Real

I am not trying to be an alarmist, but I do hope I can convince you that you have been deceived and that America has caught something. Like pneumonia, that "something" could quickly develop into a worse malady, in this case the big "C"—Communism—which inevitably leads to economic death.

By my calculations, I have concluded that most American "private" and government ventures will fall victim to a similar fate as Dubai World, Citigroup, Bank of America, General Motors, Chrysler, Enron, Wachovia, Medicare, Medicaid. Don't believe me? Then consider these stats. According to the U.S. Government Accountability Office (U.S. GAO), the government will not only be broke by 2016, but given current and future revenue projections, Social Security, Medicare, Medicaid and the new healthcare initiative will be completely and totally unsustainable, beginning in fiscal year 2017.[8] That's October 1, 2016, folks, not January 1, 2017—a few short years down the pike.

Future failures of large or supersized banks and corporations are inevitable and will soon be sending their own ripples across the waters of the "richest" nation. Why? Over a hundred years ago, many of America's leaders began to look beyond the borders of this nation and set their eyes on world markets. Thus began political pandering, exchanging the rights and wealth of the people for special interests. Morals were neatly tucked away, the gloves came off and rules were lifted, paving the way for corporate and private wealth to be siphoned from working men and women and transferred to the elites of the world.

Up to this point, the world has shown deficit practices that are clearly not growing private ventures or the wealth of nations. On the contrary, business models of the day are destroying all entities, and that means everything. The very same economic models are creating circumstances that destroy currencies. Look at the European Union, Greece, Iceland, Portugal, Spain, Argentina[9]...or read Milton Friedman.[10]

In addition to deficit spending practices, there is an undercurrent, one that causes a shift in currency tides.

This shift creates the vacuum that sucks money from the shores and leads to the tidal wave of financial devastation discussed earlier. It is not only the "red alert" budgets that lead to fiscal failure. It is not just borrowing, stimulus, or irresponsibility that result in national bankruptcy. No, the trigger, the disturbance, the catastrophic cause that sets up collapse is all of these, and all of these triggers have been pulled.

Are you familiar with the term "coffin corner"? This term is used by pilots to denote the inevitability of a crash when the altitude (referred to as the plane's attitude) changes. No matter what the pilot does to correct the flight path and even though the engines are still functioning—he's going to fly the plane straight into the ground.

A World War II retired B-24 pilot recently told me that our economy is in a "coffin corner." America has a fully functioning economy—the engines are still working and trade is still flying along. No matter the altitude, however, and no matter how much money the people and the government spend—increase or decrease of economic stimulus and bailout—there is nothing that can be done to avert a crash. Like a "coffin corner," the pilots—leadership—of the United States government have not been following the rules of aerodynamics, or economics, in this case. Now, no matter what measures are taken to correct the economy, the U.S. dollar will go down in flames.

Obedience to God Equals Wealth

For me, death is not the end of life. Death is life without God. Without divine intervention, the economy is going to die. The only thing that will save the economy is returning to godly principles.

President Adams believed in Scripture verbatim, God's Word as is, not a watered-down version. Early Americans attributed their lucrative economy to our Father in Heaven, the Creator of everything. The Day of Fasting, Humiliation and Prayer decreed by our second president acknowledges the politics of their day, the principles found in the following Scripture: "You may say to yourself, 'My power and the strength of my hands have produced this wealth for me.' But remember the LORD your God, for it is he who gives you the ability to produce wealth, and so confirms his covenant, which he swore to your forefathers, as it is today" (Deut. 8:17, 18).

Ah, now it makes sense why many people are trying to forget our "forefathers"—the Founders. Here is the bottom line, as I see it, and why Adams's selfless love for his country drove him to lead as he did. "If you ever forget the LORD your God and follow other gods, and worship and *bow down to them,* [something our forty-fourth president has done] I testify against you today that you will surely be destroyed. Like the nations the LORD destroyed before you, so you will be destroyed for not obeying the LORD your God" (vv. 19, 20).

Adams was a patriot! He believed that the nation prospered because America's leaders never forgot the Source of *all* wealth. Unlike ours, their economy truly flourished and empowered the people who gave birth to this nation to fend off America's enemies, build the nation's capitol, and feed, clothe, and house America's families while simultaneously paying off the federal debt created by war.

I wonder why so many believe that early American life was easier and less complicated than it is today or that their generation was less loving, caring and generous. Today's leaders are nothing like those men of wisdom and vision. Current leaders are quick to point out, though, that complexities of the economy are so technical that common people like us can't begin to understand the systems and processes that keep a nation afloat. Oh, really?!

On the contrary, I submit that the inner workings of an economy are not that difficult to understand. Humor a broken-down ol' carpenter for a moment. An economy is simply "the careful use of material resources: frugality, providence, prudence, thrift, thriftiness. See Save."[11]

Are you shocked? Confused? Angry? You should be, especially if you've adopted the progressive world definition of *economy*, or have listened to the viewpoint of the "refined" mind—you know, the one of "peculiar" structure. The true definition is very different from what is being taught in school, colleges and/or businesses, but it doesn't get any easier than this: Economy is "using the national resources sparingly"—in other words, as needed.

My hope is that by now the truth is beginning to set you free.

Free Enterprise—Healthy Trade

Do you, the reader, actually believe that America is a republic whose primary engine of economic prosperity is built firmly on the foundation of free enterprise, or free trade? Please permit me to take this opportunity to dispel another rumor: Government involvement in our daily lives was *not* the intent of the Framers and is *forbidden* by the Constitution! Instead, the Framers established the Constitution to protect the individual and his/her right to private ownership. Trade is part of the economy in which individuals and corporations exchange what they have in abundance for items that are in scarce supply or are not available at all.

Free enterprise is "a system in which the means of production is privately owned. A system where goods and services are 'freely traded' and profits distributed to owners, risk takers who invest 'their' own money into technologies, diversification and capital investments for the chance opportunity to make profits."[12] Free trade and free enterprise are the "unrestricted" part of any economy, meaning *no government intervention.* In other words, free trade is the exchange of goods and services without government interference or government competition, which completes the free cycle.

Under the rules and principles stated by the Framers, therefore, the government owns nothing. What does a government have to offer other than that which rightfully belongs to the people from whom it was forcibly removed to begin with? Local, state and federal governments were never intended to be anything more than watchdogs to keep the system of ownership honest and to protect America's resources from predators.

In this chapter's lead-in by George W. Bush, the president is quite adamant about two things. In his opinion, (1) the economy needs to be financially safeguarded; (2) the world is going to see the resilience of America's free enterprise system. I disagree. These two statements are diametrically opposed. First, a true economy does not need to be financially propped up or safeguarded by the government, for a nation that uses its resources carefully needs only to protect them from people who seek to steal or destroy them. Secondly, the free enterprise system, mentioned by the former president, disappeared from America a long time ago. About the same time politicians began manipulating trade in the pursuit of a progressive globalism that favors those whom leadership deems worthy or who give to their campaigns.

It only makes sense that a free economy would be the approach that a free nation like America would choose. Free—not restricted. I think the Framers would have been quick to reject any restrictive policy.

Uh, oh! I can hear the voices of opposition, still

stuck on the definition of economy given above. So let's back up so we can move forward again.

Many believe that an economy is the way society exchanges resources, or the way we create personal and corporate wealth. At least that's the argument that came up in my kitchen just the other day. For some, an economy is the way that people go about the business of exchanging one thing of value for another. Others even believe that to exchange less for more is to increase one's chances of getting ahead, or living the "American Way." This is simply not true at all. Let me say it again: "Economy is the careful use of material resources." Nothing more. Nothing less.

The problem is that most people confuse the term *economy* with the word *trade*. That is understandable, because the economy has hijacked the news ever since December 2007. "Today the economy got a shot in the arm as lawmakers prepared to sign the largest bailout package in U.S. history." Bailout? Shouldn't someone have caught that little reference to a sinking ship? But nobody's saying anything about fixing the leak. "Every politician, corporate officer, illegal alien, child, and non-taxpayer into the lifeboat first!" All the while, the string quartet is playing "Hail to the Chief"!

Here is where it gets tricky. If a healthy economy is a frugal economy, then healthy trade is also frugal, or in balance. Just as there are three types of budgets, there are also three kinds of trade: surplus, balanced and deficit.

- **Trade Surplus** is the economic condition that occurs when a nation's exports—the products they produce and sell to other nations—are greater than the amount of imports—products produced by and purchased from other nations. This is good for the surplus nation, but throws the world economy out of kilter, because if resources are out of balance, poverty can result for the disadvantaged trade partner.

- **Trade Balance** occurs when a nation's imports and exports are equal. Ideologically speaking, this is the best posture for the world. The word *balance* just has a calming and soothing effect, doesn't it?

- **Trade Deficit** is created when a nation imports more than it exports. Like the nation's budget, America's trade policies are in the "red." Not good! Not good at all! You did know that only nine of every one hundred products available is made by Americans for Americans, didn't you? This type of policy paves the path of good intentions with debt. All nations that have deficit trade policies are creating debt tidal waves, because nations that fail to sustain themselves by producing what they need only survive by spending their currency. As I mentioned earlier, the European Union, Greece, Iceland, Portugal, Spain and Argentina continue to experience the folly caused by trade deficits. Once savings runs out, debt begins. Enter the various and notorious debt instruments known as mortgage, credit cards, SIVs, CDOs, treasuries, bonds, and so on.

Would you believe that in 2008, the nation's trade deficit was almost exactly the same as the budget deficit? After our brief lesson on trade deficits, do you believe that this is a coincidence? You decide, but personally, I believe that there is a direct correlation between the two. If you are one who thinks that the economy is a crap shoot or that gambling more of our future and savings is the way to "restore our economy," you may be a progressive.

Mixed Economy

Just for fun, let's review some of the lessons learned in Civics 101. If capitalism is free trade of privately owned goods and services, then communism is a government-controlled economy, absent free trade. A mixed economy is a little of both communism and capitalism. In actual fact, a mixed economy is progressive globalism, the transition from free trade found in a democratic republic, and controlled or confiscated trade practices found in communism.

As stated earlier, the Framers set the mixed economy into existence, for America, that is. Can you now see why the Jeffersonians were so vehemently opposed to the government's mixing its business with the people's right to a free economy? They wanted a constitution that would guarantee God's gift of free will to man.

The Framers, who had come out of oppressive governments, agreed to a mixed economy only as a temporary solution to pay off the federal debt. The mixed economy was never intended to go on to become Medicare, Medicaid, Obamacare, Social Security, welfare, corporate bailouts, stimulus or anything else, for that matter.

Economies are supposed to be frugal, and we all know governments are not! So when governments create wealth out of thin air to complete pet projects such as the United States Capitol, for example, the economy becomes mixed.

My hope is that I have driven my point home. This is the "tendency" of which Jefferson spoke. Anarchies, dictatorships, socialism are all forms of communistic government, where the majority of wealth is transferred from the people. Are you with me, or are you still in the dark?

Waste Not, Want Not

Step into the light! "Waste not, want not" is the common-sense approach to economics. God and the Framers were all about practicality. Remember, the Founding Fathers kept it simple; nothing could be easier to understand than the truth about what an economy really is—just common-sensanomics.

Free trade, savings and thriftiness create true wealth. A wealthy economy thrives where people and governments do not squander, or waste, anything. Common-sensanomic nations do not commit fraud or abuse themselves, their families, their friends, environments or resources. They do not pollute their rivers and lakes or the air they breathe. They do not kill their unborn in pursuit of blind ambition or to stroke their own egos. True savings comes as a result of common-sensanomics, and savings funds humanitarian missions to foreign lands! In that order, not in the order practiced by this nation. America is guilty of great waste. Borrow, borrow, borrow, waste, waste, waste, then lend, lend, lend. Then the cycle is repeated. Notice how the nation borrows and wastes and then passes the debt off in the form of taxes, something we will discuss in detail later.

Common-sensanomics is all about making do with what you have and living within your means. That's all there is to it. But who wants to hear that doctrine when life is short and most everyone prefers to "eat, drink and be merry"?

Wastanomics

"Live life large!" "The sky is the limit!" "Greed is good!" "Take everything you can…just don't get caught!" The Bible has another take on it. God calls it greed, lust and envy. The word I've coined is *wastanomics*. You don't really need a definition since this word is self-explanatory. But this concept has become the way of life for "a new America."

America is not the only nation to suffer from selfishness and greed. This is a global pandemic. Nearly every nation in the world is feeling the effects of economic decline brought about by wastefulness. That being said, the decline of an economy can be felt in great lack—lack of material resources, lack of savings, lack of necessary goods and supplies. Wasteful nations are lazy, reckless, overzealous and their people are internationally regarded as such.

Here is another example of wastefulness. Many banks took bailout money from Uncle Sugar in the form of TARP (Troubled Asset Relief Program) in 2008. Aided by congressional deregulation, bank executives were afforded the opportunity to steal taxpayer funds. They excused this practice by explaining to Congress and to the nation that it was the change of "rules" that allowed them to loot the banks they were hired to protect. That reminds me of a joke I once heard from a banker. "You know the best way to rob a bank? Own it." Are you laughing yet?

Let me share another recent headline. At the beginning of America's financial crisis, the CEOs of the three largest U.S. automakers and their cohorts loaded up some private, corporate-owned jets and flew to Washington to beg, I mean, to explain why they needed billions of taxpayer dollars to maintain their lavish lifestyles. Excuse me again, what I meant to say was: to avoid their having to lay off thousands of taxpayers!

The reason I mention these examples is to shed light on progressive policies and procedures that give way to the conduct causing America's economic calamity. Reaganomics, Voodoo economics, supply-side economics, or whatever you call it is a wasteful practice. The aforementioned examples demonstrate that more wasteful government programs like cash-for-clunkers, new-home incentives, cash-for-old appliances, Obamacare, etc. are not helping, but rather hindering recovery. Remember, "waste not, want not." Squander and waste, spending in haste and sooner, rather than later, America will destroy her world standing along with her currency.

I do have an idea or two…but it's not going to be easy.

Solution: "Made in the U.S.A."

My mother doesn't buy anything from China. In fact, she blames America's current economic slide on the Chinese. My parents have always been part of the "made in the U.S.A." clan, so for the most part, they buy locally.

If only 9 percent of America's products are made in the States, however, then where does my mom find the other 91 percent of what she needs? First, she makes everything she possibly can with her own hands. When I was a child, she was a stay-at-home mom, who cooked, cleaned, grew all of our vegetables, was the quintessential wife, tended to her five children, and made most of what we wore by hand. She can cook up a storm, read a book, watch her favorite television show and knit an afghan—all at the same time! Yep, she's a superstar, a real American legend, and I'm proud to call her my mom.

But at one time, all of our moms were like that. They made sure we were healthy and well fed. If we got into trouble, they whipped our butts. We respected them. They protected us, taught us, patched us up. They were not our friends. No, they loved us more than that!

Once my mother's children were old enough to fend for themselves and because the dollar wasn't going as far as it used to, she went back to work full-time at the local bank.

What my mom doesn't grow or make, she hopes to find through family and friends. If they can't help her, she's off to the local businesses in little Venice—Cape Coral, Florida, that is. She shops all of the local vendors for products produced right here in America. Then, if she still can't find what she needs, she surfs the Net to see what nation "other than" communist China might have the needed items.

America must keep as many of her greenbacks as possible right here at home. This can only be accomplished by purchasing products and services within the borders of the town, city and state where you reside. You may even want to get together with some others to start a business to produce a product instead of importing it.

We must restore the local economy. Purchasing from local businesses maintains a healthy economy. God commands us to take care of the family first—that means your wife, your children, then anyone else in the immediate family. It is to be done in that order, and not the progressive priority. Then you take care of the church, and that doesn't mean simply throwing money in the offering plate as it goes by.

We are in a juggernaut. Getting away from the local economy has applied a massive, unstoppable force to the economy, and it is now crushing everything in its path—including the value of the dollars in your pocket. But if you use resources sparingly and purchase goods and services offered right here in the U.S.A., the strength of this opposing force can possibly stave off the world economic collapse.

I know, many would prefer the government to fix the problem. Sorry, but you're going to have to go it alone on this one. The government can't fix it with tariffs, duties or embargos. You must purchase everything you have the ability to purchase from the U.S.A. You must start with buying and trading with friends and family, then from local stores and vendors. If you can't find it locally, look within your state, then anywhere in the country. If you can't find it there, you must look to America's allies to help meet your needs. If they don't have it, maybe you should consider doing without. Purchasing products and services from America's enemies is as good as putting a gun or a bomb in their hands.

2024—Dollar No More

Right about now, many readers may be thinking to themselves, *Why did we ever stop trading and exchanging one item of value for another item of equal or lesser value? Wouldn't we have been better off with the barter system?*

Well, there is a lot more to trading than meets the eye. While I believe in the philosophy of "less is more," I also understand that life is quite complicated. This is certainly the case when it comes to the basic physiological needs—food, water and shelter—and other desires of civilization. Truth be known, most of us do not have the ability to provide all of our needs. Take medicine, for example. We may be able to grow our own food, fetch water from a well and build a house, but most of us can't perform a triple bypass surgery.

The need for specialization results from human inability to provide everything necessary for survival, which results in trading. With a barter system, though, people have to expend a lot of energy to find someone else that has what they need. Also, with today's technology, some people have specific skills for specialized areas, while the gifts and talents of others are perceived as having little to no worth.

Whether it is perceived or not, perception is

reality and the reality is that America chose to trade in dollars. The dollar is our currency and currency is a unit of exchange, a measure of value.[13] The U.S. dollar is portable purchasing power, something people can stick in their pockets and take with them to the marketplace to exchange for consumables. Currency—in America's case, the dollar—makes transactions in the marketplace much easier.

Why the dollar? Gold and silver are heavy to carry and even harder to divide into proper portions. Nothing else makes good sense...unless we go back to "will work for food." So, the dollar it is. Besides, it really isn't the dollar's fault that it is losing value, so let's move on to the real culprit.

Recent U.S. government reports reveal that the phrase "In God We Trust," emblazoned on the currency, will soon be all America has to trust in. The U.S. dollar currently in use is derived, for the most part, from the Federal Reserve Act of 1913. Although the United States has always used some form of currency, the 1913 dollar was worth just that. Today, however, the greenback seems to be looking a bit pale. With the value gradually slipping a little more with each passing month, it begs the question: How much is the dollar really worth, and will it ever become completely worthless?

The answer to the first question: "Seventeen cents." The answer to the second: "Nobody really knows." Taking even the most conservative estimate, over a ninety-seven-year period from 1913 through 2009, the American currency has lost 83 percent of its value, or 83 cents on every dollar. Some experts claim that the dollar bill is worth only four to five cents.[14] But the Consumer Price Index (past and present), supply and demand information, international monetary trends, imports/exports, credit expansion, current as well as future national debt burdens prove my theory.

I have been able to construct a mathematical model, which demonstrates how inflation has adversely affected U.S. currency and, in addition, projects future currency value. Mathematically, that's .8556 cents for every year the Fed has used the dollar. So, according to my calculations, it will take another 14½ years, on paper, for the dollar to become worthless.

I know, there I go again, preaching gloom and doom, but you can't dispute the facts. Math is an exact science. Here is something that can be challenged, though. Mathematically, America can enjoy the dollar until the summer of 2024, but I believe the economic grim reaper will take it from us sooner than that. I believe that the global economic forces of China, India, Russia, the Middle East and Venezuela, combined with the wastanomic policies of America and her government, should kill the dollar by January 1, 2017.

Here's why: The dollar never really changes…for the most part, that is. You hear about the depreciation of the dollar, or inflation, but what is really going on? The dollar still looks the same, feels the same, has the same president's face printed on it. Could it be that the dollar is really only worth seventeen cents? Well, yes and no.

Robbing the Dollar—Inflation

Compared to the 1913 dollar bill, today's dollar is worth only seventeen cents. It is inflation, combined with a lack of global confidence, however, that has caused the decrease in its value.

I'm only going to talk about inflation here, but keep in mind that there are other dynamics working in concert to completely destroy the dollar. Some reasons have already been explained and I will reveal even more in future chapters. No, no, no, it is not a conspiracy, but the economic forces of supply and demand that are responsible for inflation.

While inflation is good for the Fed, it is not so good for the homeowner or businessman. If the dollar becomes worthless, whom does the Fed have to pay back anyway? Well, nobody, of course. Let's face it, if I give you a dollar today, it is only worth seventeen cents, comparatively speaking, but because of inflation, it will only be worth sixteen cents around a year from now.

In America, inflation is a continuing rise in the general price level, usually attributed to an increase in the volume of money and credit relative to the available goods and services.[15] The same is true for the world. Isolated nations experience the same inflationary effects, as well. When price levels rise, each unit of measure found in currency buys fewer goods and services. In other words, one consequence of an increase in the cost of products is the erosion of the purchasing power of the dollar. Now you can see why fighting for a dollar-an-hour pay raise adversely affects the value of that dollar. It seems as though we may be fighting a battle that can't be won. But stick with me.

Supply and demand are the economic forces that inflate the cost of goods and services and deflate the dollar. *Supply,* in a marketplace—free or otherwise—is the availability and amount of goods and services for trade.[16] *Demand* is the number of people or other entities that have purchasing power and the ability to consume goods and services.[17] *Inflation* occurs when there is not enough supply to fill the demand, which almost always results from too much money being available to too many people through credit and not through the free exchange of goods and services. When governments have purchasing power, it interferes with natural market signals and can intensify inflation.

Look at it like this: If you have $100,000 and I have exactly the same amount of money, who will get the $100,000 Porsche for sale if we both show up at the same time to purchase it? Tick tock, tick tock. The answer is… nobody. That Porsche is not going anywhere until you or I put up some extra cash. Same example. If you pull out an additional grand, and I do too, who gets the car? You see where we're going, right? The Porsche is going home with me! Just kidding. The person who comes up with enough cash or credit to out-purchase the other guy will drive that baby home!

Let's run this out: If all I have is the $101,000, and you are willing to sign a loan for, let's say another $10,000 and I'm not, then the car of my dreams goes home to your garage.

This is not brain surgery, and it works the same way for every good and service everywhere in the world. Supply and demand does not discriminate. My hope is that it has become clearer that credit also intensifies inflation.

So, how has inflation gotten so out of control? Quite simply put, too many people have been artificially given the ability to compete for a limited supply of goods and services. In other words, there just never seems to be enough product to go around, and there is too much stimulus cash, easy loans, payday advances, credit cards, 90-day, 120-day, 360-day same-as-cash programs, title for cash, equity loans, personal lines of credit, grants, student loans, scholarships, stipends, welfare, food stamps, government free this and government free that programs and an unimaginable number of ways to get what people want today, without having to pay for it or exchange something of value for it. In a nutshell: Obtaining consumables without exchanging labor or something else of value has caused the dollar to crash and will stick the last nail in its coffin within the next several years.

One more major factor that greatly affects supply and demand and causes inflation is population expansion. The reality is that more people are being born, legally and illegally immigrating to this country, and most are living longer than ever before. In fact, the numbers are so great, many systems and processes will need to be changed just to keep up.

With the world increasing in numbers at an exponential rate, there is a population explosion. And governments just keep ensuring that their special interests are receiving benefits without regard to the ability to pay for the benefits received, which results in higher debt and/or higher taxes.

Deflation

I want to touch on this subject because deflation is a knight in shining armor. It is a dynamic that helps restore the value of currencies and the primary reason why the financial downturn that began in 2007 reversed its course. *Deflation* is the decrease in the price of goods and services, which results in an increase in the real value of money.[18] Deflation has the exact opposite effect on the value of currencies as inflation and can prevent economic collapse.

Forget what you have heard the government or

any analyst say. Deflation is good for the United States of America and the world. In addition, deflation can help restore the way other superpowers view the dollar.

My wife and I purchased a new car just before Christmas of 2008. It was a time in U.S. history when automobile dealers couldn't move their products. Deflation allowed us to purchase the car for $10,000 less than that same car sold for only six months later. The lesson here is this: Deflation provided me, the consumer, with the ability to purchase a product at its real value. Not so good for the owner of the car dealership, although I'm certain he didn't get scraped up much during the transaction.

After the stimulus packages hit the streets of America, though, inflation set right back in, resulting in that same car becoming unaffordable. In addition, my tax burden was lower, and Uncle Sam's assault on my family wealth was thwarted.

Now, I hope it has become clear as to why the government does nothing to end inflation but everything to accelerate it...and why the government takes no action to help deflation along. To my dear friend Don, here is the conspiracy of the Federal Reserve for the benefit of the United States Government. Uncle Sugar lost out, in my state anyway, on $1,000 in additional taxes just because the car sold for less than usual. If deflation is allowed to take hold of America, its people will be able to afford what they need without pay raises, loans or government intervention.

Conversely, if the government doesn't keep inflation on a steady track north, then tax revenues and campaign contributions will be on the decline. Am I getting through to you yet? When the Congress voted in the stimulus packages, they hit us with a triple whammy— they taxed us for bailouts, taxed us on the bailouts and then taxed us on the inflation caused by the bailouts.

Benesch Bullets

To the leadership of the United States:

- Stop mixing government activities with markets. Government purchases and influence over the exchange of goods and services short-circuit market signals, drive up costs and lead nations to communism.
- Stop stimulus spending and bailouts!
- Stop inflationary practices and focus on deflationary policies. We "the people" are on to you. Inflation is an extremely oppressive method of increasing government treasuries and campaign war chests.
- Balance trade. At the minimum, 50 percent of products available in U.S. markets must be American-made. Trade imbalance is killing the dollar and putting guns and bombs into our

enemies' hands.

- Apply the "true" definition of economy to America—"the careful use of material resources: frugality, providence, prudence, thrift, thriftiness. See Save."

To my fellow believers:

- Purchase products and services from other believers. This is an absolute must! Hire godly contractors and service providers.
- Remember, all wealth comes from God, not the government, banks, corporations or others.
- Stop listening to those who have separated God from government.
- Return divine providence to all public places.

To my fellow citizens:

- Borrow only for necessary items. This will slow inflation and cause deflation, which restores the real value of money.
- Purchase goods and services made by Americans. Do not purchase products from America's enemies. For your convenience, I have provided a list of America's allies. (See Appendix A.)
- Stop wasteful practices. Consider donating

items you no longer want or need to those less fortunate.

- Recycle. If your local, county and state do not have programs, recycle on your own.
- Change your lightbulbs over to compact florescent. The Benesch household saves $30 per month in electricity since switching from incandescent lightbulbs.
- Consider eating a left-over meal for lunch each day and one night per week. Leftovers save a family of four, on average, $10-$20 dollars per week. That's about $520 to $1040 per year, or more—money you won't have to borrow. You can laugh, but please respect this advice from my mother, passed on to her from my grandmother.

Inflation is caused by wasteful behaviors and results from not exchanging one good or service for another good or service of equal or lesser value. My hope is that you can see what really causes inflation, the harm inflationary behaviors produce and an effective cure for America's economy.

The key to true wealth is frugality, trading less for more without creating debt. Now, let's move on to one of the most contradictory, misconceived and harmful national practices.

*W*hereas the Congress of the United States, by a joint resolution of the two Houses, have signified a request that a day may be recommended to be observed by the people of the United States with religious solemnity as a day of public humiliation and prayer;...that the hearts of all should be touched with the same and the eyes of all be turned to that *Almighty Power* in whose hand are the welfare and the destiny of nations:... *[therefore we]*render *Him* thanks for the many blessings He has bestowed on the people of the United States; that He has blessed them with a land capable of yielding all the necessaries and requisites of human life, with ample means for convenient exchanges with foreign countries; that He has blessed the labors employed in its cultivation and improvement;...He has blessed the United States with a political Constitution rounded on the will and authority of the whole people and guaranteeing to each individual security, not only of his person and his property, but of those sacred rights of conscience so essential to his present happiness and so dear to his future hopes.[1]

—President James Madison
Proclamation on Day of Public Humiliation and Prayer
July 23, 1813

FROM NET WORTH TO "NET WORTHLESS"

Not long after that, the younger son got together all he had,
set off for a distant country and there squandered his wealth
in wild living. After he had spent everything,
there was a severe famine in that whole country,
and he began to be in need.

—Luke 15:13, 14

Today I sent a message to the Congress, pointing out...the
serious domestic economic crisis with which we are threatened.
Some call it "inflation"...and others call it a "rise in the cost
of living," which...means essentially what a dollar can buy.[2]

—President Franklin Delano Roosevelt
Fireside Chat 22: "Inflation and Food Prices"
September 7, 1942

"Greenbacks," "Benjamins," "dough," "moola"—no matter what you call it, cash is king. When society and governments determine that wealth should be exchanged in a measure or weight other than silver, gold or some other valuable commodity, worthless paper and coins are usually produced to represent wealth—money, or fiat currency, as it is known.

Some say that money "is a unit of account, a store of value-portable power." [3] Currency is just that. Every day, people go about their business, exchanging hundreds of millions of dollars worth of worthless fiat—an intrinsically useless object, money—for everything from batteries to Rolex watches. These same people also accept this instrument of wealth in exchange for a hard day's work. The only problem with the marketplace is that there never seems to be enough dough to go around.

In an effort to put an end to insufficiency, the world's financial geniuses have created a plan to outwit the market and bring the illusion of wealth to another level. In their attempts to achieve the unachievable, these figureheads of fortunes have given birth to credit, which has caused their family storehouses to explode with more than they could ever need.

Remember our discussion of inflation in Chapter 4—how too much money and too little supply result in the destruction of currency? Credit expansion is another culprit and results from the increase in lending for the purchase of goods and services. Keep in mind—I'm not saying that this is harmful to the value of money, in and of itself, that is. If government replaces free market activity with unnatural or artificial market forces, however, or individuals and businesses live beyond their means, you have credit on steroids!

Credit expansion is phony economic growth or what I like to call an "artificial economy." This dysfunctional economic practice occurs when government mixes with the economy by providing jobs, services and other programs to force the market and the people to behave in a specific manner. That manner is mandated by the powers that be, and those powers are part of the progressive global movement. Unquestionably, this is the reason why the dollar and the people of America are facing a calamity the likes of which this nation has never known.

Ludwig Heinrich Edler von Mises was an Austrian economist, philosopher and author who had a significant influence on the modern libertarian movement. He believed that "true governments can reduce the rate of interest in the short run. They can open the way to credit expansion by the banks. They can thus create an artificial boom and the appearance of prosperity. But such a boom is bound to collapse soon or late and bring about a depression."[4]

I know many people who believe that government involvement in the economy is necessary. I don't disagree that the helpless, the disadvantaged, the innocent and the downtrodden must be protected—but not to the extent that Bill Clinton did. By allowing those with no income to experience home ownership, he only accomplished inflation and default.

When the dollar fails, then what? Foreclosures are already at a thirty-year high. If you think we are in trouble now, just wait until the currency collapses and the survival of the fittest kicks in! The currency must be protected at all costs, and in a way that completely defies modern-day logic.

Oh, I'll bet I know what you're thinking. *You're out of your mind, Benesch! If the currency collapses, the wealthy—the bankers, brokers and financial elites—won't get paid, so they certainly wouldn't participate in expansion practices.* Not true, unfortunately. People who broker credit earn their money at the very beginning of a transaction; they don't collect during the life of a loan. Although there are some exceptions to this rule, what I am about to tell you applies to America's credit policies most of the time.

Let me give you an example. The money you borrow from banks, mortgage brokers and other lenders is borrowed from somewhere else. (We'll cover the "somewhere else" in the next section, so stick with me.) Just remember, creditors have creditors, not money.

Let's say you want to purchase a new $200,000 home, but you only have $12,000 in savings. Once you find a house and haggle with the owner to bring the price down, you will need to obtain a mortgage so that you can make the payments in monthly installments, something you can afford. You know that there will be some closing costs that will come in the form of a down payment, so let's say that the bank requires 5 percent down and 1 percent closing costs. Perfect! You have exactly what you will need to seal the deal and purchase a $200,000 home for the $12,000 cash you will bring with you to the closing table.

When you sit down at the mortgage closing, that hard-earned $12,000 for your new house won't be paid to the lender. No, it will be paid to the sharks—oh, pardon me, I mean, *professionals*—for the privilege of living beyond your means. Your involvement in the credit expansion cycle is now complete and your cash savings just transferred to the wealthy banker and/or mortgage broker. Once the transaction is complete, they will bundle your mortgage in with several hundreds or thousands of other loans and sell them to the next sucker—oops, *lender*—in some other form of credit instrument.

Even if you go broke and are unable to pay the mortgage, it won't hurt them one bit. They made their money at the closing—your $12,000—when the transfer of wealth took place. This is why interest rates continue to fall and refinance is so important to banks and brokers; the more you refinance, the more cash these organizations collect at the closings. It's that simple. You might as well not even try to out fox the foxes.

Life Cycle of Finance

It's time to tell the truth about fiscal policy. In the beginning, America was a vast land of opportunity, where people had to grow it and make it in order to survive. There were no shortcuts. Life was simple, yet seemingly unfair and brutal at times. If animals or nature didn't do you in, the common cold just might.

Life was lonely for explorers who ventured out on their own, but a family could virtually stake their claim anywhere they decided to hang their hats. Thus, the cycle began: up before dawn to feed the livestock, tend the crops, make and wash the clothes, hunt or fish for dinner, educate oneself with a book or two and the Bible, and early to bed after prayers and family time.

As the population increased, things began to get a bit complicated. The open ranges a man once called his own backyard were now shared by many others who wanted a slice of paradise.

What does that have to do with the price of tea in China? Everything, if you can't produce it for yourself. We are no longer an agrarian society;[5] instead, we count on the local grocery store to supply our food. Now the nation depends on agriculture—products grown here or imported from other countries—for its very survival. In addition, there is the need for transportation, housing, clothing and a litany of consumables which individuals can no longer produce themselves. Enter currency and the world of big finance.

The financial system starts out like this: American needs and desires drive the requirement for money. Individual and societal needs—often perceived needs rather than *real* needs—have given rise to creative financing schemes.

This is how it works: Let's use that $200,000 home purchase as our example again. The need/desire for a new house boosts the economy temporarily as the services of builders and contractors are called into play. If the purchaser of the home doesn't have the money to pay cash for it, and if that person perceives the home as a necessity, he/she will more than likely finance it. I know; I've been there, done that.

The loan starts with the lender, or what most call the mortgage broker—a business established specifically to make property loans or other kinds of loans. The lender could also be a bank, credit union, savings and loan, or a whole host of other lending institutions. But no matter what they call themselves, their objective is the same: to provide a financial vehicle to enable you to become a homeowner. To us common folk, that vehicle is called a mortgage, but in the financial world, it is also known as the Deed of Trust.

The Deed of Trust "outlines the principal loan amount (the actual cost of the home), the interest, and any other agreement that is part of a loan—which includes the payment amount and length of the loan."[6] Most importantly, it conveys ownership of your property to someone or to some other institution until the loan is paid off. Hence, the word *trust*. When an individual purchases a home and finances that home, it becomes the property of someone else—held in trust—until the home loan is paid in full (interest and all). In other words, you do not own it! It is not an asset. It is a liability, debt or millstone, if you will. It is not your net worth, but more than likely, your net "worthless."

Allow me to explain what I mean by worthless. I know of a new 3-bedroom, 2-bath, 2-car garage home in Cape Coral, Florida, that originally sold for $299,000 just a few short years ago. Today, that same home is priced at $100,000. That's about a 70 percent decrease in value. So don't let anyone convince you to get caught up in the net worth game if you are really interested in becoming an example of true wealth. People need a roof over their heads—not a millstone chained around their necks, and credit is just that.

Mortgages are pretty tricky, and it would be wise to consult an attorney before biting the bullet of finance. A Deed of Trust could cost a buyer everything, especially if it contains a "due on sale" or a "demand or acceleration clause," which changes the long-term payment arrangements—even if the borrower pays on time. I have a friend in real estate who was bankrupted as a result of these "clauses." You may even have one in your home mortgage; but as long as the economy doesn't go bust, you will probably get to keep your home. If the dollar goes south—and according to my mathematical calculations, it will—I would suggest that you pack up your china and silverware, because big brother—oops, I mean big *business*—is coming for the house.

Remember, every time a financial instrument is created, a very large fee is paid to the institution that creates the credit/debt instrument. This is also one of many ways government bailout and stimulus money enter the economy. The government really just pays figureheads of fortunes to pay employees—out of credit expansion proceeds, your tax dollars—to push paperwork on their behalf. Now that's taking the lemons of life and making lemonade!

This cycle is repeated over and over again—so many times, in fact, that during the foreclosure run in 2009, the Cook County Sheriff in Illinois refused to serve eviction notices, because no one could prove who really owned the homes or rental properties being foreclosed.[7] Even the figureheads of fortune don't know which one of them owns many of the "mortgage trusts."

That being said, the goal of the financial and political elite of America is to make sure that the original credit instrument—in this case, the $200,000 home—winds up in some type of government security, such as a revenue bond—in other words, onto the backs of the taxpayers. You see, financial heads of fortune have figured out how to get "the people" to finance their cars, their homes and everything else, without ever having to put out a single dime of their own money. In fact, they use the taxpayers, or at least their promise—and, incidentally, that of their children and grandchildren—to perpetuate a system that is actually nothing more than a loan to the people by the people.

In other words, homeowners are really just borrowing money from themselves. If that doesn't make sense to you, you might be a progressive.

Americans are the lender of last resort, and the government has created several vehicles to ensure that this will happen. We're chasing our tails for nothing. Does stimulus now compute? Have you ever asked yourself why we are paying those fat cats on Capitol Hill, Wall Street and the Fortune 500 for something that really belongs to us? How stupid! The mortgage broker and every other financial layer is just a façade for Americans to lend money to each other.

The Epic Bubble

These days, it seems that credit, not money, makes the world go round. Before you, the borrower, can borrow money for that house and car, special credit vehicles must be created in the form of collateralized debt obligations (CDOs), structured investment vehicles (SIVs, first created by Citigroup, 1988), bonds (private and municipal, many of which are tax-free), Treasury notes (T-notes, one way the U.S. government borrows), and so on. Many of these credit instruments are known as derivatives, which is just a word that signifies certain credit instruments that derive their value from another financial security, such as interest rate swaps or credit default swaps (CDS).[8] If you are in a bank and hear "credit default swap," duck!

Please keep in mind that, unlike your home mortgage, derivatives back other forms of credit instruments and not hard assets. Allow me to put it like this: If you gave someone a promissory note for ten thousand dollars to pay for a motorcycle and then gave them another ten-thousand-dollar promissory note and used the first one as collateral, that's a simplified example of a derivative. The first promissory note is backed by an asset, and the second is backed by nothing at all. This is the world of the financial and political elite. I hope you can now see why the elites of the world have become disconnected from the way the rest of us have to live!

This is important, so please pay special attention: **There is over $57 trillion in outstanding debt in the United States of America alone.** You've seen this number earlier in this book, but it bears repeating since it appears to me that many people are either brain dead, numb or oblivious to its significance. Most of the $57 trillion is in the form of some type of credit expansion—derivatives, SIVs, etc.

Why should this number be significant to you? Because it means, for example, that you don't own your house. The bank doesn't even own the bank. The same goes for City Hall. In fact, over 90 percent of ongoing stimulus projects are not cash-and-carry capital improvements. "So what?" you ask.

Let me put it this way: If a new $37 million prison project or municipal water project failed, who would get the asset to cover the default on the loan? The financially elite holding the bonds, that's who. In other words, China,

France, Germany, Canada, Saudi Arabia, Dubai, United Arab Emirates and who knows how many others. And because most of the project is funny money/credit, they will pick up City Hall for about one-tenth of its value, when it is all said and done. Sometime in the not-too-distant future, some king, emperor or dictator may be determining your water bill for you…from the desert!

Listen up. During the S&L crisis, banks and all of their assets, which includes savings account balances, were sold to financial elites for as little as $1,500. That's one thousand five hundred dollars. One figurehead of fortune invested only $1,000 to purchase fifteen failing S&Ls. The government reimbursed him $1.85 billion in federal credit expansion subsidies.[9] I could have afforded several banks; how come I wasn't offered that opportunity? Easy. It's because I'm not a king, an emperor or part of the elite class in America or the world. If I were, I probably wouldn't be writing this book; someone else would be doing it for me, and I would be paying him with your tax dollars.

But here is where it gets even scarier for me. The world has over $600 trillion in derivatives and other credit,[10] and less than 3 percent of those loans are backed by hard assets.[11] That would be like getting a mortgage without having to secure the loan with your house. Somewhere, someone has just signed a piece of paper to take what you now own if the credit system ever falls apart.

Within a few short years, in an effort to pull the

world out of its current dilemma, it is believed that a new debt amount called the "quadrillion" will be ushered onto the financial scene. Like the dissonant sounds of a first-year aspiring Mozart, credit creates noises that make the most sympathetic cringe and beg for mercy, because if there is something a crotchety creditor hates more than empty pockets, it's a person who fails to pay his bills.

"Bookies" for Banks

Now is the perfect time to explain what happened to the "economy" in December 2007 that triggered what some have called "Great Depression II." As I have already said, the credit instruments we have talked about have no real hard assets backing them. Your home mortgage was re-packaged with other mortgages before you moved in and was sold to brokerages, which combined them into one derivative form or another and sold them as bonds. Then these bonds were gathered together and sold as another credit instrument, and so on, until one day the bond-rating agency—something like a "bookie" for banks and other credit organizations—stepped in and said, "These credit vehicles are worthless."

Take the Katrina disaster, for example...or the fires in Southern California...or the oil spill in the Gulf Coast...or the floods in Nashville...or "the inevitability of war." Some natural or man-made disaster can rip through an area and take out whole blocks, neighborhoods or cities, destroying the hard assets that originally created the package. After a war, hurricane, tornado or other catastrophe, every financial transaction that found its roots in a package of mortgages is now worthless. You may be saying to yourself, *Well, that's why there is insurance.* Yes, and insurance companies are taking premium payments and purchasing derivative packages.

When the financial markets began to have problems, it was because one of the largest bond rating agency analysts reported to his/her boss and the U.S. government that many of the credit issues outstanding would more than likely default in the near future. So the bonds and credit instruments were downgraded, which required refinancing of several "creative" financial agreements…well, who wants to finance manure anyway? Currently, many credit obligations have just been parked into government-created "stimulus" programs. But that's just not enough to prop up the big world of finance.

Now there is the need for new government initiatives like health care and cap-and-trade bills to sustain finances from everything from credit cards to home mortgages. Do you really think that a government that would wreak financial terrorism on its people gives a hoot about their health care, liberties, freedoms, welfare or anything else? Or are you, like me, on to the fact that "progressives" serving on both sides of the political aisle have given in to the insatiable appetite for spending their way into the re-election halls of political idolatry. This is treason...

The apparent goal of this progressive government is to continue credit expansion, which leaves no doubt as to its outcome....at least, that is the correct conclusion of the expert on credit expansion—Ludwig von Mises.

If we are truly going to keep ourselves safe from the calamity of credit, though, we must avoid irresponsible behaviors that lead to insolvency and cause bankruptcy.

Bankruptcy

Many blame the fall of nations on lack of regulation. No, no, no, not so. It is the lack of self-control that leads nations down the slippery slope of financial calamity.

What calamity are you talking about now, Jim? I'm talking about the one that comes with not being able to pay the credit expansion bill. Bankruptcy provides U.S. court protection to those who become insolvent— unable to meet specific financial obligations—and is available to individuals, corporations, farmers, fishermen, municipalities, and public agencies—including foreigners.

So you didn't think the government could file bankruptcy, did you? You may have even thought that all of this financial collapse talk wasn't even possible. The point I want to make about the bankruptcy of the United States of America is not that the president goes to a hearing to put his creditors on notice that Washington, D.C. can no longer pay its debts. The way a nation washes its creditors is through the collapse of its currency. You are the United States and the dollar is America's currency. China, Germany, Great Britain and Japan are the creditors for the federal government—and you, in case you missed that point.

I want to share a little-known, or little-discussed, fact. Every currency, since the first person wrote on a clay tablet, has failed because of fiscal irresponsibility. Just like the behaviors of today's Congress. Over the past several thousand years, nations have used many different currencies to represent wealth. All of them have failed— 100 percent of them, no exceptions! When a currency fails, it results in national bankruptcy, which means that other nations no longer accept the bankrupt nation's expression of wealth, or value of exchange.

Let's review the six types of bankruptcy:

1. **Chapter 7** is a personal, sole proprietorship, partnership and corporate liquidation of assets to pay creditors, commonly called "a wash." I'm not going to get technical, nor am I giving any legal advice here; any reader considering bankruptcy should consult with an attorney. This is strictly information that is provided to suggest what happens when individuals, corporations and governments are unable to pay their bills. The courts stop collection of the debt you owe. Your debt is not forgiven, but state laws govern bankruptcy and provide for the federal courts to stop

all collection procedures and release people from the responsibility to pay back creditors.

2. **Chapter 9** is for municipalities and public agencies. Courts have tremendous latitude to do as they wish to resolve issues when government organizations lack the ability to pay their bills.

3. **Chapter 11** provides corporations with collection protection from creditors during a flexible period of time, which allows corporations the ability to get back on their feet without completely liquidating or shutting their doors. There is a requirement that at least some debt—usually a very small part—must be paid. General Motors washed tens of billions of dollars in their Chapter 11, which included the shareholders.

4. **Chapter 12** is a special bankruptcy provision for family farmers and family fisherman to hold off creditors for a specific period of time, which allows these people extra time to make up for years of drought and other natural calamities.

5. **Chapter 13** is almost exactly the same as Chapter 11, except that it is designed for individuals and other non-corporate, or government entities, and family businesses not covered by Chapter 12.

6. **Chapter 15,** which is the most recent and frightening financial turn of events, involves cross-border disputes. My hope is that you see the "globalism" here. The bankruptcy code has recently been changed

to allow foreigners not only to default on their debts to the United States and her citizens, but to be given protection by our courts and Constitution. U.S. citizenship is no longer a requirement to receive the benefits for which you and I pay. The problem is that foreigners aren't required to be accountable. I can see the future world court taking shape and exposing Americans to the foreign "injustice" of other communist nations.

Here is the most important point: Every individual, corporation, public agency and so on is eligible for bankruptcy protection. No exceptions. The reason is that most everyone falls prey to creditors at some point. Although not everyone needs to be protected by the courts, if there were no regulation, there is no limit to what creditors would do to debtors. Debtor prisons were very popular at one time, and with bankruptcy protection, the United States is a territory that can never be victimized by unscrupulous financial elites.

Personally, I am struck by the Holy Bible's take on debt: "Let no debt remain outstanding, except the continuing debt to love one another" (Rom. 13:8). God also intended for debt to be paid or forgiven every seven years, and for us to treat others as we ourselves would want to be treated if we were ever unable to pay our bills. Keep in mind that given the current fiscal direction, spending, monetary policies and the irresponsibility of

U.S. government and world officials, America is sure to become bankrupt—probably by October 1, 2017, but definitely during the next decade. There is nothing the government is doing to stop it!

Credit allows people the ability to have what they want without having to pay for it at the moment. On the other hand, credit is destroying your dollar, and contrary to what the current president and previous presidents have said, their actions are killing America's currency. As Washington stated in his Farewell Address to the Nation, "Use [credit] as sparingly as possible." Keep in mind that the dollar has been losing better than ¾ of a cent per year and is worth only about seventeen cents. The only way to reverse this trend is to put an end to inflation, create conditions of deflation and begin using resources responsibly or as needed.

Irresponsibility is the reason the dollar doesn't go as far as it used to, why foreclosures are so high, and why the government is intervening in the economy. Wasteful and irresponsible people seem to be the new breed of American, nothing like our strong, stalwart forefathers.

The Good News

I know that much of this book is not sugar-coated. Like castor oil, the truth can be hard to swallow. But America is mortally wounded. I don't know how else to say it. Her moral fabric is ripped to shreds. She is badly scraped up from all of her fights. The dollar is on the brink of collapse. Lady Freedom has lost her luster. The republic...well you know how I feel about that. Even worse, in my opinion, is that the nation is moving so close to communism that most people know it is just a matter of a step or two before we're there.

So where's the good news, Jim? The good news is that this nation is poised to become greater than ever before! We have learned some very valuable lessons during the past two hundred years; and with the combined intellect, strength, love, and understanding of our citizens, we can forge ahead.

America is the land of milk and honey, silver and gold. Here we have everything we could possibly need. God created this nation for His children. With His blessings, there is no end to the wealth, success and good will America can bring to the world.

I propose the following strategies to restore the dollar and bring prosperity back to "the land of the free and the home of the brave":

Benesch Bullets

To the leadership of the United States:

- Set up separate fund accounts to receive revenue and distribute specific budget items. Taxes for Medicare go directly to Medicare costs—Social Security, the same. This will not increase revenue, but it will increase government transparency, accuracy and stewardship, which will cut down on the potential to hide, waste, steal and abuse taxpayers' hard-earned dollars.
- Reduce United States government employee salaries to equal the average salary of "the people." This is arguably around $48,000 per year. Reducing legislative, judicial and other government salaries should incentivize public officials to become more responsible and cut down on the need for more credit expansion to pay "public servants."
- Restructure all future credit expansion policies to reflect a seven-year cycle. America has loans like that already. Most car loans and some balloon mortgages are less than seven years. Loans going forward must be structured for less time and not more time.
- Forgive early 401k withdrawal penalties.

Because U.S. leaders have betrayed their promises, citizens should now be allowed unrestricted access to their own savings—401k—to pay off debt: house first, then cars, credit cards, etc. This additional revenue will aid in refreshing the credit system.

To my fellow believers:

- Stop pushing party platforms. God knows what is best for His people, not Republicans, Democrats or any other political party.

- Recruit and support godly candidates for all branches of government and for leadership roles in America and throughout the world. "Godly" does not necessarily mean that the candidate is a deacon or elder at the local church! Be willing to do your homework and closely examine all candidates' true beliefs: what they do, not just what they say.

- Start acting like a true believer. WWJD—"What Would Jesus Do?"—bracelets are cute, but it is time to stop wearing Him at the end of your sleeves and start allowing Him to direct your every action.

- God said, "Follow all these commands I am giving you today. For the Lord your God will bless you as He has promised, and you will lend to many nations but will borrow from none. You will rule over many nations but none will rule over you" (Deut. 15:5, 6). You can't do that if you are bound by debt.

- Be good stewards. All things belong to God, not to us. We are just Christ's tenants on this earth.

To my fellow citizens:

- Make fewer trips to the mall. Slow down! It was the slowdown in consumer spending in 2008, not the stimulus, that thwarted another great depression.
- If you are a true patriot, act like it—even when everyone else doesn't.
- Spend no more than twice your annual salary for a home purchase. If you make $50,000 per year, the mortgage amount should be no more than $100,000 and so on.
- Spend no more than 40 percent of monthly net—take home—salary for "all" monthly credit obligations. This includes the mortgage, car and credit card payments.
- Do not support incumbents—especially if they have been in office for more than two terms. Consider removing them—at the local, state and federal levels. Even if they are not

openly corrupt, they have done nothing to end progressivism and prevent communism.

- Research, research, research—especially when it comes to financial matters! It has been said that "knowledge is power" and will save you hundreds, thousands or even tens of thousands of dollars.

You, the legal citizenry of this sovereign nation, are more valuable than any asset you own. You are more precious than silver and gold, but your spending habits have drained your worth and left you "net worthless."

You can choose to live within your means and vote for others who agree with you, which will ensure that you retain your freedom. Or you can continue to live beyond your means, voting for those who are determined that you will become wards of the state, which will inevitably lead to...AMERICOM.

Our relations with foreign powers are of a friendly character, although certain interesting differences remain unsettled with some. Our revenue under the mild system of impost and tonnage continues to be adequate to all the purposes of the Government. Our agriculture, commerce, manufactures, and navigation flourish. Our fortifications are advancing in the degree authorized by existing appropriations to maturity, and due progress is made in the augmentation of the Navy to the limit prescribed for it by law. For these blessings we owe to Almighty God, from whom we derive them, and with profound reverence, our most grateful and unceasing acknowledgments.[1]

—President James Monroe
Eighth Annual Message
December 7, 1824

AMERICOM

A tyrannical ruler lacks judgment,
but he who hates ill-gotten gain will enjoy a long life.

—Proverbs 28:16

Where economic conditions are such as not to make
Communism seem an attractive alternative...
It is true that fear sometimes perverts true patriotism
into fanaticism and to the acceptance of
dangerous enticements. [2]

—President Dwight D. Eisenhower
Eisenhower Doctrine, January 5, 1957

Contrary to what some people believe, there is only so much money to go around. Believe it or not, there is also a limited amount of credit. We have seen that these financial tools require the trust of the people. I also believe that I have proven "beyond a reasonable doubt"—as they say in the legal world—that fiscal irresponsibility leads to financial bankruptcy.

Earlier, you learned that victory comes with great pain and that there is no better example than the War Between the States. Although America had emancipated an entire culture, *that* war, as is true of all wars, came at a great price—loss of life, dwindling trust and a devaluation of currencies.

After the war, the fractured states continued to struggle financially, running headlong into the Long Depression when people here and abroad lost confidence in this country. No wonder. Our young nation had just torn herself limb from limb. Remember, currency has no value other than that which people are willing to give it. Could it be then that the real reason America's currency is rapidly declining is because foreign countries have lost faith in the "greatest nation"?[3] Is the erosion of the world's trust a result of America's moral misbehavior, which this author believes has bankrupted the nation's soul?

As a consequence of the Civil War and the "credit expansion" that comes along with war, the Long Depression, recession upon recession and the failing trust factor, America's leaders were forced to find a new currency. The big problem was this: They issued the new currency dollar for dollar with the old, which in large part brought about another depression.

The Great Depression of 1929 resulted from the marketplace trying to adjust the real value of America's wealth with the perceived or credit value. That was exaggerated. The dollar never had a fighting chance to begin with, so it has been struggling ever since. When nations do not save for the inevitability of war—and let me add two others: natural disasters and market imperfections—their currencies suffer from the credit expansion to pay for these events. These, combined with the excesses of daily living, can kill the dollar!

So here we are, with bankrupted souls, bankrupting our currency. There are no quick fixes, folks. To make matters worse, for the past one hundred years or so, America has changed her course from a republican to a progressive form of government.

The Land of Plenty

Upon leaving office, James Monroe, fifth president of the United States, thanked God for a successful and productive nation whose tax structure was not only adequate to sustain itself, but was also able to provide for the future and pay off debt brought about by war and economic development. That generation emphasized savings. They were frugal and ever mindful of safeguarding the republic. We are not!

Instead, we have forsaken our patriots and have taken matters into our own hands. America has worked herself into a frenzy to export everything—agriculture, manufacturing and mining, along with our equal and human rights. In addition, we have done so without exporting God's principles. How can that be possible if "equal and human rights" are guaranteed to citizens by the Constitution and were recognized by the Framers as God-given?

Modern-day presidents concede that things aren't going too well and are, in fact, creating economic and political conditions that have given way to a new form of government. President Eisenhower foresaw this danger and warned America that the fear created by failed leadership was perverting true patriotism into fanaticism and the acceptance of dangerous enticements. One of those "dangerous enticements" is communism.

As a reminder, America, communism is a black hole—a form of government that becomes all-consuming and all-powerful, swallowing up all wealth and resources and frivolously transferring them to elites and groups of people deemed more deserving or needy.

Societies with power-seeking factions all too often support a quick fix and rush to control and repair. In fact, stimulus, trickle-down economics, Social Security, government health care and welfare are all programs designed by well-intentioned hearts. Yet, it is not the hearts but lust for power that has manipulated, misused and destroyed the good initially sought in these types of social and human service programs. In spite of the progressive globalist effort to create a perfect world, America finds herself in a bigger mess than if her leaders had left well enough alone.

The desperation of our current economic conditions may make communism seem an attractive alternative. But, remember, communism is a tyrannical government, and the Book of Life warns that these types of rulers lack judgment. In fact, under communism, government leadership is the ultimate drug cartel, providing a "high" in the form of handouts. Today it's "free," but tomorrow it will cost you everything. The alternatives do *not* justify the means. Be careful of the leaders you give up your freedoms to follow.

It is true that the nation is in need of repair. But we need leaders with good judgment—leaders who will stop transferring wealth and, instead, store it up.

The Storehouse

From ancient times, God instructed His people to bring a "tithe"—one-tenth of everything they grew, made, hunted or earned, along with other gifts and offerings[4]— to the storehouse. A storehouse is a room, a building, or some other physical structure where people may place a portion of their agricultural produce, commerce and manufactured goods to keep for a "rainy day." These provisions were intended for the use of those who were widowed, orphaned or disabled and for their caretakers, teachers and so on.[5] I can see why some liberals hate the Bible. God only requires 10 percent tax and honest scales.

The storehouse approach is similar to people filling their pantries with bulk items purchased at discount stores. The storehouse was also a place where people of the church community could turn for assistance during hard times—something like the times we are experiencing right now—to keep God's children from being enslaved by the evils of a godless globalist government.

All humans are called to serve one another and to help those in need, but don't confuse goodwill with communism—a means by which a tyrannical government takes from those who have earned or inherited wealth and property and redistributes the larger portion to those who have not earned the right to any share at all. The storehouse was never intended to be a place of provision for those who are not hard workers, thrifty and frugal. In other words, savings by some were never to be ransacked by those who abuse their resources. To take from the thrifty and distribute to the wasteful is communism and grows out of progressivism.

There was a time when the government mandated savings accounts (storehouses) for an individual family's "rainy day." They called it Social Security.

Social Security

Many social welfare programs were founded under the storehouse principle. These programs were created to serve only individuals and their families in the event that something happened to the wage earner. Social Security was never intended to care for individuals who have not helped to fill the storehouse.

The Social Security Act was written by a committee on economic security, not a social welfare commission. Its intent was to provide a small subsistence to encourage older workers to retire, freeing up work for younger workers during times when employment opportunities were scarce.

In America, Social Security was established after the Great Depression and during the recession of 1935. As part of Roosevelt's New Deal, this act limited what were seen as dangers in the modern American life—including old age, poverty, unemployment and the burdens of widows and fatherless children. Today, these benefits fund retirement, disability, survivorship, and death and serve as a loan mechanism to pay for a part of America's excesses. More recently, unemployment has been given its own tax category called SUI and FUI—state and federal unemployment insurance, which was designed to float people for six months or less.[6] Borrowing against Social Security is still one way the federal government supports the jobless. Today, employment, unemployment and hundreds of other programs—all hidden within Social Security—are killing this well-intentioned program and redirecting your retirement storehouse.

The Ponzi Scheme

It is true that your Social Security storehouse has been ransacked, and now Congress has nothing left to do but scheme. How does the government manage to get away with this? They learned it from a master swindler by the name of Charles Ponzi. Figureheads of fortune use this scheme to finance multi-million-dollar yachts, fast cars and a lavish lifestyle that people like you and I can only dream about.

Charles Ponzi was born in 1882, died the same year China became a communist nation (1949), and is known as one of the greatest swindlers in American history.[7] Thus, the term "Ponzi scheme," which is "essentially an investment fraud wherein the operator promises high financial returns or dividends that are not available through traditional investments. Instead of investing victims' funds, the operator pays 'dividends' to initial investors using the principle amounts 'invested' by subsequent investors. The scheme generally falls apart when the operator flees with all of the proceeds, or when a sufficient number of new investors cannot be found to allow the continued payment of 'dividends.'"[8] Sounds a little like derivatives, or perhaps Social Security, doesn't it?

Surely people would not allow this to happen, would they? They're just too smart. Really? Smarter and richer people bought into the Bernie Madoff scheme.

For many years, Bernie Madoff got away with the financial equivalent of murder by breaching the trust of America's credit and securities system.[9] In addition, a U.S. Securities and Exchange Commission complaint alleges that R. Allen Stanford and James M. Davis "executed a massive Ponzi scheme through entities under their control."[10] The list of banks, financial institutions, management companies, investment advisors, brokers and many others that participated in this scheme is shocking. But what is even more appalling is the "Ponzi scheme" being perpetrated by Congress and the president on the American public.

Congressional Ponzi Schemes

Here's how the Congressional Ponzi scheme works: The government collects 6.2 percent FICA tax from your gross wages up to a certain amount. In 2009, the government capped FICA at $106,800 in annual earnings, an amount that fluctuates. In addition, Uncle Sam collects the same amount from your employer. Earlier, I told you that this "employer contribution" is really your additional contribution to your retirement, but suit yourself—you don't have to believe me. I, on the other hand, haven't changed my mind.

Let's assume you make $600 per week. (That's the real "average" American take-home pay, not the government's statistic which claims that the average

American pulls in $923 every week, or approximately $48,000 a year. Are you kidding me?) Your FICA tax burden would be $37.20 per week, or $1,934.40 per year, and your employer would pay on your behalf exactly the same amount, totaling $74.40 per week, or $3,868.80 per year.

Now, let's run this out, without figuring in inflation (which doubles the cost of goods every ten to twenty years) or an increase in wages. At the current retirement age of 65—if a person began work at 21—that individual will have accumulated $170,227 in his/her lifetime to pay for Social Security retirement benefits. Given the current average benefit, he or she will collect $1,153 per month. At that rate, the retirement funding will last about 148 months or a little over twelve years. With a life expectancy of 77½ to 80 years, Americans are collecting benefits from six months to 2½ years longer than they have paid into the system.

At first glance, the problem seems to be that Americans are not setting enough aside for Social Security. If so, then the government must be paying the first set of investors on the investments of others. Uh, oh...Social Security is a scam? Well, it is by the Ponzi definition: "A widely known description of any scam that pays early investors' returns from the investment of later investors." I didn't define this term; your government did. If it is, indeed, criminal activity, it needs to stop immediately! Not later, but sooner. All employed people must begin to put aside their fair share and stop relying on future generations to provide for retirees.

If you just dismissed the whole thing because it is government-sanctioned, then you are a progressive globalist...or a communist. At the very least, you are permitting your fellow citizens to be enslaved. You are the reason Social Security and welfare are broke. You are not on the side of freedom-loving Americans because you are helping to destabilize the retirement safety net of future generations.

Maybe you believe that the interest on FICA tax money should cover the spread. Well, that would be great if those funds were in a savings account collecting interest. Instead, the so-called guardians of the Treasury are redirecting those funds for their own interests—oh, excuse me!—for welfare, Medicaid, junkets[11], new office furniture for Congress, pay raises for Congress, White House grand balls, ad infinitum.

To quote the Federal Bureau of Investigation: "Avoid Ponzi schemes!..." [12]

These same public officials have spent that money on war, war and more war. In addition, they have been giving it away to foreign nations, as well as to people who don't want to work. Instead, shouldn't they be ensuring that the storehouse is full for retirement? Have I mentioned war?

To the preceding generation, may I point out that you have spent my future and my children's future? Shame on you! To my grandchildren's generation, I need to make an apology and give you a heads-up. First, I ask you to forgive us for spending your inheritance and your children's and grandchildren's inheritance. Secondly, I beg you: Do something to stop this insanity!

I'm not saying that we should not care for our aging, disabled, widowed and orphaned. It's our moral duty to care for them. Like so many other things, however, we are going about it in the wrong way.

Welfare Forever?

Many are growing weary of those who think that just by being born in America—a phenomenon known as "anchor babies"—or by illegally immigrating to this country, they are entitled to drain the lifeblood of hardworking American taxpayers. We don't mind giving the poor fellow a leg up, but I assumed that Congressional cannibalism was illegal.

In 2008 and 2009, I served as the chair of the Nashville Mayor's Economic Development Committee on Poverty. My committee heard numerous reports from city, state and private leaders. One report, however, still haunts me. A director of Human Services for Tennessee told us that during the 1990s' welfare reform debates on Capitol Hill, the time limit to receive welfare benefits was reduced to five years.

In fact, President Bill Clinton signed welfare reform sponsored by the Republican Congress in 1996.

The Personal Responsibility and Work Opportunity Reconciliation Act, as it is known, included sweeping reforms that continue to go unenforced. Fourteen years later, many 1996 welfare recipients are still receiving welfare. Apparently, the progressives told them, "Don't worry. We don't plan to enforce this law."

Welfare now includes, but is not limited to health care, food stamps, child care assistance, unemployment benefits, job training programs, cash aid, drug and alcohol abuse aid, free school lunches, housing assistance, homelessness assistance, tuition assistance, job retraining and others. These benefits are paid to people from all over the world without regard to citizenship.

For example, if an illegal alien mother enters the United States without permission and sets up a homestead, she can enter her children in school, where they receive a free education, along with free lunches and breakfasts if the school offers that type of program. In addition, the mother will receive housing, food stamps, health care and one of those stimulus jobs for her children to navigate the welfare system. The cost to America will vary, but this woman will more than likely receive somewhere around $15,000 to $20,000 in benefits per year.[13] Of course, this amount might not sound like a lot of money to a government employee earning six figures, but it would be a lifesaver to many out-of-work U.S. citizens who are not collecting a dime.

Since Lyndon B. Johnson's Great Society initiative,

America has spent somewhere between $5 and $12 trillion on welfare assistance.[14] What concerns me even more is the fact that Congress has provided no accounting to the taxpayer to reflect the exact amounts paid. The closest estimates, accepted by the federal government, put the cost of welfare reform at $5.1 trillion from February 1964 until fiscal year end 1992.[15] Hmmm. Half the debt of the nation...at the time of this printing.

In 2008, the president and the United States Congress, along with every governor and state house in the entire country, were spending $24.5 billion in welfare/unemployment and $23.03 billion in Medicaid per month.[16] That's $47.53 billion per month, or $570.36 billion per year in humanitarian aid to U.S. citizens alone. That does not include all other aid, hidden in every budget line item, to support welfare. To date, my estimates indicate that America has spent over $11 trillion on the war on poverty.

Let's face it. Some limited welfare is necessary, because people get down on their luck and someone needs to be there to help them up. A hand up is a kind and generous gesture on the part of American taxpayers. Although welfare was reformed to help people get back on their feet, the big problem is that many recipients feel entitled to government aid, resulting in some families living on welfare for three and four generations.

In fact, after the horrific events of Hurricane Katrina, the government issued emergency credit cards.

These heartfelt taxpayer funds were to be used to feed, clothe and house those "in need for many months." Instead, many of the "needy" took those funds and stormed neighboring electronic stores, buying out every big-screen television available.

In the report cited earlier, the director stated he feared that during this economic downturn, welfare recipients would have to be told that this "really" would be the last year of eligibility. Apparently, the government expects us to follow the rules, but at election time, your representatives will break every rule in the book. To them, the end justifies the means. Time to collect your television set so you can watch their campaign commercials on the big screen!

Perpetuating Poverty

When I was a kid, my father and mother both worked full time to support the family. They were a team and although we never had much, it was more than enough. We were grateful just to be Americans.

By now you probably feel that you have heard more than you ever wanted or needed to know about inflation. But allow me to let you in on the real ugliness of the matter. Inflation causes the poor to become poorer. Let me put it another way: As the purchasing power per dollar decreases, poverty increases.

The purchasing power of the dollar is a much

greater problem than leadership wants to acknowledge. The term *poverty* seems elusive, because poverty is subjective and the definition changes. Depending upon how people and society view their roots, what their moral standard might be and whether they are willing to accept the status quo, individuals may either succumb to a pity party or rise to meet the challenge to overcome their circumstances.

Back when I was a boy, even if my tennis shoes had big holes in them, I wouldn't get new ones until my birthday. My mother wasn't much on fashion fads so I wore hand-me-downs. My siblings and I qualified for subsidized school lunches, but my mother always packed our lunches to avoid embarrassment. Not that being poor is anything to be ashamed of, but our family value system required that we do everything we could for ourselves before asking for help. Not so today!

The government-owes-me attitude is pervasive in every area of our society—from the dock worker to the illegal alien to the president of General Motors. I was brought up during a time of 12 percent-plus interest rates and high inflation. These economic conditions didn't make life easy. In fact, during the past forty-plus years, inflation has made families poor and forced mothers into the workplace. My mother wouldn't have gone back to work when she did if her additional income hadn't been necessary for the family's survival. This also devalued the worth of my father's ability to make a living wage because at one time in this nation a man's wages was all that was needed to provide for his family.

Inevitably, America's deficit spending is not only destroying the value of the dollar, but it is expanding poverty. Politicians go to extremes to ensure that the truth about inflation, poverty, real American wages, unemployment and the ineffectiveness of welfare programs are hidden, misinterpreted and confused.

In fact, the cost of goods keeps rising, but the paycheck doesn't. Government has put a hold on Social Security increases, yet has increased the excessive pay of our Congress. Non-union carpenters who were making $15 per hour fifteen years ago are making the same $15— if they're lucky and still have a job today. This is what I mean when I say that people are becoming poorer. It is not their fault that their government sent wealth-building jobs to foreign nations and began trickledown economic policies that cause inflation.

The big question is this: When America can't borrow and both the man and woman of the house work full-time jobs, then what? Perhaps government will slowly increase the hours of a work week, or maybe they will begin allowing three or four people to marry so that there are more breadwinners per family. We may have to survive by sleeping fifteen to twenty people per two-bedroom house like many of the illegal aliens in our country.

If people continue to permit progressivism to flourish, communism will follow.

"Keeping Up with Comrade Jones"

Communism is socialism, liberalism, dictatorship fascism and anarchy. Don't mince words with me. Communism is "a theory advocating elimination of private property. A system in which goods are owned in common and are available to all as needed. A doctrine based on revolutionary Marxian socialism and Marxism-Leninism that was the official ideology of the Union of Soviet Socialist Republics. A totalitarian system of government in which a single authoritarian party controls state-owned means of production. A final stage of society in Marxist theory in which the state has withered away and economic goods are distributed equitably or collectively."[17]

The fatal flaw in communism is that the party in power is considered superior to the rest of society. In other words, these are the elites. The class system is never removed, because everyone else is considered to be equally poor. Now "keeping up with the Joneses" is a cinch. Under this model, the elite tier is redistributing middle-class wealth to the poor. It is now possible for communists and their progressive globalist conspirators to create an equal society in half the time it would take to build up the poor with sustainable employment.

These dictators and their fellows take more than an equal share of wealth, food and shelter. They do not participate in the division of labor and do not get their hands dirty. The elites use factions—special interests,

PACs, lobbyists, dividers, and so on—to fuel dissension among state and national leaders. In addition, they create tension among the poor, middle and rich classes; between political parties; between labor and management, and so on. Communism may sound good, but human governments tend to be abusive, and this is the most serious oppressor of free individuals and families. Communism is the ultimate tyranny.

Stages to Communism

Laziness (lethargy) leads to despotism, which leads to the several stages of progressivism, which eventually becomes communism. I will show you how:

1. Existing leadership loses fortitude, strength and confidence in their ability to lead a nation.
2. Lack of leadership prowess gives way to greed and corruption and panders to special interests, PACs, lobbyists, labor groups and so on.
3. A new group of rebellious leaders shames previous leadership and labels them and their supporters "wicked and evil."
4. Evolved leadership uses the "rule of law" as their ranks begin to grow in numbers, strength and wealth, gaining ever more control of society as court precedence begins to shape a new politically correct order.
5. New Deals, welfare, Social Security, poverty initiatives,

Great Societies and trickledown economic programs cause government to grow larger and larger as a nation's tax structure drains the wealth from the upper-middle, middle-middle and lower-middle classes and redistributes that wealth to an authoritarian elite, those less fortunate, the poor, the downtrodden and special interests.

6. The national currency begins to decrease in value as credit expansion policies are manipulated to create an overall false sense of wealth and lethargy among the citizenry.

7. War is waged by measured response initiatives, called diplomacy, and conflicts are left unfinished by a series of truces and withdrawals.

8. Manufacturing, agriculture and mining operations are exported as part of a "for-the-better-good" global peacekeeping initiative.

9. As the nation begins to struggle with debt brought about by credit expansion and jobs losses created by a severe trade imbalance, authoritarian leaders begin to splinter—within political party ranks—and a progressive global initiative is born.

10. Education and entertainment are expanded and given an agenda that greatly differs from the traditional family values, and heads of families do nothing to slow or stop it.

11. Government begins to control religion, as this is viewed as a source of the people's strength and

must be manipulated. Because America was founded upon godly principles, all worship in public places is controlled, and references to God are outlawed.

12. Progressive leaders seek support from foreign governments to gain a foothold over opposition leadership. "There is strength in numbers."

13. Society is convinced that its history is littered with failures and injustices, and reparations must be made to those who have suffered at the hand of national injustice.

14. Minority and special interest groups are given preference over the original majority; the majority are further shamed into accepting the fact that they are worthless unless they buy into "A New AmeriCom" and assist with social transformation.

15. When national currency becomes almost worthless and credit expansion has run its full course, there will not be enough people working to provide adequate support for individuals and their families.

16. Government seizes control over banking and financial institutions and markets as they are forced to provide government surety in order to sustain institutions, individuals and their families.

17. Government begins to control a majority of the activities of everyday life and the government jobs sector begins growing, amassing an almost unstoppable power base; the people become increasingly dependent upon the government for direction in everything.

18. Laws and new government measures are put in place in overwhelming strength, control and numbers in an effort to confuse the masses, setting the final stage to seize control.

19. Prisons, jails, city centers and government construction increase at a faster pace than private development as leadership struggles to stay ahead of rising unemployment.

20. Public officials rewrite plans for a state of emergency on national and state levels, giving employees, police and fire departments, public health, and government contractors and subcontractors unprecedented and unconstitutional power. Government proclamations allow "whatever- it-takes" actions to maintain control over the masses. All of those acting on behalf of the "new government" are given immunity to prosecution for what would have originally been considered crimes.

21. The president signs a proclamation declaring a state of emergency. On October 24, 2009, President Barack Obama issued a Declaration of National Emergency under the purview of flu pandemic. A declaration may be modified as necessary, however, as long as one is in place.

22. The nation's governing directive is suspended—in America, that is the U.S. Constitution and Bill of Rights—and a temporary governing charter, usually one of martial law, is created as the cornerstone of

the new system of justice and social order.

23. Authoritarian leadership enslaves a section of the population—in China, it was 25 million high school-aged youth up to age twenty-four—to provide a cheap source of labor for the production of agricultural and manufactured goods. Consumables will stabilize the economy and stave off the possibility of rebellion on the part of those who were raised in the old way of life and might present roadblocks to "progress."

24. Those members of society not enslaved are more or less put on an equal pay structure. There is still a tiered level where doctors, lawyers, and other professionals earn more than truck drivers, but there is not a large disparity between the income of a brain surgeon and that of a street sweeper.

25. The "rule of law" becomes the stick that threatens to imprison anyone else that has not been enslaved and to prevent possible insurrection.

26. All private property is confiscated and becomes the property of the People's Republic of AmeriCom. This includes intellectual property, patents, trade secrets, etc.

27. Education is restructured to focus on the new society. Children will be segregated from their parents' influence, and their careers will be determined by the government for the best interests of the government.

28. Those who can remember "the way it used to be" will not be assisted with medical problems and will be

required to attend "end-of-life" counseling sessions. Death will be promoted to benefit society.

In the past century, each of these stages has been repeated time and time again, resulting in the takeover of free nations around the world. In America, we are already at Step 21. What are we going to do about it? Are we going to continue down the progressive road we are on and end up with our own form of communism, or are we going to change direction?

Benesch Bullets

To the leadership of the United States:

- Collect FICA taxes and deposit them in a trust account for retirement, disability and survivorship use only.
- Immediately cease conducting Social Security affairs as a Ponzi scheme.
- Assist in creating disadvantaged-and disability-friendly work programs and end quotas.
- Restrict welfare programs to provide for basic life needs—education assistance, housing, food, child care, clothing and all other basic needs—to a maximum of five years. (Cell phones, big-screen TVs, cable and the like are not necessities.)

- End welfare assistance to individuals and families who unlawfully enter America.
- Implement a U.S.A. citizens-first work initiative, in which U.S. citizens who are ready, willing and able to fill a job opening must be hired before an alien can be solicited.
- Adopt a national morality.
- Swiftly punish those who make a mockery of justice (e.g., the Ted Stevens corruption trial).
- Abolish double standards and class discrimination/diversity/privilege.

To my fellow believers:

- Give a minimum of one-tenth of your total (pre-tax) provisions—income, gifts, crops, bonuses, inheritance, time—to your church or synagogue.
- Create a church storehouse to care for members of *your* congregation who are widowed, orphaned, disabled or disadvantaged, and to provide for emergencies.

To my fellow citizens:

- Create a storehouse in your neighborhood to provide each member of the community with one month's supply of food, water and basic medical supplies.

- Adopt a national attitude toward "earning the right" to replace the "right of entitlement."
- Initiate work programs to put an end to the low wage cycle. Low wages perpetuate poverty.

History suggests that under the guidelines of this nation's sages and patriots, if a people abide by godly principles, the economy and society will flourish. While Social Security, welfare, the war on poverty, Medicare and Medicaid are all well-intentioned programs, those of the progressive and communist mindset have destroyed their inherent benefits.

The AmeriCom agenda promotes these trillion-dollar, heartfelt programs, which rob the storehouses... one tax at a time.

[God who rules over all] has again favored us with healthful seasons and abundant harvests;...The receipts of the present year have amounted to near $2,000,000 more than was anticipated at the commencement of the last session of Congress.... It is, indeed, a general law of prosperous commerce that the real value of exports should by a small, and only a small, balance exceed that of imports, that balance being a permanent addition to the wealth of the nation....So far as the object of taxation is to raise a revenue for discharging the debts and defraying the expenses of the community, its operation should be adapted as much as possible to suit the burden with equal hand upon all in proportion with their ability of bearing it without oppression.[1]

— President John Quincy Adams
Fourth Annual Message
December 2, 1828

7

TAXAQUENCES

Give everyone what you owe him: If you owe taxes, pay taxes; if revenue, then revenue; if respect, then respect; if honor, then honor.
—Romans 13:7

The present tax structure is a disgrace to this country.[2]
—President Jimmy Carter, Debate with President Gerald Ford
September 23, 1976

I don't want this message to get lost, so let me say it right up front: All tax burdens, no matter who they are intended to benefit, wind up being carried on the backs of the working class.

To the working men and women of the nation, you are the backbone of America, the very reason this nation exists. You have enabled her to achieve great heights in commerce and industry, and you will either help her resist the temptations of communism or propel her toward that alluring pit. Frankly, though, I don't know how any true son or daughter of this republic could ever vote for a tax increase, which is an invitation to oppression.

Well-intentioned or not, that is pure selfishness. Period! With every tax approved, Americans lose a little more control over their destiny and surrender the decision-making process to a closed circle of elites who care little or nothing about the masses.

The power to tax—now that's ultimate control. It was the issue of taxes that led this nation to declare her independence from the tyranny of a dictator, King George III of England.

In 1913, the year America's republic was lost, progressives restructured government by adding the Seventeenth Amendment to the Constitution. This single act seized political power from the states by taking away election rights granted by the Framers. This amendment extinguished state representation within the federal ranks on Capitol Hill, dramatically shifting the governmental equilibrium so eloquently crafted by certain men of virtue. To make matters worse, federal globalist power brokers confiscated state wealth by creating a monetary "Frankenstein," known as the Federal Reserve.

Passage of the Sixteenth Amendment that same year established the current income tax system and has given rise to a multitude of taxes that have spiraled out of control. These unjust and excessive taxes have been inflicted on the working middle class of America and will continue to oppress the people.

Tax Attack

Federal income tax, state income tax, state unemployment tax, federal unemployment tax, entertainment tax, hospitality tax, real estate tax, personal property tax, gasoline tax, liquor tax, gambling tax, cigarette tax, luxury tax, inheritance tax, license plates, wheel tax, city vehicle permit, city dog license, emissions tax, electricity tax, natural gas tax, corporate tax, capital gains tax, deed tax, telephone usage tax, fishing license, hunting license, trappers license, business license, drivers license, import tax, export tax, state sales tax, county sales tax, vehicle title fees, vehicle transfer fees, self-employment tax, pension tax, severance tax, gift tax, stock transfer tax, tire disposal tax, battery disposal tax, landfill tax, air travel tax, airport use tax, city building permits, county building permits, state fire permits, septic permits, burn permits, county impact fees, environmental impact fees, city impact fees, toll booths, toll bridges, parking meters, Social Security tax (FICA), Medicare tax, education tax, business property use tax, dividends tax, and coming soon, U. S. government-sponsored health insurance tax, cap-and-trade, firearms ownership tax, ad infinitum.

All of these taxes are paid by you, not by your employer, illegal aliens, college students or anyone else. To add insult to injury, every product you purchase contains embedded taxes—a layered tax structure which creates a multitude of additional taxes. Even the government admits that the working men and women of this nation pay embedded taxes to the tune of about 22 percent[3]—and that's before your purchase is taxed again at the sales counter.

For example, if you purchase a $10,000 car, $2,200 of the sale price is tax. Then the $10,000—which already includes tax—is taxed again. In my state, that's another $950 for a total of $3,150 or 31½ percent tax. If I sell the car, let's say for $9,000, the new purchaser pays $885 more in taxes. If he sells the car, it is taxed again…get it?

Did you know that you paid embedded taxes when you purchased your last house as well? Would you believe that 22 percent of your home purchase was taxes? For every $100,000, new homeowners pay $22,000 in embedded taxes. That's right! Without embedded taxes, a $100,000 home would only cost $78,000. Or take a $200,000 residence, which, if it weren't for embedded taxes, would only require a $156,000 mortgage.

Here is another sad truth. Sooner or later we all move on to greener pastures. At the time of our passing, we will leave to our heirs the family home. When that happens, the government will require our children—our heirs—to pay some type of capital gains tax if they elect to sell the home outright. Or, if those who inherit the home decide to keep it—to rent, or live in—they will pay inheritance tax. Would you believe that if the children elect to sell the family residence, the next purchaser will pay approximately 40 percent of the total purchase price in taxes...and that every plank in that house has a horror story to tell?

The Tale of a Two-by-Four

A tree grows in the forest. Before the tree can be felled, the lumber company must be licensed, zoned and granted a permit—all of which are taxed. Next, a gasoline chainsaw must be purchased; there are taxes on both the saw and the gas to fuel it. The saw is then transported by a vehicle that was taxed at purchase, as was the vehicle's license plates, inspections and so on. These big rigs require their owners to pay huge taxes, nothing like the smaller amount people pay for their cars. The tree is cut down and taken to the mill. Now the lumber must be planed and cut into planks.

The mill saw is taxed as well as the mill itself— business-related and employee taxes, including FICA, Medicare, Workman's Comp, FUI and SUI (federal and state unemployment "insurance"). The electricity to run the mill is taxed; the saw blades are too. The tree is cut up into two-by materials, one-bys and veneers for plywood and such. These are taken to the lumber store, and the mill pays taxes for the sale of the finished product. Finally, the lumber is sold to the builder, who pays taxes on the sale, marks it up and pays taxes on that; his services and those of the realtor—the same. All of that is built into the final price of the home and passed on to you.

Ah, the life of a two-by-four. This is the same for every nut, bolt, nail, wire and everything else that was necessary before you turned the key and walked across the threshold of your new house.

The Tax Deduction

Home ownership used to be the American dream. Now it's the American tax nightmare! My research has revealed that the road we are traveling down has no guardrails to protect the consumer, and the asphalt pitches and curves with such tax frequency, it is only a matter of time before the rain-soaked taxaquences cause us to slip off the pavement and down the mountainside.

With this thought in mind, I decided to do a little digging into the rumored tax advantage surrounding the discussion of mortgage interest payments. If you are a homeowner, you know what I'm talking about. Just as the road has dangerous, unprotected tax curves, we have been convinced that there are some nice smooth straightaways that come in the form of mortgage tax deductions. This is Big Brother's way of making up for the curves, of course. Just like the misinformation concerning debt, we have been sold a bill of goods about mortgage payment tax deductions as well.

Consider this scenario for the mortgage mentioned in Chapter 5. Historically, financial advisors have encouraged people to carry a mortgage on their homes.

After all, you don't want any more than 40 percent of your hard-earned dollars going to Uncle Sugar—so it makes sense to take out a mortgage so that you can deduct the interest, right?

Well, not exactly. Let's look at that $200,000 mortgage. At 4¼ percent fixed rate interest, amortized over a thirty-year period—without insurance or real estate taxes—you will pay $354,196.72 over the life of the loan, of which $154,196.72 is interest.[4] That breaks down to $5,139.89 per year in interest alone—roughly half the loan amount.

Now, here is where it gets slippery, so hang on. If you didn't own the home and, let's say, rented an apartment or—the smart thing—paid cash for a smaller, less expensive home and didn't have the interest payment to deduct from your taxes...and if you fell into the 18 percent tax bracket, you would pay $925.18 in taxes— which makes better sense than paying $5,139.89 to the lender!

If you did not finance a home and rented instead, you would not pay the hefty $154,196.72 in interest to the lender. The savings, or increase in your net worth over that thirty-year period, would be a grand total of $126,441.31! Let me put it another way: The savings in interest payments would increase the length of your retirement by another eleven years, or would increase your monthly retirement payment by $1,153.00 for eleven years.

Now, here is the beauty of my plan versus the

financial advisors' plan. If you were saving the money you were paying and earning the same 4¼ percent annual interest instead of paying it, at the end of thirty years you could have a $256,810 nest egg. To avoid paying taxes, most Americans run to the opposite extreme—taking advantage of a rigged tax structure that only works for the top 5 percent.

The Top 5 Percent

Oh, wait, there go the voices of opposition once again. *But, Jim, the top 5 percent of society, comprised of Big Business and the wealthy, pay 95 percent of the tax burden in America.* Government has the ability to tax; Big Business has the ability to pass those taxes on to the working class.

Here's how it works. Let's look at the high-paid field of entertainment. If a movie star or an athlete is married and earns $10 million per year, that person will pay about $3,604,892.50[5] in taxes, right? Wrong! The cost of the tax burden is passed on to you in admission, paraphernalia, etc. Got it? Yes, the celebrity pays the tax, but he increases his fees to cover that tax. You are the real taxpayer. Have you noticed the price of a movie these days? I just took my family of four and spent an outrageous $80 for the movie tickets, popcorn and soft drinks. Did I just say that entertainers passed their tax burden on to you and me? (By the way, don't forget the embedded taxes on all those items.)

According to the U.S. GAO (United States Government Accounting Office), in 2008, 39½ percent—or $1.146 trillion—of the $2.982.6 trillion 2008 U.S. budget was paid by middle-class personal income taxes. I know what you're thinking, so hold on! Employee/employer FICA taxes, totaling $910 billion, were paid.

But, Jim, employers pay half of that amount, don't they? Keep your shirt on because that's just not true! Only $391 billion were paid by corporations and other revenues. "Other revenues" are fines we working stiffs pay above and beyond the unbearable—court costs, bankruptcy fees, traffic violations on federal land, and the like.[6] In addition, when 2008 state and local tax revenues were paid, Americans had forked over a show-stopping four trillion, eight hundred and sixteen billion, three hundred million dollars for government expenditures.[7] That's almost five trillion dollars in taxes for 2008.

Let's not forget George Bush and the Republican deficit of $458.6 billion[8] for that year, to make up the difference between tax revenue and Capitol Hill's champagne tastes. *Aren't the Republicans much more fiscally responsible than the Democrats?!* A warning to you Dems: Don't you dare even think about jumping on this bandwagon!

Pay really close attention, because this is the truth about taxaquences. In 2008, taxes on America's revenue, paid by corporations, was really collected by corporations and paid directly to Uncle Sugar for redistribution. Here is the part no one wants you to figure out: Those taxes were added as a part of product "mark-up," or margin. So, who really pays the corporate tax if it is embedded in the price of a product? That's right—you, the consumer!

Remember the $80 movie? You'd do the same thing, wouldn't you? I mean, we have to chain—oops! I mean pass on—the tax to the next guy.

What Jefferson feared has now become our culture: "If we run into such debts, as that we must be taxed in our meat and in our drink, in our necessaries and in our comforts, in our labors and our amusements... [we will] have no time to think, no means of calling the mismanagers to account; but be glad to obtain subsistence by hiring ourselves to rivet their chains on the necks of our fellow-sufferer....This is the tendency of all human governments."[9] Does "riveting the chains" make more sense now?

So it's not the top 5 percent, after all. If the business or corporation you work for pays the employer's portion of FICA, but counts it as your total compensation on their balance sheets, who pays the tax? Again—you!

Tax by Cop

Then there's "Tax by Cop." That's the fines, court costs and fees paid in the form of traffic tickets and other citations—the bulk of which are paid by people like you and me. There go those voices again: *If people didn't break the law, they wouldn't get tickets.* Sure enough, but let me share a true story, one that might cause you to be a little less trusting of your beloved peace patrol, who are just "doing their duty."

As a police officer, I have been certified in all kinds of methodology and technology—from the breathalyzer to emergency medical assistance, from radar to "hot" pursuit. I have arrested people for everything from speeding to drug trafficking, from reckless driving to pot smoking, from wives shooting at their husbands to driving while intoxicated, from bar fights to murder! I know why the justice system exists. I also know that many government agencies have begun using the laws of the land as revenue tools—or what I have called "Tax by Cop."

You've seen it on television—rogue governments, crooked cops…the whole nine yards. There are such things as quotas, both verbal and written. Believe me, if you are a police officer, you had better bring in the bad guy or turn in your badge.

I remember my breathalyzer training using the old "Widmark Formula," a calculation for determining a person's blood alcohol content: the Horizontal Gaze Nystagmus Test—watching how smoothly the eyes track objects—the Nose Touch, Walk and Turn, and so on.

As an MP in the State of Virginia, I also worked with the State Police Tac (Tactical) Teams (SWAT). I, along with my fellow military police officers, was certified on the Smith & Wesson Model 900, now relegated to the

DUI Hall of Fame.

It was a crude device and one that could be manipulated in such a way that operating it was an issue of integrity. The device was so untrustworthy that the U.S. government required all federal law enforcement agencies to use the much more expensive, all-electronic, hands-free (for the most part) Smith & Wesson Model 1000.

I was proud that the government agency I worked for was so concerned with individual rights that it would implement the use of a "failsafe" device to check the blood alcohol of those suspected of drunk driving...that is, until I found out that the 1000 could be manipulated as well. All you had to do—especially if it was the end of the month and you needed another DUI to keep your badge—was to dump a little fluid out of the ampoule. Less chemical solution requires less alcohol to be present in the blood for a positive reading—and poof—an instant DUI conviction! Where do cops come up with these shortcuts to "justice"?

The breathalyzer manufacturer knew that the 900 had an integrity flaw, so they fixed it in the 1000...well, almost. You can laugh now! See, the 1000 was a plug and play, but it was necessary for an officer to hold the tube the suspect blows into, read the results and load the solution; that is where the system falls apart. Kind of like the prosecutor who withheld evidence in the Duke Lacrosse case. As I have said before, there are no lengths to which desperate people will not go, or what ambitious politicians will not do just to be elected or re-elected.

Yes, it is true that radar clocks everything from the squad car's heater fan to the rain, and no, aluminum foil in the hubcaps does not fool the radar. But don't get caught speeding in inclement weather. "Tax by Cop"—what a convenient way for local, state and federal government to get into your pocket while your neighbor thinks that Big Brother is just making America a safer place. I would never trust my future security to the tools of law enforcement nor to the government's system of jurisprudence.

I entered the field of law enforcement, expecting to protect the safety of my fellow citizen, but found myself using a radar gun to collect tax revenue for the government. I wanted to make an impact, and now I don't have to. Someone beat me to it!

Impact Fees

What are impact fees? They are fees paid to cities and counties by developers, builders and homeowners who build their own homes. These fees represent the financial impact that new houses have on a community—forcing an increase in schools/sewer/water/police/fire demand, adding wear and tear to roads and, in many cases, calling for road expansion projects.

Now wait a minute. Aren't the taxes we pay for schools, roads, police and fire protection used to cover our "impact" on these services? Don't we pay for infrastructure maintenance and repair in our monthly water and sewer bills, property taxes and much more?

Listen to what one of the Framers had to say on the matter: "So far the object of taxation is to raise revenue for discharging the debts and defraying the expenses of the community, its operation should be adapted as much as possible to suit the burden with equal hand upon all in proportion with their ability of bearing it without oppression."[10]

So what is this "impact fee" all about anyway? To pay for the excesses, that's what. To provide health care for drug dealers and welfare for people who refuse to work. To make sure that CEOs don't just make millions, but tens of millions! To pay Congress to throw their furniture away every couple of years. To design prisons that aren't used—Two Rivers; to plan urban developments that are never completed, and to build bridges to nowhere.

When I built my father's home in Cape Coral, Florida, he paid over $5,000 in impact fees. In addition, he paid $2,000 for a building permit, plus a couple of hundred dollars more for re-inspections throughout the construction process. You're probably thinking, *Wow, he must have a very large home!* Well, it seemed that way as we worked side by side in the heat and rain, building that house with our own hands for eight months.

Actually, it is an average 3-bedroom, 2-bath, 2-car garage home on a single lot. Believe it or not, the impact fees and permits alone were over 3 percent of the total construction costs. If I had charged my father to build his house, he would have paid an additional $10,000 for a builder's portion of income taxes. Keep in mind: Taxes get rolled into the total cost of a home.

Impact fees are like a double tax—property taxes used to pay for things that are now taxed twice. These fees are so controversial that I know of one local city council which met in the middle of the night. They purposely did not hold the meeting in a public forum to prevent the citizens' outrage that was sure to come. Of course, the tax ordinance passed unanimously. Surprisingly, though, the people didn't do anything about it, and now they pay plenty for new homes in that community.

Almost everywhere in the U.S.A., government imposes these double taxation schemes in the form of impact fees. While there is no way to avoid these fees, once approved by local government, is there a way to avoid unnecessary taxes? Simple. Just get yourself a nonprofit status.

Tax-Exempt in America

One exception to the tax attack summary mentioned earlier—when it comes to transferring property, cash and wealth—is known as the 501(c)(3) tax-exempt organization.[11] Want to open up a tax-free business? Go 501(c)(3), but be warned. This tax-exempt form of business creates an entity that surrenders individuality, autonomy and free enterprise to the government. Second only to oppression by taxation, one can count on total control by submitting to the U.S. government. In other words, if you would like to operate a business that is virtually tax-free and you're not part of the elite monopolies, a billionaire or a large corporation, 501 is the way to go.

Just decide what kind of business service you would like to offer, submit a government-approved nonprofit charter, and you will discover the government grants and programs that are available for you. But don't mention God, or you'll lose your grant opportunity. Take the city council of Columbia, Tennessee, for example, when during a recent council meeting, City Manager Boyer informed everyone present, including the mayor and city council members, that a ministry requesting reduction in rental fees for the Macedonia Community Center "would have to drop all religious education [teachings on God and Jesus Christ] from their program if they are going to be under contract with the city because we cannot use tax money to pay for religious programs."[12] The 501(c)(3) ministry, Word of Life, could do anything they wanted, but they had better not preach the Word of God or speak about Jesus Christ!

What is very concerning for me is that churches and ministry organizations are not eligible for public funds as religious organizations. Yet, if the ministry performs the same secular duties as other organizations and are willing to agree not to talk about God or Jesus while performing these duties, they can get their hands on public money. Sadly, some churches and ministries do just that—leave God and His Son out of it—or they talk about Him anyway behind the government's back.

This, of course, gives the government 100 percent control. If the government decides to clamp down—and at some point, they will—churches and ministries will have to do what they are told or face returning the funds they have accepted. This is certain to bankrupt many. I am sure some progressive will argue the point. You know— the end-justifies-the-means group.

Allow me to tell you about some other tax-exempt segments of our society. Of our total population of 336 million citizens and illegals residing in America, only 109 million are paying taxes. That means that fewer than one of every three people living in this country, receiving benefits and using our schools, etc., actually pays for those privileges. In fact, many are alive, period, because those 109 million tax-paying citizens support the other 227 million.[13]

Of the 227 million, I know that 38 million are retirees who have contributed, at least in part, to their retirement.[14] Interestingly, many retirees are included in that 109 million who are paying taxes—such as my mother, who had to go back to work just to make ends meet. So she collects retirement, but she pays taxes on her fresh revenue. No rest for the weary, Mom.

Tax Incentives

Somewhat like 501(c)(3) organizations, tax incentives are another way the government directs people's behaviors. Incentives reward certain individuals and entities for doing what Big Brother requires of them. If individuals buy a certain type of car, they may receive up to $4,500 from "cash-for-clunker" programs. Purchase a new home and the reward is as high as $8,500. Energy-star washing machines, refrigerators, and computers can generate a basketful of cabbage. That's right, total government control, paid for by the 109 million taxpayers mentioned above.

Incentives are great for the people receiving them, oppressive for those paying them. If you are both receiving and paying, you probably think it is a wash. Think again. After all, doesn't someone have to give before another can receive?

Here comes big government to the rescue, so forget about hard work. Our president has heard the loud cries of the middle class, so he is going to fix it. He has announced "phat" tax incentives and tax breaks for the middle class. I am announcing that this is a big "phat" lie. Where do you think they get all of this money they throw around on Capitol Hill?

Incentives are a "nice" way of demanding specific behaviors, such as recycling and green energy initiatives. Most tax incentives, however, go to very large corporations for relocating their businesses to regions of the country where the government needs to pick up the pace and where stimulus program money is distributed, such as the cap-and-trade initiative coming soon, currently being run as pilot programs for certain power company elites. Right now, there are incentives in the states of Michigan, New York, California, Illinois, Florida and counties with unemployment over 30 percent. Feed me, feed me, Big Government, and let me slap the chains on my brother for you!

The Republican Party is best known for throwing money around in this manner. However, the Democrats have picked up on this little jewel and are experimenting with it to see how it works for their next election cycle. The belief is that incentives stimulate the economy by taking money from hard-working men and women of the middle class and giving those dollars to everyone—from the regular guy to the poor to the richest of the rich. I would not argue against the fact that everyone deserves it, but America must stabilize the tax system, and tax incentives do quite the opposite.

There is too much money from credit in the system, causing consumables to become unaffordable and increasing the debt of the nation. Taking money from the government to make purchases and pay down debt leaves more debt and interest on that debt for someone else to pay. Trust me when I say that you won't be doing yourself a favor if you take money in the form of tax incentives from the federal government.

"It's Mine!" "No, It's Mine!"

I can still hear the children's voices. Three little girls are skipping rope, chanting a rhyme. Four on the merry-go-round are singing. In the distance, two are fighting over a football, and 535 on Capitol Hill and their constituents all over the country are shouting, "It's mine!" "No, it's mine!"

Once taxes are paid, that money belongs to the Treasury, where its intended use is "discharging the debts and defraying the expenses of the community"—not paying for this little whim or that little desire. This is something nobody is taking seriously at all. We're no longer children playing on the playground. We're all grown up now, with children of our own who will not have a nation unless our leaders and all our people begin to treat the Treasury like the responsible nation-building mechanism it was created to be.

In America, there are several groups of people with quite different views as to how tax proceeds should be spent:

1. The citizens who pay taxes and involve themselves in every aspect of society, including humanitarian efforts, community development, the government, and so on. These are genuine American patriots who care, the very reason America has retained remnants of greatness. They are a dying breed, however. Fewer and fewer people go above and beyond what is

required, and there is a growing number of citizens and non-citizens who pay less and demand more.

2. Those who pay their fair share of taxes and don't care what happens next, as long as they are comfortable. These are part of the "I've-done-my-part, now-don't-bother-me" crowd. Understandable. Life has a way of hardening the hearts and souls of many.

3. The "If-I-pay-money-in taxes, it-still-belongs-to-me" bunch, the "It's my money and it doesn't belong to anyone else unless I say so," or "It's mine, and if I don't use it, then nobody else can." These feel that the money they pay in to the government should be there for them to use when they want or need it or that their contributions should go to a special interest of their choosing. Some of these people even believe that the taxes they pay throughout the year should be returned in full or that they have earned additional income credit (EIC) from others.

4. Finally, there is the growing group of people, aliens included, who collect every last dollar they can from the U.S. Treasury without ever having lifted a finger to help others in need or to pay off the debt of the nation. This is most concerning for me because they are currently the loudest voices, and they ensure that candidates who make sweeping campaign promises are on the Hill, providing for them. (For those who doubt the veracity of this statement, see the results of the 2008 general election.)

The last group has always polluted the world, continuing to pull society down to their level of laziness.

The Framers knew what taxes were to be used for, and they set up our tax system to represent a republic—not to sustain a dictatorship, anarchy, progressive or communistic government. The system may have the appearance of the Robin Hood effect, where the government supposedly takes from the rich and gives to the poor. But it does not work that way. In the words of Jimmy Carter, "The present tax system is a disgrace to this country."

What about the Constitution?

If you are still with me, there is one more thing that is troubling about taxes—the more we give, the more they expect. The *we* referred to here are hard-working, middle-class Americans. The *they* is everyone else—government officials and all those who work for the government—representatives, legislators, senators, the elites, special interest groups, lobbyists and even the president himself. If you don't believe it, you could be a progressive.

Did you know that there are approximately 1.2 government workers watching over and regulating every American factory worker, truck driver, union member, delivery person, mail carrier, retail professional and so on? Don't get me wrong—these are well-intentioned people, but they are creating a worldwide supervisory board that costs you a lot of money to feed, clothe, house and pay. And you thought your boss was a bear who didn't cut you any slack. Don't feel too bad though. Your boss has 1.2

government workers telling *him* what to do also.

Taxation has evolved into something it was never intended to be. The Framers ensured liberty when they chose to free this nation's citizens from the all-consuming, communist-style government of the crown. Our forefathers avoided policies of big taxes that cause oppression and protected Americans from future leaders who might seek to return the country to tyranny. How did they accomplish this? With Constitutional provisions:

"**Article I, Section 8.** The Congress shall have Power to lay and collect Taxes, Duties, Imposts and Excises, to pay the Debts and provide for the common Defense and general Welfare of the United States; but all Duties, Imposts and Excises shall be uniform throughout the United States."[15]

You can see by the language that the Framers sought parity—everyone was expected to pay a "fair share," and that's what was meant by "uniform." When America's first Congress met, they followed a rule book that kept them honest and provided limits and boundaries for taxaquences.

Now, in America, the original language and intent of the Constitution has been changed through multiple amendments beyond the Bill of Rights, causing the republic to be replaced with a progressive globalist government. The Sixteenth Amendment to the United States Constitution, ratified on February 3, 1913, reveals the emerging progressive mindset. Notice the blatant changes: "The Congress shall have the power to lay and collect taxes on incomes, *from whatever source derived, without apportionment among the several states, and without regard to any census or enumeration.*" [16]

In other words, Congress has given itself the authority to take 100 percent of every dollar you earn and 100 percent of your property. I hope you can see the discriminatory tax policies of today's progressives who seek to exploit working men and women through taxation. This power, granted to the government in 1913, is slowly and surely consuming our wealth.

At this rate, Americans will all be working for the government as they are "reduced to mere automatons of misery, who will have to affix the chains of oppression to the necks of their fellow sufferers" just to feed, clothe, house and provide medical care for their families. I guess that's okay if you are pro-AmeriCom.

If not...if you're as disgusted with the current cultural tax crisis as I am, then my suggestion is that we return to the original "rule book."

Benesch Bullets

To the leadership of the United States:

- End redistribution of wealth! Repeal the Sixteenth Amendment, restore **Article I**

Section 8 of the Constitution and impose taxes in a fair manner.

- Use tax dollars in the manner prescribed by America's forefathers—that is, only for discharging the nation's debts and defraying costs of the community.

- Outlaw impact fees to avoid double taxation.

- End tax incentive programs, which give government too much control over individuals and businesses, impeding freedom and liberty.

- Initiate a ten-year tax moratorium to stop tax increases and the creation of any new taxes.

- Evaluate the state of the union during the tenth year of a tax moratorium and implement tax cuts between 1-5 percent of income, sales and other taxes. This cycle must be repeated every ten years until the debt of America is paid in full and her currency is back on a renewed course of trust and growth.

- Seriously consider replacing the mixed tax system of income and sales and implement a "Fair Tax" bill similar to the one now before Congress.

- Cease "tax-by-cop" tactics. Hiding taxes in law enforcement initiatives is downright disgusting.

To my fellow believers:

- Do not put 501(c)(3) grant money before God. Churches are not required to become 501(c)(3) organizations to receive tax-exempt status.
- Do not follow the government, follow God.
- Look to other believers for assistance and counsel in time of need instead of leaning on the government.

To my fellow citizens:

- Stop allowing the government to control behaviors through tax incentives. Do not participate in redistributing wealth. In other words, refuse government bribes.
- Insist that illegal aliens pay taxes.
- Cease accepting campaign promises to spend tax dollars on certain initiatives.
- Outlaw Robin-Hood actions of the government. Stop looking to the rich and middle class for financial gain.
- Promote the teaching of true patriotism. "Ask not what your country can do for you—ask what you can do for your country."[17]

The nation's leaders have studied their constituents and, like a puppet master, have learned how to manipulate the strings of their necessities and cravings, their strengths and weaknesses, their ambition and overweening greed. Taxation provides gatekeepers with the strings of control to champion the cause of factions.

America's tax policies were never designed to control the people, but were intended to discharge the debts and defray the expenses of communities—roads, clean water, security. The Framers were wise men of virtue, but today's leaders are not. Taxes have become oppressive, because rulers who lack judgment use them to lift up their special interests, without care, concern or regard for the people who pay for them.

Like abused children, the nation's taxpayers have adapted themselves to this political abuse as a sign that leadership is a caring and loving guardian who is "just doing this for your own good." In addition, the "rule of law" has punished the nation's workers and extended the overreaching arm of government through taxation. This type of control will eventually transform the careers of our dreams into the nightmare of the "chain gang."

In my present position I could scarcely be justified were I to omit raising a warning voice against this approach of returning despotism....It is the effort to place capital on an equal footing with, if not above, labor in structure of government. It is assumed that labor is available only in connections with capital; that nobody labors unless somebody else, owning capital, somehow by the use of it induces him to labor....Now there is no such relation between capital and labor as assumed, nor is there any such thing as a free man being fixed for life in the condition of a hired laborer. Both these assumptions are false, and all inferences from them are groundless. Labor is prior to and independent of capital. Capital is only the fruit of labor, and could never have existed if labor had not first existed. Labor is the superior of capital, and deserves much the higher consideration. [1]

—President Abraham Lincoln
First Annual Message
December 3, 1861

CHAIN GANG

We command you, brothers, to keep away from every brother
who is idle and does not live according to the teaching....
"If a man will not work, he shall not eat."

—2 Thessalonians 3:6, 10

The Taft-Hartley bill is a shocking piece of legislation.
It is unfair to the working people of this country.
It clearly abuses the right,
which millions of our citizens now enjoy,
to join together and bargain with their employers
for fair wages and fair working conditions.[2]

—President Harry S. Truman
On the Veto of the Taft-Hartley Bill, June 20, 1947

According to government statistics, as of January 1, 2010, 15.267 million people were unemployed. That's 10 percent of the working population of the United States.[3] Frightening, isn't it? The total number of people out of work has never been so high in our history. Not even during the Great Depression. Yet, what if I told you that this figure is not accurate and that the actual number is more like 26.2

million[4] and rising, or a staggering 17 percent?![5]

How could the government so misinform the people? Easy! When government wants circumstances to appear better or worse than they really are, they simply bend the truth or up the stats. For example, if you want to scare people to the point of taking preemptive military action against another nation, tell them: "The first time we may be completely certain he (Saddam Hussein/Iraq) has nuclear weapons is when, God forbid, he uses one."[6] At the same time, have your Secretary of State address the U.N. Security Council: "In fact, they (Iraqi regime) can produce enough dry biological agent in a single month to kill thousands upon thousands of people. Our conservative estimate is that Iraq has a stockpile of between 100 and 500 tons of chemical weapons agents. Even the low end of 100 tons of agent would enable Saddam Hussein to cause mass casualties across more than 100 square miles of territory, an area nearly five times the size of Manhattan."[7]

Another illustration of misinformation as told to me recently by one of our big city's leaders behind closed doors: "If you want to cut poverty in half, just redefine the term *poverty* by lowering the dollar amount that defines poverty so that the poor don't appear poor anymore."

The same is true for unemployment. If you want the people to think that America's jobs situation isn't as bad as some people say, tell them a "lie"—that 15 million are out of work rather than 26 million. You see, for reporting purposes, the only people the government considers to be unemployed are those who presently receive benefits and not those who have fallen off the unemployment rolls because they couldn't find another job. For the past three generations, many have landed on welfare or have been forced to settle for jobs serving coffee instead of managing bank loan departments. In addition, many workers have had to seek part-time instead of full-time employment, because full-time work hasn't been available and unemployment benefits have expired.

You know what else your government isn't telling you? They're not telling you that the rise in unemployment is their fault. That's right! Officials have created obstacles to wealth-building jobs and are the cause for unemployment being out of control. The only jobs that are being created are government-controlled projects. No other company is hiring.

Barack Obama was elected to straighten out the economy and to put Americans back to work. Today's leadership touts their excellence—"a good solid (B+)"[8] —and advises patience on the part of the people, claiming that economic recovery will be slow and painful. Just a friendly reminder: After the Great Depression, during Roosevelt's first year in office, he stated: "There were about 10 millions of our citizens who earnestly, and in many cases hungrily, were seeking work and could not get it. Of these, in the short space of a few months, I am convinced that at least 4 million have been given employment or, saying it another way, 40 percent of those seeking work have found it."[9] It seems that our current leadership is seriously derelict in comparison.

After months of research, I have discovered the truth about how jobs are created in America. It is a system that I call the "chain gang," previously used by prisons to create and organize work for the benefit of wardens and state officials. Big business and progressive leadership, however, have devised a similar plan to greatly increase their private wealth by forcing the "chain gang" mentality on American workers. Under the current economic development model, we are all prisoners.

This kind of philosophical behavior didn't begin or end with previous administrations, but finds its deceptive roots buried deep in America's corporate and political history, all the way to the Oval Office.

Two Rivers

In April, 2006, Two Rivers Port Authority for the City of Hardin, Montana, was established to pursue economic development activities—government-sponsored and sanctioned credit expansion work projects. The Two Rivers Authority entered into an agreement with Municipal Capital Markets Group, Inc., and Herbert J. Sims & Co. to purchase over $27 million in Senior Lien Project Revenue Bonds—government debt obligations for private and public gain.

Here is a real-life example of credit expansion and another illustration of where derivative issues can start. Proceeds from a bond sale were used to construct the Two Rivers Regional Detention Facility, a posh, privately designed 464-bed secure facility that was to be operated and managed for the Two Rivers Authority by CiviGenics-Texas, Inc. This bond amount included the first two years' worth of debt service (mortgage payments, for us common folk). Ha! That's just like your borrowing the mortgage for your home and the first couple of years' worth of payments, with no capability of ever paying back the bond. (This payment process, in fact, played a major part in the "sub-prime" lending debacle that Congress has yet to address.)

According to the audit, the organizations listed here, along with a "select" few builders and private correctional facility operators/managers, created a consortium that have proposed several projects like this one—some with construction costs as high as $50 million—throughout the United States. They propose to use revenue from the project to pay back the bonds— hence the term "revenue bonds"—as well as produce local jobs for the city's inhabitants.

The auditor who reviewed this deal knew something was wrong. However, his written pleas were ignored by state officials, bankers and the federal government as they have cheated financial trust by exploiting supply-side economic policy. In other words, the nation's gatekeepers, agents and protectors let America down. These officials knew that the risks to repayment of the bonds included:

- Future need
- Occupancy assumptions
- Inability to sell or lease the project in the event of a default
- Restrictions on prisoner eligibility
- Default remedies might be unenforceable (which means no one is accountable to pay back the loan, except the taxpayer)
- Repayment risk
- Damage/destruction to the facility [10]

Did you get that? Your government not only knew the risks, but it also created a debt that would not be reimbursed to the people of this nation, even if the project failed to pay back the debt. How can a financial system survive if collection is impossible? Well, that's simple. It can't.

The prison builder made off with just under $20 million. Here is part of the upfront payment scenario I explained in an earlier chapter in another flavor. You don't honestly believe the "builder" is a puppet on a string, do you? Though many projects of this type are necessary to develop, maintain and build nations, they have become vehicles for your government to pump artificial sources of cash into the economy...and give a false sense of job security. Two Rivers-type projects have become the primary way for your government to hide the fact that their trickledown economics have failed.

The prison at Two Rivers is now complete. It's a joke though. In spite of all of the warnings from state officials, there are no prisoners housed at the facility. Yep, it's vacant. Throw up the vacancy sign, fellers, we need some prisoners here! Everyone from the Development Authority president, to city, state and county officials have begun finger-pointing. Why? Because the deal is in default, that's why. Just as the auditor had warned. This is an unbelievable circus, and as Barack Obama himself has said about the debt of this nation, "We are all complicit." If Roosevelt, Johnson, Carter, Reagan, Bush I, Clinton and Bush II were professors in the art of trickle-down economics, Obama is the teacher's pet.

General Motors recently perfected a similar scam with government stimulus when they took bailout money to keep the corporate officers' bonuses intact under the auspices of "saving" jobs and then filed for bankruptcy protection not long afterward. You are aware that the old General Motors has been replaced with a new one, aren't you? This is the quintessential example of what I have redefined as "tricky-down economics."

Two Rivers has failed, and you and I will be forced to make it right through additional taxes, because there is no way we can count on the same people who created these problems to fix them, now can we?

Maybe legislators will need to pass some more laws, which will create new criminals so Hardin can begin filling the Two Rivers Detention Facility. Create enough new laws, and they'll have to build an addition onto this prison. Yeah! We're talking lots of new work now. Those dirty no-good criminals will get what they deserve, and the City of Hardin will have more jobs. Hey, I have another idea, let's enforce existing laws against greedy and corrupt CEOs, executives and legislators and put guys like these tricky-down economists behind bars. We'll fill the new prison in record time!

Dollar-an-Hour

Pay raise, that is. That's all we heard around my house when I was growing up—that, and health and retirement benefits. When I was a boy, my father worked for the largest package delivery company outside of the Post Office. He drove a tractor trailer, one of those big rigs. Dad was also a steward for the Union before working his way up the ladder, where he eventually became a labor leader. As a steward, he was the first line of defense for employees. My father always said, "Management is out to get the guys." Those were his very words.

He was good at his job too. He must have saved 15,000 jobs during his driving career, including saving his own neck a few. The boss man, well, let's just say he was always gunning for Ed Benesch, and firing my father for sticking up for the men was kind of like Christmas. It came around once a year.

That dollar-an-hour discussion was most important, because the cost of living inevitably goes up, forcing people to earn more money just to make ends meet. Ah, and let's not forget taxaquences. They drive up the cost of living as well. Oh, I'm sure you've heard the stories. "When I was a kid, a candy bar and a Coke cost a dime." Man, I've gotten so old, I have some of those same stories!

You know me by now, so hang with me while I explain the dollar-an-hour effect. On January 8, 2010, the U.S. government claimed that the average worker in America made $18.80 per hour.[11] That's $624.16 per week, or $32,456.32 in 2009 for a forty-hour workweek. Now, we know that's not true—the front-line American worker, such as a bank teller, earns less than $10 per hour while her boss earns on average $8,461 per hour.[12] This example demonstrates how the numbers get skewed.

Let's take a closer look at why people need at least a dollar-an-hour pay raise. Let's use the out-of-control gasoline crisis that occurred in late 2007 which will be revisiting the American worker sometime in the near future. Gas went up as much as $3-$4 per gallon everywhere in the nation and was as high as $6 per gallon in some places. That's inflation. That's what destroys currencies, economies, families and the living wage. That is why Americans are always hopelessly pursuing pay raises. In the case of the 2007 scenario:If a person used forty gallons to get to and from work each week, the rise in gas prices adversely affected the budget by adding \$120-\$160 per week.

I hope you might understand a little better why a person might need a dollar an hour more to afford what was once affordable. In this case, a person would need a \$3-\$4 per hour raise just to break even. I also hope you now see why asking for a pay raise isn't about greedy employees or unions, but about ensuring that the working men and women of this nation don't go broke just to put gas in the car. This really angers me, because I personally know people who had to make the decision between putting gas in the car and putting food on the table. I know many others who packed their credit cards and even took out second and third mortgages just to make ends meet.

A dollar an hour is not going to fix it, though. Two dollars an hour? Three dollars? Five? I can't give you a figure that will fix America. But the rise in the cost of living is one of the most serious problems facing the American worker. You see that the inflation cycle is put in motion by the aforementioned example. The \$3-\$4 per hour pay raise that is required to offset higher gas prices is eventually reflected in every consumable product and service. Can you also see that the taxaquences are much higher and that the government Treasury increases, while yours decreases? This devalues the dollar, which demands more credit, causing us to surrender more power to the government until communism swallows a nation alive.

The "Company Store"

Maybe you're too young to remember the company store. I know I am. As a student of history and in the interest of setting the record straight, let me tell you what I've learned. At one time, coal was a large source of America's energy. I have remodeled houses that still had the coal chute, so I believe it when people say homes were once heated with the stuff.

In fact, coal mining was big business. Everything from home heat to power plants and steam locomotives ran on coal. It was a time when the miners lived in camps on the mine sites or on adjacent property. Having once built a large bed and breakfast in Montego Bay, Jamaica, where the workers rode to work on donkeys and lived at the work site in a tool shed, I can relate to those camps— and I'm only 46 years old, not 146.

At these mining camps, the owners of the coal mine provided a company store for the convenience of the workers, or did they? We had a similar arrangement in Jamaica, but we just picked up what the guys needed when we were in town and they paid us no more than the items cost. Owners of the coal mines, however, marked up their prices—and were proud of it!

These unscrupulous businessmen charged so much for products at the store that the coal miners couldn't afford to pay for their basics in cash. So, in lieu of money, the workers charged what they needed on store accounts.

Not that the mine owners needed the extra cash. They were greed-driven men who were never satisfied with the profits of the mine.

What is even more interesting is that the coal miners believed in God's plan: "Let no debt remain unpaid." When a miner could no longer work because of age, illness or infirmity, his kid went to work for the boss to pay off his father's debt. Since conditions never improved from one generation to the next, the debt became perpetual for the mining families.

Nothing changed until the union rescued the working man from the clutches of the mine owners. America's workers have the dreaded unions because of the evils of the dreaded corporations.

Since those early days, union leadership has worked to improve working conditions—health care for all, safer environment, minimum wage and CEO salary caps. Now the government is taking over. What will the unions do now? If they continue to push for dollar-an-hour pay raises, they will be fighting a losing battle. Their efforts will never outpace inflation.

In their attempt to create the ideal workplace, however, union leadership has adopted the progressive cause. Organized labor usually supports Democrats. On the other hand, I know many of these union leaders personally, and I know that they truly love and care about America and the members they represent, but I don't think they see the communist beast at the other end of their progressive agenda. So the unions just keep struggling.

Sorry, but I have to say this: Leadership of the AFL-CIO, Teamsters, SEIU, AFGE and so on, are missing the real problem. While they are fighting for a living wage for the American worker, corporations have shipped manufacturing, mining and agricultural activities to foreign and slave nations. Now, imports have consumed most of their jobs, leaving their brotherhood to shop at the new company store—government welfare.

Remember, I was raised in a union household. I know the logic and I have seen the horrors. I believe that union leadership could have prevented the trade imbalance that exists in this country, if they had really wanted to. After all, they thwarted the evildoer at the coal mines!

Fiscal irresponsibility, credit expansion, debt caused by trade imbalance, progressive globalism, communist enticements and taxes are the real reason dollar-an-hour pay raises are necessary, and the very reason they will never be enough. Now the dollar is struggling to survive and losing its value because the union never tended to the threat of foreign labor. This very threat will continue to steal jobs away from union membership until union leadership stops it, and the only way to stop it is for America to become a producer again, not just a consumer.

The new and "improved" company store is coming to your place of business. What we need is a modern-day industrial revolution.

Modern-Day Industrial Revolution

Every morning I scan the news, looking for signs of hope. This morning was no exception. I read that government hasn't changed and that Congress just keeps on recklessly spending deficit dollars to fix a systemic problem that isn't going away until the United States increases sustainable employment—domestic manufacturing, agriculture and mining.

If unemployment is over 26 million and rising, the truth is that any ol' job is not going to be enough to rescue this nation. We will need 26 million sustainable new jobs before any president can award himself a B+ going on an A-.[13]

One thing was different about this particular morning, because I live in a state that seems to have been chugging along without too big a hiccup—Tennessee. To my chagrin, though, I found further evidence that we haven't avoided the inevitable collapse brought about by big government. Today, March 24, 2010, Governor Phil Bredesen announced that the state will mail out more than 1,000 layoff notices to state employees this week and that their jobs will be eliminated "for business reasons amid bleak budget conditions."[14]

Keep in mind: Government only creates work that is dependent upon tax revenue and credit expansion to keep those jobs afloat, nothing like sustainable employment. Up to this point, I have thrown around such words as *jobs, work, manufacturing* and so on almost synonymously, but there is a very big difference. Sure, any job can put a roof over the head and food on the table, but not just any job ensures that the economy sustains itself, grows and prospers. No, a nation needs employment opportunities that create national wealth by exporting domestic goods and services. Creating a handful or even a few million domestic jobs won't be enough.

Domestic manufacturing, mining, services and agriculture must account for 51 percent of everything we purchase. Did you know that America only produces 9 percent of her consumer goods? Consumer goods are known as durable or capital goods—products that exist or remain in the same state for an indefinitely long time.[15] Some examples are plant equipment and durable machinery, industrial and residential construction equipment, automobiles, washers, snowmobiles and so on.[16] All types of manufacturing—cigarettes, pencils and such—are great for economic growth and sustainability; manufacture of durables, however, is vital to a nation. Simply assembling an automobile on U.S. soil does not qualify as domestic manufacturing, even though a car is a durable good.

Secretaries, authors, construction workers, restaurant employees and medical professional careers fall into the category of service industry jobs. Regarded as absolutely necessary, service jobs cannot sustain an economy although they can build, maintain, and repair people and durable goods.

President John Quincy Adams said, "It is, indeed, a general law of prosperous commerce that the real value of exports should by a small, and only a small, balance exceed that of imports, that balance being a permanent addition to the wealth of the nation."[17] If we are to take his words at face value, of the total workforce for December, 2009, America should have employed 42,533,140 in manufacturing. This nation only employed 11,630,000[18]—a manufacturing shortfall of 73 percent or 30,903,140 workers. Where are all of the employees, you ask? The answer is service, government jobs… and the unemployment line.

I believe by now that most readers would agree that we must produce, produce and produce durable goods for domestic and foreign consumption and stop relying on foreign goods and foreign labor. America must immediately start growing her own food, mining her own natural resources, converting those resources into finished products and begin exporting/selling them all over the world. This nation will not get ahead as long as she continues to import more than she exports.

It's time to pitch in and assist in regaining America's prosperity. We must be willing to sacrifice by purchasing at least 50 percent of all of our goods and services from other Americans. How do we do this? Community development.

Community Development

Just as the word *bank* used to denote a safe place to store our money, so the term *economic development* once represented the building of America. Let's take a closer look at this phenomenon to discover the real truth.

As you probably noted in the Two Rivers case, sustainable employment was traded off for temporary jobs. Economic development may build up a community in the short term, but it is much like a drug addict who needs a "fix" to achieve a desired state. Economic development is a "high." In the end, government knowingly charges the taxpayer to pay off their "dealer." Economic—government—development is a "fix" and nothing more—a short-term answer that causes long-term problems called unpaid debt. The worst part is that there is no intention of paying back the debt created by progressive leaders who, in reality, are just looking to transform the nation into servitude by using the long arm of the law.

On the other hand, community development is a permanent solution and not a quick fix, unlike the new city center projects, convention centers, new prisons and new city hall projects that drive economic development. Towns, cities and states must begin to wrap a community around sustainable employment found in domestic manufacturing, agriculture and mining.

These community development authorities can

restore order, inspire community participation and return control to the people, where the Constitution intended it to be. Community development is all about bottom-up, not top-down revitalization. In construction terms, community development begins with "counting the cost" to ensure that there is enough cash to fund the entire project, that the foundation is built on stable ground and that any debt financed can be paid off within seven years—because that's all the time we've got left! The old building may look new, but sooner or later, it will crumble. It may be tempting to go the quick-fix route, but wouldn't it be better to take the necessary time and energy to build a new community on rock-solid sustainable fundamentals?

A community development begins with a vision for growth and a blueprint from which to work. The plan provides citizens with clearly defined milestones and an agenda that is in the best interest of the community. Here are some guidelines we are currently using to create a homeless veterans' community development:

1. Establish growth curve and set a maximum community population.
2. Incorporate advanced, green and renewable technologies.
3. Guarantee adequate agriculture—fruits, vegetables, meats—to provide for all nutritional requirements of life.
4. Initiate mining of and/or trade in agriculture

for natural resources necessary to build and maintain the development.

5. Produce products consumed by the community and for export.

6. Ensure service jobs to maintain the community development.

7. Elect "rulers"—*leaders who are mature, wise, honest and virtuous people of integrity*—who put the people of the community before their own ambition.

Recently, Nashville, Tennessee implemented a new "surefire" economic development plan that assures voters that "more than 3,000 construction jobs will be created during the four years the [city convention] center will be built—1,000 to 2,000 workers will be on site each day."[19] I love the total shot-in-the-dark "guesstimate," which is par for the course for U.S. leadership today. In other words, they proudly tout the 3,000 jobs the new center will bring to locals, and in the very next breath, tell the real truth— 1,000 to 2,000 workers on the job each day. According to my math, that's 1/3 to 2/3 fewer jobs than we are told in the beginning. What politicians refer to as "political correctness" and "puffing," my mother and father always called "lying."

This plan is also estimated to cost Music City somewhere around $595 million, but if city leaders want parking for the visitors—and surely they will—an additional $40 million will be required. The grand total, not including additional land and the convention hotel that is sure to follow, should be around $635 million, not $595 million.[20] Are you beginning to see the pattern of lies? Or are you a progressive who thinks that "puffing" is just good politics?

Allow me to tell the truth without "puffing." The Nashville Music City Center, as it is being called, will cost $188,333 to $200,000 per job, if you use the bold 3,000-person figure. Keep in mind that Music City is actually you, the taxpayer. I wonder how many illegal aliens the city will employ as cooks, housekeepers, painters and the like? That's a great way to ship more greenbacks…out of the country!

Wait, I have another idea. Just give 3,000 people $200,000 each and tell them that they need to make it last for the rest of their lives. They won't have to work ever again. Isn't that the goal of the communist welfare state anyway? There won't be any job injuries. That's a good thing, isn't it? Oh, wait, that won't work. Then there won't be any taxaquences, which are needed to fly America's royalty to exotic places—oops, I mean, to fly government officials to meet their girlfriends in Argentina!

Wake up! How much longer are people going to give in to jobs servitude by following the economic development bunch? How much longer are you going to be able to pay for a privilege that Abraham Lincoln asserted was our right? How much more of your children's futures are you willing to put on credit before you have enough homes, cars, clothes, vacations, computers, televisions, furniture, toys, golf lessons and entertainment? How much is enough, America?

When are people going to realize that the progressive agenda is what ails the nation? When are progressives going to acknowledge that despotism is robbing the country of its future and its promise? When are people going to stop promoting monopolies and big business and start looking out for small business?

Small Business—Big Impact

Why haven't those creative credit expansion and derivative deals been made available to the little guy? How come House bill H.R. 4173 only tends to "too-big-to-fail" businesses when, according to the U.S. Small Business Administration (SBA), small businesses:

- employ just over half of all private sector employees.

- pay 44 percent of total U.S. private payroll.

- have generated 64 percent of net new jobs over the past 15 years.

- create more than half of the non-farm private gross domestic product (GDP).

- hire 40 percent of high-tech workers (such as scientists, engineers, and computer programmers).

- consist of 52 percent home-based and 2 percent franchises.

- made up 97.3 percent of all identified exporters and produced 30.2 percent of the known export value in FY 2007.

- produce 13 times more patents per employee than large patenting firms; these patents are twice as likely as large-firm patents to be among the 1 percent most cited.[21]

Small business has no real lobby on the Hill, and they lack the ability to provide large campaign finance support, generated by massive stock bonuses and outrageous pay that CEOs, executives, and directors make in big business.

It doesn't make good sense that Congress virtually ignored the number-one source for new jobs when dealing out large corporate bailouts during '08 and '09. I just feel it necessary to restate the truth: Small business creates 64 percent of new jobs in America, not big business or government...yet! The bailouts were intended to put people back to work, but the real jobs creation machine received almost nada, zilch, zip from any of the stimulus plans. For me, this is all the proof I need to demonstrate that America's leaders have an agenda separate from the majority and are not interested in restoring the free economy. If they were, they would have distributed 64 percent of bailout money to small business!

I know that small business loans are risky and that 50 percent of them fail. So what? Look at GM. Chrysler has failed twice in my lifetime now. Amtrak has a revolving door with the bankruptcy court. Over $100 billion in bailout money in 2008 and 2009 went to American International Group (AIG) alone. The list of supersized corporations that have failed is as long as many politicians' rap sheets.

Unlike many big businesses, small businesses don't fail because the owners aren't incredible cooks, fine craftsmen, exacting builders and so on. Small business owners have a gift, or calling, if you will. These people are great at what they do, but in most cases, running a business is not what they do best. After all, big business students are the people who go to college to learn how to be big business leaders. Small business owners, who usually grow up in their trade or devote their lives to a skill, are not always experts in creative financing and credit expansion—skills required by their counterpart, big business.

Ivy League schools prepare big business students for the takeover of other corporations; they don't even teach them to be good businessmen and women. Instead, these iconic institutions teach the future of big business how to leverage stock, legally squeeze the life out of employees for the least amount of money, avoid unionization, build cars like the Pinto while legally limiting liability, import products that are illegal to produce in the States (i.e., lead-based children's toys) and beg Congress for bailout dollars, all at the same time.

I'll let you in on a little secret. I was talked into going to an SBA function in Nashville once. I still have the silly little chip they gave me and wasted our hard-earned tax dollars on. But you know the insane part? That was more than six years ago, and I am still waiting for a callback. How can they help businesses if they refuse to do them the courtesy of a follow-up? Is there a membership fee or a bribe I have to give someone—oops, I mean a large campaign donation? Did I forget to tell them that I am a disabled American veteran? Oh, wait, maybe that's the problem. "No loans for patriots, only foreigners here on expired visas."

Abraham Lincoln carried the forefathers' courage, wisdom, and Creator's will into the war of emancipation. Lincoln abolished slavery and held off the persistent rule of despotism. Yet in the past fifty years, progressive leadership has promoted slavery and bowed down to the world leaders of despotism.

President Lincoln was a true American. Republican leaders, be forewarned: "Labor is prior to and independent of capital. Capital is only the fruit of labor and could never have existed if labor had not first existed. Labor is the superior of capital, and deserves much the higher consideration." Those are the words of the former leader of the Republican party, not mine.

Leadership must respect and honor the sacrifice of labor, the fruits of which should not spoil by perpetuating the low-wage cycle found among those classed as the working poor. Moving forward, America must emerge from her financial folly and assume her rightful position as an honorable leader of the free world.

Benesch Bullets

To the leadership of the United States:

- Create an FBTA (Fair Balanced Trade Agreement). America must only purchase products from nations that purchase products made in the U.S.A. Focus on trade balance.
- Suspend NAFTA (North American Free Trade Agreement) and CAFTA (Central American Free Trade Agreement). Eliminate NAFTA and CAFTA and any other foreign trade policies that give preferential treatment to foreign manufacturers, agriculture, mining and service providers who do not reciprocate in a balanced policy with the United States.
- Charge duties and taxes to all who sell their products in the United States.
- Implement a U.S.A. citizens-first work initiative, in which U.S. citizens who are ready, willing and

able to fill a job opening must be hired before an alien can be solicited.

- Stop stimulus spending for large corporations—bailouts interfere with the little guy's ability to compete and confuse free market signals—or at least ensure that small business receives 64 percent.
- Shift current government focus from too-big-to-fail—monopolies, large corporations—to the real business backbone of America, Small Business.
- Cease and desist Two Rivers-type economic development projects and replace them with community development initiatives.

To my fellow believers:

- Support individuals and groups that require others to reciprocate and work hard. "In the name of the Lord Jesus Christ, we command you, brothers, to keep away from every brother who is idle and does not live according to the teaching you received from us....We were not idle when we were with you, nor did we eat anyone's food without paying for it. On the contrary, we worked night and day, laboring and toiling so that we would not be a burden to any of you. We did this, not because we do not have the right to such help, but in order to make ourselves a model for you to follow. For even when we were with you, we gave you this rule: 'If a man will not work, he shall not eat'" (2 Thess. 3:6-10).

- Encourage and help others by offering a hand up, not a hand out. Handouts discourage hard work, replacing Protestant work ethos with the philosophical "right of entitlement."
- Participate in community development planning.
- Do not place earning wages and careers above God.

To my fellow citizens:

- Work hard!
- Engage community leaders to develop a "comprehensive community development plan" including sustainable employment initiatives. If your community doesn't have a plan...
- Don't rely on state and federal officials to create jobs.
- Put your best foot forward at the office. Smile, maintain enthusiasm, make suggestions and follow workplace SOP (standard operating procedures).
- Support local agriculture, manufacturing, and

mining. When their products aren't available…

- Purchase products and services from local businesses that sell products made in the U.S.A. If they are still unavailable…
- Consider producing a product made in the U.S.A…. or doing without.

At the very beginning of this chapter, I exposed the ugly truth that 26.2 million Americans were actually unemployed and that government officials deliberately, with malice aforethought, misled the public. I have also explained that the government is the reason for this season of unemployment. Their willful and reckless spending, wasteful handouts and blatant disregard for small business have caused big business to grow into monstrous monopolies that, like communist government, consume all wealth and resources, stealing them from their rightful heirs.

Union leadership confronted despotism at the company store. But they have also sold out to special interests, progressive leadership and foreign labor. Organized labor may fight for the rights of workers; at the same time they are selling the brotherhood down the river of communism, replacing God-fearing, hard-working Americans with a labor force that is blind to America's heritage.

Barack Obama signed a proclamation declaring a national emergency in the form of a "flu pandemic," but he neglected the real threat to the nation's job security. According to U.S. government reports, in 2008, 15.6 percent of America's workforce was foreign born.[22] These foreign-born workers have replaced Americans and account for almost 100 percent of this nation's unemployment.

The impending national epidemic—the job-killer and wage-destroyer that will lead to the ultimate demise of labor—is not the flu, but an "aliendemic!"

In the first place, we should insist that if the immigrant who comes here in good faith becomes an American and assimilates himself to us, he shall be treated on an exact equality with everyone else, for it is an outrage to discriminate against any such man because of creed, or birthplace, or origin. But this is predicated upon the person's becoming in every facet an American, and nothing but an American....There can be no divided allegiance here. Any man who says he is an American, but something else also [hyphenated American], isn't an American at all. We have room for but one flag, the American flag....We have room for but one language here, and that is the English language...and we have room for but one sole loyalty and that is a loyalty to the American people. [1]

—President Theodore Roosevelt
Letter to the American Defense Society
January 3, 1919

ALIENDEMIC

*You shall not murder.…You shall not steal.…You shall not
covet your neighbor's house. You shall not covet your neighbor's
wife, or his manservant or maidservant, his ox or donkey,
or anything that belongs to your neighbor.*
—Exodus 20:13, 15, 17

*The commandment given us is clear and simple:
"Thou shalt love thy neighbor as thyself."* [2]
—President Ronald Wilson Reagan
"Evil Empire" Speech, March 8, 1983

I can hear my pundits now: "Benesch, you are a racist
who doesn't care about or understand the plight of the
poor, the disabled and the downtrodden."

Nothing could be further from the truth. I'm
only third-generation American. My family hails from
a nation that no longer exists—Bohemia—because
big government and war destroyed the once great
superpower. Now called the Czech Republic, the former
Czechoslovakia is made up of my homeland, Bohemia,

Moravia-Austrian-Silesia, Upper Hungary (present-day Slovakia) and Carpathian Ruthenia.[3] Prague is the capital of the Czech Republic, located in the heart of the former Bohemian nation.

I'm tired of being told that Americans are second-class citizens to world diversity! My grandfather was the illegitimate son of an immigrant woman and the first American-born citizen in our family. He served his country in WWII as a United States Marine. From the muddy foxholes of Okinawa, he fought many battles against the Japanese.

My grandfather was a tough son-of-a-gun, a patriot who spilled blood in order to preserve this nation's freedoms. I never heard him ask for a thing, but he was willing to risk everything to protect and preserve his new country's honor. I deeply miss my grandfather. Semper Fi, Joe!

Roots in Bohemia, Branches in America

No one handed over our protestant culture and riches to other people just because we wanted to achieve a communist humanitarian utopian society. In fact, world wars remapped my family's homeland numerous times, eliminating Bohemia from the European countryside. Some theories conclude that the Beneses were renamed "Benesch" as fascist occupation and the Second World War erased our family title, expelled our citizens and confiscated our property and our wealth. Like America today, the left and the right tore the Democratic Republic of Bohemia apart, and elites filled their pockets full of our family heirlooms.

I know a lot about diversity, poverty and being downtrodden. Webster makes matters worse by defining Bohemian as "vagabonds and gypsies and suggests that Bohemian is often spelled with a lower case 'b'."[4] How would you like to be known as a "bohemian-wanderer"? That is how some refer to persons of my nationality.

Allow me to share with you how my family has handled the adversity of diversity. First, may I tell you what my family did *not* do? We did not march in the streets of Chicago carrying our Bohemian flags. We did not hire the American Civil Liberties Union (ACLU). Although I do joke from time to time with my father about returning to the motherland and setting things right, we haven't started a civil war. We did not create fraudulent documents so that we could steal from America's savings or increase her debt burdens. My family doesn't whine, file lawsuits or complain to the United Nations. We have not petitioned the U.S. government to right the wrongs or lobbied Congress for reparations.

Instead, my family went to work doing whatever anyone would hire us to do. We continue to make sure that we pay our taxes and that we help family, friends, the communities and states where we reside. Most importantly, the first-, second- and third-generation

Benesches dropped the hyphenated label "Bohemian-American", joined the United States military, pledged our allegiance to the U.S. flag and gave an oath to protect and defend the U.S. Constitution from all enemies—both domestic and foreign. I am proud to report that the fourth generation is equally committed. Two of my nephews serve in the armed forces—one in the Navy and one in my alma mater, Army.

Now for the flip side of that coin. We are instructed in Scripture to love our neighbors…but to let them walk all over us? I don't think so! My family understands tyranny and oppression. We have no intention of going through that again or allowing modern-day immigrants, aided by progressive globalists, to help themselves to our possessions. Benesches are Americans who came from the adversity of diversity and live peacefully in the land that once protected the free. We have our priorities in order and plug along, just trying to hang onto our postage-stamp piece of America.

Keeping Our Priorities Straight

Poet Emma Lazarus wrote:

> Give me your tired, your poor.
> Your huddled masses yearning to breathe free.
> The wretched refuse of your teeming shore.
> Send these, the homeless, tempest-tost to me.

I lift my lamp beside the golden door![5]

Now a beloved part of the Statue of Liberty, these words stand as a testament to those who desire to make a fresh start, share in *and defend* our cherished freedom, liberty and justice.

Yet, the floodgates of progressive prosperity remain wide open to anyone who will come to America to work for cash under the table. What is the cost to legal citizens of this nation? *Your* job, *your* home, *your* car and *your* representation, because factions seem to have declared those of us in the majority as second-class citizens. I know that many Americans tend to focus on our neighbor to the south, but truth be known, even Great Britain's citizens enter the U.S., having no intention of ever going back home.

I have one such friend who traveled to America on a work visa. He spent the next seven years learning how to be a hard-working and taxpaying bona fide American, including paying his $595 citizenship fee and an $85 fingerprint fee. That's right. You have been duped about the costs of becoming a citizen as well. There is nothing difficult or cumbersome about becoming a U.S. citizen, and the fee is the price of a 32" flat screen television and not the thousands of dollars immigrations lawyers charge their clients to skirt the system, break rules and evade the "no murderers or criminals allowed" naturalization prohibitions.

How hard could becoming a citizen be? An immigrant must reside in America for five years (three, if married to a citizen), read and write basic English, not be a felon or fugitive, be a person of integrity—not one who entered America illegally—know basic civics and U.S. history, not be involved in drug or human trafficking, pay the required fees, pay income taxes, pledge allegiance to the flag, and sign up for selective services like every other American must.[6]

The daughter of a friend followed her father to this country, the land of opportunity, several years after he earned his citizenship. Before ever boarding a plane to America, she had decided that she wanted to naturalize.

After arriving in America, she began the "difficult" process of becoming an American citizen. She has now taken all of her classes and fulfilled almost all naturalization requirements. She could easily become a citizen. After all, that's why she came here, isn't it? There's a catch, though.

It seems my friend's daughter has her priorities out of order. She, unlike her father, chose the television set over her citizenship. That's right. A 32" Dolby surround sound, 1080 pixels, HD color TV over becoming a bona fide red, white and blue daughter of the United States! She must be thinking, *What good is it to be an American if you can't have the television to go along with the Green card?*

I believe I have just found another example of greed—imported version. Apparently this young lady lacks morals, values and ethics. Maybe that is the problem—"privilege over principle." To be quite honest, I hope Immigrations and Custom Enforcement (ICE) picks her up and sends her packing real soon. Oh, and confiscates her television set to cover the costs of deportation as well!

If you have just discovered that you are a progressive, then you should skip over the balance of this book and go straight to the Conclusion. A progressive still might find America's history to be a good joke or at least entertaining. If you are not a progressive, then please allow me to share some thoughts on language expectations/necessities.

English First

"These people are a matter of great concern to us.…Few understand our language, so we cannot communicate with them through our newspapers. They are not used to freedom and do not know how to use it properly. … They bring in much of their own reading from their homeland and print newspapers in their own language. In some parts of our state, ads, street signs, and even some legal documents are in their own language and allowed in courts. Unless the stream of these people can be turned away from their country to other countries, they will soon outnumber us so that we will not be able to save our language or our government."[7] It was Benjamin Franklin who uttered these words.

I'm sure I'll catch some flak over this, but I believe that Americans should learn more than one language. After all, how can we be expected to love one another and give our all if we can't understand or communicate with each other?

Why can't we learn multiple languages? Just think of the doors that would open for us if we could communicate with everyone. New business deals would open up and the "sky would be the limit." If I were president, I would initiate a minimum standard for children to learn two primary languages, beginning in kindergarten. Sign language would be an additional requirement. Under my leadership, high school graduates would speak and write English as well as any other language of their choosing, and seniors would be able to sign the day they earned their diplomas. It is important for Americans to be well connected with foreign visitors and with the citizens of nations we visit.

Up to the mid-1900s, Americans spoke a language—not necessarily English—but the language of their country of origin. Children of immigrants often learned English before their parents. My grandmother, whose parents came to America from Germany, speaks both English and German fluently. Today, those languages have been allowed to die out with our grandparents. My father never learned German; nor did I. We regret that.

Front and center today, however, is the question of

Spanish. I want foreigners to visit the States; but if they intend to stay, they must learn the national language—English. This requirement is already in place and is part of the reason why immigration takes time. Aliens must speak and write the English language well enough to read road signs and other important information communicated and spoken in English. The fact that aliens already speak the language of their country of origin is a plus and should be required.

Let's clear up the road sign and English-first issue. Congress would like to replace every road sign in America, in our law libraries and in all public documents to reflect both English and Spanish—and not for the reasons you may think. Replacing every sign and document in the United States would require a lot of purchase orders—a great excuse for the World Bank to lend America money for what it calls "humanitarian reasons." That's right, stimulus is the reason for U.S. congressional and state officials to push for America to relinquish her hold on the English language. It has nothing to do with a kinder and more understanding nation, and everything to do with jobs and progressive globalism.

I know the aforesaid is a bold statement and accuses the government of further culture-cleansing. But my last remark is supported by progressive President Bill Clinton's global actions that I have identified as an initiative to eliminate English-first.

As a final act of sovereign rebellion aboard Air

Force One, Executive Order 13166, entitled "Improving Access to Services for Persons with Limited English Proficiency" requires all federal agencies to relieve aliens of their responsibility of learning English.

This single act of "America-second" has opened the door to considerable federal and state litigation, expanded bureaucracies on all levels of government, greatly increased welfare as hands-on jobs have been handed over to migrant workers, increased translation requirements and stimulated a whole host of stimulus initiatives similar to those mentioned above. All of this comes at a colossal cost to the American taxpayers, who are not only losing their livelihoods and lifestyles to globalization, but are being forced to pay to become third-class citizens of the world as well.[8]

Jak jsem ekl. Nejdletjším dvodem pro anglitinu-první, je pro nás vdt, pro sebe pravdu, e nám pomáhá udret naši nezávislost a naši svobodu, kterou jsme Americané ztratí-li progresivní globalismu je povoleno i nadále svobodu vzkvétat.

Now that I have communicated my thought in Czech—the language of my family's origin—please allow me to translate into English:

"The most important reason for English-first is for us to know for ourselves the truth that helps us retain our independence and our freedom, which we Americans will lose if progressive globalism is allowed continued freedom to flourish."[9]

The Cost of Cheap Imports

Let's tackle the issue of cheap imports or the pursuit of cheap consumer goods that seems to be the centerpiece of illegal immigration. Estimates total somewhere between 11 and 33 million people who have been smuggled, born (anchor babies), sneaked, driven, flown, shipped or otherwise entered America illegally or who have stayed beyond legal permission. They come from all over the world, not just from Mexico.

How do I know how many aliens have come to America illegally if the statistics are unreported? Well, I can't tell you exactly, but if I take the facts we do know and apply the math, I can come close. For example, we know that President Ronald Reagan's Immigration Reform and Control Act of 1986 (IRCA)[10] gave legal citizenship to about 3 million illegal aliens.[11] In addition, the 3 million who were seeking citizenship ballooned into more than 11 million during the decade that followed. That's an increase of 3.3 times in ten years. The math works out like this: Let's say that the increase remained somewhat constant at a multiplication rate of 3. From 1996 until 2006, that would be 3 x 11 or 33 million. Keep in mind: IRCA permitted legal entry to 3 million and not the flood that followed.

It is the pursuit of consumer goods and services, especially those goods and services that can be purchased at a low cost to Americans, that continues to drive discussions concerning the benefits of illegal aliens. To some, cheap imports and cheap labor are the "goose that laid the golden egg," because consumables are more affordable and business is more profitable as a result of the aliendemic. These same individuals seem to consider the resulting carnage—tuberculosis, AIDS, bed bugs and who knows what other diseases—to be the price we must pay for affordable products.

To even begin to understand how an aliendemic infects a nation, we must go all the way back to the beginning of the book. True wealth, or the lack of it, forces a nation's people to look at affordability, instead of nationality. If Americans possessed true wealth, cost wouldn't be an issue.

Americans must know that there are consequences for allowing tens of millions of people from other nations to illegally tread the countryside with impunity. I have discussed many of the consequences already, but allow me to recap.

When a nation crosses the balanced trade threshold, the economy enters into debt storm. Cheap consumables, in lieu of more expensive homemade and home-grown products and services, always lead to economic collapse, high taxes, greed and a broken system of justice. These social and economic consequences result in progressivism and communism and the destruction of national currencies, which perpetuate poverty, homelessness and a state of disrepair. So consider the destiny of your nation the next time you pick up a tube of toothpaste made in China or invite two or three illegal aliens into your neighborhood to care for your landscape.

You may also want to consider the significance of the unknown. Who are these people coming to America? What are their motives? What kind of morals, values and ethics do they possess? Do you want them marrying your children and fathering your grandchildren?

Allow me to share a bone-chilling personal experience. While working as the project superintendent for one of the world's largest construction companies for the Catholic Church, I was required by the priest to hire people of diversity. One such person, referred to us by Catholic Charities, was an illegal alien I'll call Juan.

Juan was a good-looking, hard worker who spoke very little English. He came from Costa Rica, claiming, as best he could communicate, that he had come to the land of opportunity to achieve his dreams—money, a wife and children. Who could blame him? After all, that's exactly what I was pursuing when we met. Juan had a driver's license and Social Security and Green cards. He had all of the necessary documents and qualities of the perfect employee—or so I thought.

When the company I worked for completed its projects in Nashville, Tennessee, I went on to Arab, Alabama, and Santa Cruz, California. Juan got a job with one of my friends who owned a Tennessee construction company.

Juan was working out well, making good money and passing time with my friend's bookkeeper, Liz (fictitious name). Liz wound up marrying Juan, who fathered a beautiful baby girl with auburn hair like her mother.

Several years had passed when Liz called me one day. "Have you heard from Juan lately?"

"No, I haven't," I responded.

Then she laid a bomb on me. "Jim, Juan went back to Costa Rica for his father's funeral. His father died of a heart attack about thirty days ago, and I haven't been able to get in touch with Juan since."

I'm sure you know how this story ends. As it turned out, Juan, the perfect employee who had come to America to make a better life for himself, actually came to escape justice at home. You see, Juan was a common criminal who had fled his country while awaiting trial for murder! That's right, I had a murderer on the job. My skin still crawls whenever I think about Juan. He lied, cheated and stole to get away with murder! How did he do it? He sneaked into Tennessee after hearing that we were giving away drivers' licenses, and once you had a state-issued driver's license, it was easy to obtain a Social Security card and Green card. Poof! Instant citizenship for 300 bucks.

Whatever happened to Juan? He's far away from Nashville, serving fifteen years to life in a Costa Rican prison. You know who takes care of that child of his, all the way through college, don't you? That's right—the hard-working, tax-paying Americans who took the time to make sure there are laws against illegal immigration so that more Juans don't show up in this country. His paperwork? I'm glad you asked. All courtesy of another criminal, aided by the State of Tennessee, who saw fit to provide a guy who couldn't even speak, read or write the English language, with a driver's license. Way to go, Volunteers!

I want you to understand that I am not opposed to the citizens of Mexico. They are a great people. I respect their work ethic, their family values and their love for God. I am, however, opposed to governments that perpetuate the cycle of poverty. We must counter this corruption wherever it is found by first protecting America's sovereignty.

Mexican-American War

I am not referring to the war that began on April 25, 1846, and ended with the signing of a peace treaty on February 2, 1848. Rather, I want to discuss the war that began on America's streets right about the same time United States boots stepped onto the Iraqi field of battle.

As of August, 2009, 4,250 members of the U.S. Armed Forces had fallen as a result of combat-related incidents in the Iraq War.[11] Since the beginning of that war (March 2003, which translates to seven years or seventy-eight months), an average of 607 soldiers per year—or 54 soldiers per month—have given their lives in the pursuit of freedom, liberty and the defense of America.

Would it shock you to know that in comparison with the number of soldiers killed on the battlefield of Iraq, approximately 10,050 to 14,028 Americans gave their lives in the pursuit of cheap labor? During the same time frame, studies reveal that between 1,435 and 2,004 Americans were killed annually by illegal aliens, right here on the streets of America. That's three times more deaths than in the Iraq war. There's a war going on right here at home, and nobody is saying a thing about it! Between 129 and 180 people are killed every month by illegal aliens— oops! excuse me, I mean people who are just trying to make a better life for themselves and their families. Well, forgive my naïveté, but what does murder have to do with gainful employment? [12]

Oh, that's not all. For each illegal alien residing in the United States of America, the government redirects your taxpayer dollars to law enforcement, ICE, courts, interpreters, transportation, Social Security, welfare, food stamps, additional infrastructure, roads, housing, schools, health care, inpatient hospital care, outpatient hospital care, emergency hospital care, prenatal care, social services, unpaid taxes and interest on all of the above. In addition, you get to pay the difference in automobile accident insurance, because we all know that illegal aliens don't have that, either, and are not held to the same standard of accountability for personal property damages as legitimate citizens.

Indulge my anger a little longer. I know a guy who has a gambling problem. He has borrowed money from me many times. You probably know someone like this who borrows and borrows and never pays you back or pays sporadically until the payments stop altogether. He called again the other night, looking to bum $500 off me for two weeks. I finally did him the best favor he will ever receive. I told him to quit gambling, and he would never have to borrow money again!

My advice to America is the same: Quit gambling! Progressive globalism is a gamble. America was established upon principles that are no longer embraced. If we continue to sit at the blackjack table, the double-dealers of diversity will eventually take all of our winnings—the car, the house and our kids too.

That brings me to the reason why illegal immigration just can't be tolerated any longer. I understand that America wants to rescue the world, but allow me to reason with those who can be reasoned with.

- "You shall not murder (Exod. 20:13).
- "You shall not steal (v. 15).
- "You shall not covet your neighbor's house. You shall not covet your neighbor's wife, or his manservant or maidservant, his ox or donkey, or anything that belongs to your neighbor" (v. 17).

These commandments from the Original Land Owner of America say it all. Don't come to this country against the will of the land owners and begin murdering, stealing, lying, cheating and coveting, then expect a warm welcome, a great job with all of the benefits and free citizenship. Deliberate, self-centered violation of the law is nothing short of evil.

Representatives, leaders and others who stand by doing nothing to confront these evil acts and, worse, aid in illegal activity are nothing less than conspirators and accomplices to murder, rape, theft and unlawful confiscation. No wonder the Founding Fathers didn't frame a progressive globalist or communist nation. Anyone who commits these acts of atrocity against honest, hard-working Americans deserves to be in prison, not in Congress!

People who break into America without permission; fraudulently obtain fake documentation; pawn anchor babies off on our nation; steal Medicare, Medicaid, welfare and education; crash their uninsured vehicles into citizens' vehicles and do not lift a finger to aid other Americans are not here to help. They are murdering, stealing, coveting and harming this nation. They are America's enemy, not her neighbor and not her friend.

As my experience with Juan demonstrates, illegals may possess false documentation, provide a source of so-called "cheap imports" and seem to complement America. But don't get caught up in the crossfire of immigration...

or you could become one of 129 to 180 people gunned down every month in this aliendemic!

Benesch Bullets

To the leadership of the United States:

- QUIT BREAKING THE LAW!
- Stop illegal immigration.
- Do not give citizenship to common criminals who have already proven that they cannot be trusted to become honest, hard-working, contributing Americans.
- Deport all people caught in America who are not authorized or show proper documents.
- Confiscate U.S. currency found in possession of foreigners in foreign lands. It is illegal to possess America's currency outside of the contiguous United States.
- Enforce America's laws "equally!" Discriminatory practices are despotism.
- File charges of treason and murder against all U.S. officials aiding illegal immigration, even if a violator is the President of the United States or a member of Congress. They are responsible for over 10,000 American deaths since March 2003! Prosecutors would charge a bank robbery getaway driver for murder if

a bank employee or patron were killed during the crime, even if the driver didn't pull the trigger. So charge the accomplices to illegal immigration as well.

- Stop making a mockery of justice. Illegal immigration is a very serious problem, and our justice system cannot afford to lose what virtue still remains.
- Strictly enforce the Benesch 50/50 Immigration Plan: a fifty-year prison sentence—without the possibility of parole—and a $50 million fine for CEOs, directors and corporate executives who ignore or violate current immigration laws.
- Protect America's borders and enforce her sovereignty.
- Protect American citizens from all threats, especially foreign.

To my fellow believers:

- Teach the Scripture, verbatim.
- "Thou shalt love thy neighbor as thyself" (Lev. 19:18 KJV). Require the same from others. Allow me to dispel Christian political correctness. To love your neighbor is not to let him murder, steal and covet. That is aiding and abetting sinful and wretched criminal activity and is not genuine love.

- Read 1 Corinthians 13:4-13 for the definition of love, and you will find that my last bullet is true.
- Stop following the world and lead America by example by maintaining obedience to the Word—that's "world" without the "L."

To my fellow citizens:

- Peaceably assemble and exercise the First Amendment. Petition government for redress to end government-subsidized illegal immigration.
- Stop looking to government to fix problems. If your neighbors hire illegal aliens, correct them.
- Read the Declaration of Independence so that you will know exactly why America's forefathers removed the dictator's chains, and you will see for yourself that America once again resembles the anarchy from which we were freed.
- Stop patronizing restaurants, contractors and other businesses that hire illegal aliens. These are criminal enterprises.

In our attempt to rescue the world and consume cheap imports, we have caused an aliendemic that has infected the nation, allowing Americans to be murdered and financially destroyed. All of this pain and suffering just so a few can feel a sense of accomplishment while even fewer grow their personal bank accounts.

Affectionately regard and heed the word of President Theodore Roosevelt: "We have room for but one flag, the American flag...We have room for but one language here, and that is the English language...and we have room for but one sole loyalty and that is a loyalty to the American people."

Upon further consideration, I am more determined than ever to end the aliendemic destroying America. For if neighbor sells out neighbor for personal gain, it will be greed, not compassion, that sears this nation's soul.

We have now lived almost fifty years under the Constitution framed by the sages and patriots of the Revolution....Our Constitution is no longer a doubtful experiment; and, at the end of nearly half a century, we find that it has preserved unimpaired the liberties of the people, secured the rights of property, and that our country has improved and is flourishing beyond any former example in the history of nations. In our domestic concerns there is everything to encourage us; and if you are true to yourselves nothing can impede your march to the highest point of national prosperity....The lessons contained in this invaluable legacy of Washington to his countrymen should be cherished in the heart of every citizen to the latest generation...and artful and designing men will always be found who are ready to foment these fatal divisions and to inflame the natural jealousies of different sections of the country. The history of the world is full of such examples and especially the history of republics...The paper-money system and its natural associates—monopoly and exclusive privileges—have already struck their roots deep in the soil; and it will require all your efforts to check its further growth and to eradicate the evil. The men who profit by the abuses and desire to perpetuate them will continue to besiege the halls of legislation in the general government as well as in the States and will seek, by every artifice, to mislead and deceive the public servants. [1]

—Andrew Jackson
Farewell Address to the Nation
March 4, 1837

GREED: NEVER ENOUGH!

Watch out! Be on your guard against all kinds of greed;
a man's life does not consist
in the abundance of his possessions.

—Luke 12:15

Greed is self-centeredness to the detriment of others.[2]

—James Edward Benesch
In a speech to the Maury County Rotary Club
December 31, 2009

The U. S. GAO states that a minimum of 7 percent of all government revenues are lost to waste, fraud and abuse. Other estimates set that number as high as 12 percent.[3] In fiscal year 2010, that will add up to over $268.1 billion, or right at 60 percent of the 2008 budget deficit. At the less conservative number of 12 percent, we can see that waste, fraud and abuse could account for as much as $459.6 billion, or more than the entire 2008 budget deficit! If you take the welfare estimates and combine them with the waste, fraud and abuse of my lifetime, one could conclude that the entire federal debt could be attributed to lying, cheating and stealing.

A United States Department of Transportation audit report, released on January 7, 2010, revealed that the Kentucky Department of Transportation has awarded $24 million in federal stimulus contracts to companies associated with a prominent figurehead of fortune—a road contractor—who is currently accused of bribing the previous Kentucky Secretary of Transportation for state contracts.[4] Of course, there would never have been a problem to begin with if the Secretary appointed as the gatekeeper had been a person of integrity and love of country and if a lot of money in the form of credit expansion initiatives hadn't been available. Instead, this shows yet another example of figureheads whose reckless anti-patriotism is killing our country.

Oh, I can hear those voices now. *But, Jim, out of $787 billion in stimulus money, you'd expect some theft, wouldn't you? You know, we can't catch everyone. Why jeopardize a worthy system for a piddling $24 million?* Actually, this is the kind of reasoning I would expect from the progressive mindset. But allow me the opportunity of addressing the opposition while giving the working men and women of this nation a heart attack.

For those who remember the S & L scandal, the average bank robber—excuse me, the average CEO *banker*—received one-fifth the prison term of the common bank robber. Maybe it was because he was wearing a Gucci suit instead of a mask.

Power Corrupts

On a cold winter's evening in 2009—January 27, to be exact—in Brentwood, Tennessee, I watched the president's State of the Union address. My fellow Americans, we have been betrayed! Misstep upon misstep, one selfish act after another, the course of America has been set.

I must admit that if I were the guy in the White House or even the previous resident, I, too, would have created stimulus programs to revive America. To let this nation fall? Not an option.

Truth be known, I would have created sustainable community development, employment and small business initiatives instead of wasting trillions on city centers, corporate bonuses and billion-dollar banker bailouts. I would have revitalized the county seat of America with homeland mining, agriculture and manufacturing. With the billions of dollars in bailout money given to AIG alone, I could have built fifty community developments for two million people each. That's sustainable employment and food for one-third of the entire population of the United States of America for the next thirty years.[5]

We have it backwards, folks. We are propping up corporations that have already failed; some, multiple times. That's not only abnormal, it's insane! Those businesses haven't failed because the large companies lack wealth or unions have sucked them dry. Rather, they have failed because the guardians and gatekeepers have stolen their wealth.

In all honesty, we must spend a lot of dollars to balance trade, not frivolously perpetuate continuing imbalance. With honesty and integrity, we must right the wrongs that have led America to this economic crisis. We must challenge the pervading mindset instead of pander to it. We must engage this nation in reform and not change. But we must seek reform in a responsible manner and avoid even the appearance of favors to old friends, campaign contributors, special interest groups and political factions.

Favoritism is communism—actions of greed buried in the corrupt hearts of men who are more concerned with how things are done on the Hill than with the prosperity of the common men and women of this nation. You can take this to the bank: Main Street always bears the burdens of the abuse of Wall Street and Pennsylvania Avenue.

Greedy and corrupt people lack wisdom to discern and virtue to pursue the common good of society. Greed corrupts all and is the reason why 79-81 percent of the world is living in poverty—less than $2.50 USD per day— and over 385 million more live in abject poverty—less than $1.25 USD per day.[6] Although for the past fifty years, progressive globalism has claimed to promote positive change, present-day estimates support my claim that this "kinder and gentler" movement is in reality killing fifty thousand people per day or eighteen million per year—genocide on a scale that has never before been seen in history![7]

Words from the Father of the Constitution

"History records that the money changers have used every form of abuse, intrigue, deceit and violent means possible to maintain their control over governments by controlling money and its issuance."[8] Known as the Father of the United States Constitution, James Madison co-founded the Democratic-Republican Party. Madison served two terms as the fourth president and was deeply concerned with the amount of power the Constitution granted men in positions of authority.[9]

Leaders responsible for America's independence and national sovereignty in Madison's time were different, though. They were patriots. Madison was one of those men who believed that "the aim of every political constitution is, or ought to be, first to obtain for rulers—men who possess most wisdom to discern, and most virtue to pursue, the common good of the society—and in the next place, to take the most effectual precautions for keeping them virtuous whilst they continue to hold their public trust."[10]

Lobbyists are the enemy of the United States Constitution and do just the opposite of what the Framers mandated. In fact, special interests bribe, intimidate and manipulate America's elected officials and rob the nation of leaders who possess wisdom to discern, virtue and public trust. For Madison, selfish ambition had no place in America. For him, leaders of factions, or special interests, posed an imminent threat to the republic he represented. Madison's manifesto pays tribute to national integrity, trust and prosperity. For the forefathers, service to country came second only to God. The Framer of the Constitution proclaimed that patriotism—service to and maintenance of God's principles as reflected in the Republic of the United States of America—was the *duty of every citizen*, but was the *responsibility* of America's *rulers*.[11]

Trading Democracy

We have let America's greatest generation down. We have not only allowed but have, in some cases, sullied the reputations of our elected officials. Oh, don't get me wrong, leadership has been complicit, sometimes leading the charge. Please forgive me...

Let me re-emphasize: "The aim of every political constitution is, or ought to be, first to obtain for rulers—men who possess most wisdom to discern, and most virtue to pursue, the common good of the society—and in the next place, to take the most effectual precautions for keeping them virtuous whilst they continue to hold their public trust."[12]

Keeping them virtuous, now that's the trick...and

seemingly impossible for those of us who have personally witnessed what happens on Capitol Hill. I have worked with some of the most powerful leaders in the free world. You would think that there are some real debates going on there, but that's just not true. Oh, sure, one can observe the hearings, but some of them are pure theater. During those hearings, debates and speeches on the floor, America's representatives aren't considering how they will vote, just making it look as if they are.

Let's say a member of Congress has a large campaign contributor who wants to leave a legacy in the form of a museum—by the way, this is a true example: The contributor doesn't expect to pay for the museum himself. Why should he, when he runs in circles that have the ability to steal—oh, excuse me, I mean to provide jobs to the community—by spending America's tax dollars to build the museum?

It shouldn't come as any real surprise to you that elites have the means to ensure that their guy or gal gets the bucks needed to be elected, or reelected. Oh, sure, they spend a lot of money on campaigns, but it is only a fraction of what a nice museum costs. Elites call this risk- or good money management.

Then, after election, that congressperson writes a bill for the museum, which is then submitted to the House of Representatives or the Senate. To be perfectly honest, no other congressman will support the bill. What good would it do their constituents? Well...maybe if they have struck a deal to support each other's pet projects. And so it goes until there is a large enough contingent of congressmen—a "majority," 218 members of the House of Representatives and 51 senators—who "gang" up or team up to push their private agendas.

This nation used to be built on entrepreneurialism, hard work and innovation. Not so anymore. Instead, it is being dismantled by misuse of your tax dollars, lethargy and democratic manipulation! Sad to say, but a majority of the Congress is involved in manipulating democracy for personal gain, meaning election or re-election. It's that simple.

I liken the congressional process to the stockyards or an auction with an auctioneer. "Who'll give me twenty? Twenty...now thirty, thirty? Forty...fifty? Going once, going twice...sold! To the gentleman in the cowboy hat!" On the Hill, it goes something like this: "Who'll give me health care? Health care...health care...for gay rights, abortion and same-sex marriage...going once, going twice...sold! Okay, now I have jobs that come with a bridge to nowhere in Alaska...for support on the stimulus bill...."

Your rights, freedoms, careers, family values and children's futures are being bartered away. If you don't have something to offer your representatives, you'll walk away with nothing when you leave the square. Leaders of today care nothing about what Madison, Washington and God think is right for this country. America's leaders are literally "trading democracy!" This epitomizes greed and corruption.

Why is government giving in? Because, once again, "history records that the money changers have used every form of abuse, intrigue, corruption, deceit and violent means possible to maintain their control over governments by controlling money and its issuance."

To each and every American citizen, your local, state and federal governments have given you over to the financial figureheads of fortune. Your lives are scripted and directed. Your nation is being victimized. If you continue to do nothing to thwart the evils of greed and corruption, you will be sold at auction, along with your children.

Living Excessively

Now let's take a look at the figureheads of fortune and the greed and corruption they represent. Jack Welch ran General Electric for two decades. After he retired, he received $2.5 million in perks, unlimited personal use of a company jet and bodyguards for his book tour, exclusive use of a luxury apartment that normally rented for roughly $80,000 a month and had a resale value of more than $11 million.[13]

Divorce documents filed by his ex-wife also include use of a G.E. owned Manhattan apartment; seats to NY Knicks, U.S. open, Wimbledon, Red Sox, and Yankee games; satellite TV and security services at his four homes; all costs associated with the New York apartment (wine and food, laundry, toiletries, newspapers); dining bills; car and driver for the couple, communications and computer equipment at the Manhattan apartment and at their homes in Connecticut, Massachusetts and Florida; security personnel and limousine service when the Welches traveled; and four country club fees.[14]

Welch acknowledged that "in these times when public confidence and trust have been shaken, I've learned the hard way that perception matters more than ever." and gave up most of the perks. He didn't apologize, however, telling the newspaper that the benefits were part of a contract that helped GE keep him at the company longer.[15] Lucky GE! Nevertheless, he never could have pulled it off without the board of directors.

Think this CEO deserved his outrageous compensation and retirement package? On August 1, 2000, GE common stock was worth $60.50 per share. By the time of his retirement in 2001, the stock had begun its southern migration and fell 31 percent to $42.17. Welch did a lousy job at best during his last year. Since Welch's retirement, GE has performed pitifully and the stock has fallen as low as $5.72 per share. I don't know about you, but I hold him accountable.[16]

"One last note, his estimated worth is right at $720 million." (according to the nytimes article, he has a prenuptial agreement which provided some protection for his $900 million fortune.) How much of that do you think he managed to skim off GE—in unearned and unmerited bonuses? How many of you, like me, believe skimming is the reason the corporation has struggled throughout the years following his retirement? In my opinion, $720 million could have gone a long way toward keeping GE financially healthy.

How about John Thain, the former head of the New York Stock Exchange, who was hired by Merrill Lynch in late 2007? Soon after his appointment, Thain spent $1.2 million to renovate his new office, two conference rooms and a reception area. New furniture included a $35,113.50 "commode on legs." For a toilet?! I could have found him a grand toilet for under a grand! That amount would have paid a nice salary to one of over 15 million who currently can't find work. In addition, Thain spent $68,178 for a 19th century credenza—that's two more jobs—and $87,783 for a pair of guest chairs[17]…that's a total of three jobs. You know what is really scary? This guy grew up just a couple of towns over from me.

Goldman Sachs's CEO earned an enormous salary of $70.324 million in 2007.[18] His salary alone would have provided 1,427 workers with a job earning $48,000 per year. That's not a bad living! Occidental Petroleum Chief Executive Ray Irani was compensated $77.628 million in 2007,[19] which makes him one of the highest-paid executives in America.

Those were not the only ridiculous salaries

paid in a year marked by corporate scandals, citizen bailouts, bankruptcies and unprecedented shenanigans. Leadership is continuing to propagate this lifestyle.

The following list reflects the actual figures for the top ten corporate annual salaries for 2008.

- Blackstone Group, Stephen Schwarzman, $702.4M

- Oracle, Larry Ellison, $557M

- Occidental Petroleum, Ray Irani, $222.6M

- Hess, John Hess, $159.6M

- Ultra Petroleum, Michael Watford, $117M

- Chesapeake Energy, Aubrey McClendon, $114.3M

- XTO Energy, Bob Simpson, $103.5M

- EOG Resources, Mark Papa, $90.5M

- Narbors Industries, Eugene Isenberg, $79.3M

- Abercrombie & Fitch, Michael Jeffries, $71.8M[20]

Their combined salaries total $2.2175 billion! With these salaries, you or I could have employed 46,197 people, or we could have built two self-sustainable cities accommodating two million people each.[21]

Don't get me wrong, I do understand that those

who actually started or inherited businesses should be able to earn whatever they feel is appropriate. It's not mine to judge under those circumstances. In the example above, however, these managers are simply figureheads and have done nothing to earn what they made. In other words, they have no ownership. In fact, this group of CEOs is smack dab in the middle of the "right of entitlement" bunch.

Allow me to put it another way: In the early 1900s, CEOs earned approximately ten times the average employee's earnings. Today, the average worker earns $48,000 per year, so that would equal $480,000 per year for a CEO. What is wrong with making that kind of money? Keep in mind, I'm not pointing my finger at those who have built and own their companies—the entrepreneurs—but I am pointing to those who are the agents, gatekeepers, guardians or employees of those corporations. You do know that Lee Iacocca agreed to work for virtually nothing until he got Chrysler back on its feet after it fell—the first time, that is.

Now, hold onto your hats: Today, the average Fortune 100 CEO earns 479 times more than the average American worker, or an average of $23 million per year— between $16 and $32 million.[22] Stephen Schwarzman, the top-paid CEO in 2008, took home $702.4 million, but for those who invested in Blackstone Group—the financial advisory and asset management firm he leads—they lost 68 cents for every dollar that they invested in his company.[23]

In other words, the highest paid CEO runs one of the biggest losers on Wall Street. Abraham Lincoln must be rolling over in his grave.

Confronting Evil

In 2008, the earnings of top-paid CEOs averaged $80 million in direct compensation and perks. Do you want to know what is worse? These exorbitant wages were paid to corporate failures by the government thievery program called "stimulus," creating trillions of dollars of debt to be repaid by you and the next several generations!

In fact, these corporate failures were already bankrupt, about to be fired and the companies dissolved. But their cronies in Washington, D.C., handed them your 401k. Because of the bailout, the corporations reported a boom year, so many top CEOs will receive as much as $70 million in windfall bonuses.

Thieves protecting thieves! And CEOs aren't the only pirates of corporate treasuries. No, they are joined by CFOs, COOs, chairmen and many other corporate executives who feel as if they, too, are entitled to have hard-working Americans foot the bills for their lifestyles. This is one of the most incredible thefts in corporate American history—and they stole it right before our eyes. They should all be arrested and sent to prison until we pay off their multi-trillion-dollar debt.

With the first two hundred Fortune 500 CEO salaries alone—not including directors' and executives' pay—we could cure homelessness in the United States. Did you get that? I said, we could fix homelessness... permanently. We have discussed this at great length with America's leaders, but they really don't want to cure the scorns of society, because perpetuating them keeps citizens off balance...and the money flowing. My father always says, "Jimmy, they have to keep the money moving. That's how they skim it!"

Going Public

Still not convinced that there is something wrong with greed in America? Maybe you're one of those who believes that CEOs, directors and executives are entitled to pillage and plunder corporate treasuries. After all, they own and run those businesses, right? Wrong! For those of you who still think like this, what part of "public" in "publicly traded" do you not get?!

A corporation is a separate entity. That means that a corporation requires agents, gatekeepers, guardians and other professionals to act on behalf of the entity; and the law requires that those individuals must act "in the best interest of the corporation" and not themselves as agents.[24] Allow me to put it like this: CEOs, directors, and executives are *servants* of the *publicly traded* corporation.

I introduced you to this concept in the "Chain Gang" chapter.

Once again, I want to dismiss the notion that my discussion revolves around any company, corporation or business that is privately owned and/or its stock is held by a single principal. Also, private businesses do not have debt. If a corporate entity or business can pass debt off through default, and the taxpayer may at some time be responsible, my point is that business is not private. Do you remember the discussion earlier on money and where it derives its value and trust? Yes, from the people of this nation, not from a bank or the federal government.

Private businesses also do not have outstanding bonds, pension funds, 401k retirements, publicly issued stocks and so on. Instead, those kinds of businesses are "public" entities whereby the corporation and public must be safeguarded from the abuses of the "money changers" and those without "virtue." If such people are the agents for a corporation, that business entity is doomed. Greed and corruption always victimize the innocent. If the victimizers are given a pass or law enforcement officials turn the other way and overlook corporate criminals, then jurisprudence becomes a mockery of justice.

Public corporations must uphold the public trust. The problem with public corporations is that one bad step and they could become owned by the state, because it is the state of incorporation that is the last legal guardian for these entities. Just as when parents fail to care for their children and the state steps in, so, too, when the people who are appointed to safeguard corporate wealth fail to do so, the corporation becomes a ward of the state. Sure, the state appoints foster parents to care for children and trustees to look out for the interests of other entities, but this only means that the state controls every move made.

Who backs, or provides, funds for the state? That's right, the people. Are you now beginning to understand how awkward America's business structure really is? Is the opinion of the forefathers more understandable? Can you now see why the Framers were vehemently opposed to "banks and the corporations that grow up around them?"[25] America is unstable, is teetering on the edge and at any time could fall into communism. At that time another set of tyrannical leaders will assume leadership, finish taking this country's wealth from its citizens and give it away to our enemies.

Oh, they are doing it now! If you own stock in a publicly traded company, you need to verify the CEO and executive salaries. If they're making more than ten times the average wage of the employees, then sell your stock, because these sharks are stealing your money!

RICO

Speaking of sharks, here's a law that prohibits schooling of these man-eaters. Called RICO (Racketeer-Influenced

Corrupt Organizations), this law was originally intended to confiscate illegal proceeds from criminal activities such as drug distribution, prostitution, gambling and the black market. RICO was given life to offset the costs of prosecuting mob bosses and reimbursing the people for their crimes. Unfortunately, even the good intentions of this law have been corrupted by politicians who have figured out that RICO is a great way to increase government treasuries to pay for congressional greed.

Let's look at the State of Illinois because they have a long list of mob-type legislators, even governors, who have been convicted of defrauding the people by many different means. At first glance, one might think that RICO would be useful to aid the people in recovering ill-gotten gain from their rogue leaders. That isn't the case, however. Illinois might convict corrupt conspirators, but they do little or nothing to right the wrong.

On the other hand, you had better not possess fireworks or go fishing without a license in the Land of Lincoln. If caught, police will confiscate your car, boat and cash; but Rod Blagojevich—the Illinois governor caught up in the U.S. Senate seat scandal—will not lose anything, even if he serves time. Sure, he'll probably get convicted—I have read the complaint—and one of his co-conspirators has already confessed and has agreed to testify against the "governor," but there will be no justice for Illinoisans.[26] Yes, he will pay what judges and prosecutors love to call "restitution," but please don't believe that.

I know that corrupt officials everywhere in the country are convicted, but Americans are never "restored" or given just restitution. No, there will be no confiscation of property to reimburse the people for the tens of millions the U.S. government has already spent to investigate this guy over the past five years. Nor will there be a repayment of the tens of millions being spent to prosecute his case. Instead, a lot of sick individuals will watch the former governor on "The Apprentice." What a shame! I used to like and respect the Don, but not anymore. Listen up, Trump. This country is in big financial trouble, so there is nothing entertaining about those who have brought about America's financial tidal wave.

RICO is a powerful tool; yet it, too, often goes unenforced against the Madoffs of this nation. Prosecutors confiscated some, but not all, of his assets and cash. In fact, Bernie's wife was even allowed to keep millions of dollars that her husband had stolen.[27]

You've seen the cop shows and know the face of crime—those shirtless guys being wrestled to the ground and cuffed in the dirt by the police, but our courts are doing nothing about the $200 French-cuffed Blagojeviches. The guys who steal the wealth of this nation get their own television shows. To many, crime is those shirtless guys, while the French-cuffed criminals hold court on Capitol Hill.

Term Limits

Government officials seem to go after the Gotti, Gambino and Genevese families, but not government mobsters! So, many are talking about limiting the amount of time congressional bosses run the "American Family."

Term limits are a great idea and a possible solution for curbing greed and corruption. The president of the United States is limited to two four-year terms, although this has not always been the case. Franklin D. Roosevelt was elected four times as president, served three full terms, and died while in office during the first year of his fourth term. Two years after his death, Congress passed the Twenty-second Amendment, which limited the length of a president's tenure.

Most state governors are limited to the number of terms they can serve as well. But legislators, U.S. representatives and U.S. senators can serve indefinitely. Take Ted Kennedy, for instance, who was elected to the U.S. senate nine times for a total of forty-six years prior to his death in 2009.[28] That's almost a half-century. Senators are elected to serve six year terms while U.S. representatives are elected every two years for two-year terms. Like senators, they can serve as long as their health holds out.

As I said, term limits are a great idea—senators and representatives will only be able to cause so much harm before they are naturally forced out by an act of

Congress. I'll go along with that. Will that really stop the progressive globalist agenda, stave off communism or force this nation to behave like a republic?

Why so much focus on limits, because if there is one thing I can tell you about Capitol Hill, there are no limits. Congressional members can speed, run red lights, flee justice and literally get away with murder—all in the same evening. Why? Because "The Hill" is a kind of millionaires' social club. At one time in American history, it was a boys' club; but now they allow women, who seem to be equally as abusive, greedy and corrupt as their male counterparts.

Limits aren't going to fix the problem on the "Hill"; it will only create limits as to how long the members can commit greedy and corrupt acts as senators and representatives. Most Capitol Hill club members move on to the private sector after serving a few terms. After all, the private sector is much more lucrative than civil service. If Congress limits themselves to terms, they will just wind up back on the Hill as lobbyists, advocates, lawyers, advisors, cabinet members, sub-contractors, contractors, directors, ambassadors, university and college presidents.

In Congress, many members prove that they can be bought so they can qualify for the higher-paying jobs they are promised when they reach their limit—or ours!

What Do Morals Have to Do with Politics?

I heard it again today.

Part of my routine every week is to pick up food to help feed two hundred at-risk youth who go hungry in a town near mine. While standing at the checkout counter, I overheard the cashier and the woman in front of me discussing abortion. When I was ready to pay for my groceries, I noticed that the cashier was wearing a cross around her neck. "Excuse me," I asked politely, "but I believe I heard you tell that woman you were pro-choice."

"Oh, yes, I believe in abortion," she replied, then quickly added, "I'm a Christian though. Well, a feminist, to be exact, but I believe in the Bible and the goodness of God, too."

What?! This woman is no Christian! I thought to myself. *She's a progressive!* She wasn't through with her diatribe....

"The woman who just left is pro-life. She's afraid that our tax dollars will be spent on abortions, and that's just not true! I know because I've read the entire thousand-page health care bill, and abortion funding just isn't in there."

Hmmm, I thought to myself, *the bill is actually over 2,000 pages and the feminists are not being straight,* but I held my tongue and listened a while longer. What came out of her mouth next let me know that this was no ordinary believer. "...and just because candidates are pro-choice shouldn't mean that we Christians can't vote for them."

Despite the cross around her neck, this woman was a christian, spelled with a lower-case "c," if you know what I mean. I was wearing my ministry pin; and as she scanned my items, I could see her gaze darting to the cross in its center. When she finished talking, I knew what I needed to say. Calmly and matter-of-factly, I asked, "You have read the health care bill, but I am interested to know…have you read the Scriptures?"

"Of course!" she exclaimed. Then suddenly she became quiet, appearing overwhelmed as she continued to scan the items.

In fact, from her demeanor, I suspect that she was experiencing conviction, right then and there, as she began to realize that the Lord's commands contradict her beloved movement. Her next words, spoken in a subdued tone, were more of a frantic apology. She must have said, "I'm sorry! I know abortion is wrong!" at least a dozen times before I paid and left the store.

Today, there are very few people who openly support the Word as they get caught up in their so-called "politics." I believe that this cashier knows the truth; but left exposed and unprotected, people like this woman feel helpless and all alone. When abandoned, believers are faced with the tough choice of fighting the world or just going along with it. This is known as the Roman Effect. "When in Rome, do as the Romans do."

For this young lady and everyone who thinks as she does, let's take a moment to review the definition of politics, because it is obvious to me that many Americans just don't get it.

I've said it before: Politics is an unsystematic approach and a process by which groups of people make decisions. Though the term is most often applied to civil governments, it is a term with a much broader interpretation. Politics are reflected in policies with regards to our beliefs and are shaped by the view, behaviors and actions of governments as well as corporations, religious and academic institutions and other non-governmental groups.

Our beliefs are derived from individual experience, morals and values. Though experience, morals and values are beliefs belonging to individuals, groups emulate a combination of individual experiences. Group beliefs affect the process by which decisions are made and they lead to and stem from the manner in which people rule over or govern others.

In fewer words, our beliefs *are* our politics!

Greed—self-centeredness to the detriment of others—has sunk its roots deep into America's politics and into every institution. Obviously, from the cashier's comment, the roots of greed have even cracked the godly foundation of the Church as well. Greed isn't just about money. No, its ugliness even kills the unborn because it corrupts hearts and minds, consuming virtue and all that is good and honorable.

Greed and corruption were also the number-one concern for voters in the 2006 mid-term election and the third most important issue to voters in the general election of 2008, after jobs and the economy.[29] Morals, values and ethics have *everything* to do with politics and whether this nation will return to its former greatness or fade into obscurity.

The Criminal Cost of Greed

I have a friend whose son is a musician. Like many musicians, he carries his guitar everywhere he travels. One day he parked his pickup truck in a large parking lot. While his truck was unattended, a common thief broke out the side window, reached in and helped himself to the $1,300 guitar. I have a list of 535 suspects.

The crook was found and arrested after he pawned the guitar at a local pawn shop for a measly $100. As it turned out, the criminal was a "poor, drug-addicted" man who just "needed" a fix. At least, that is how the defense attorney made it sound in court. Whether you agree that the criminal is actually a victim or not, individual greed and corruption are confiscating America's wealth at a pirate's ransom.

Since the guitar was worth $1,300 and the criminal sold it for $100, that's a total loss to the owner of $1,200. The average theft costs this nation dearly in police protection, training, equipment, surveillance, loss and damage to property, courts, incarceration, probation, parole and so on. This one example of a $1,300 stolen guitar cost America about $30,000! That's just for protection but doesn't include loss of work, missed payments, car repairs, car rental and rise in insurance costs.

In 2008, there were a total of over 14 million crimes committed, or 4½ percent of the U.S. population, illegal aliens not included. It is estimated that another 7 million crimes were *not* reported, for a total of 21 million, or almost 7 percent. That means that the average crime in America costs you, the hard-working men and women of this nation, $50,000 per crime annually, or $700 billion. In fact, the total of all crimes—reported and unreported—is estimated at over $1 trillion and could total a migraine-causing $2 trillion in 2010.[30] What is it about "Thou shalt not steal" that people don't get? Oh, excuse me, we can't legislate morality!

If greed and corruption were eliminated in America, we could easily end poverty and fully fund accountable welfare initiatives without creating a debt footprint. Do you still think we should continue to look the other way when greed and corruption are the cornerstone of crime and the progressive globalist agenda?

Benesch Bullets

To the leadership of the United States:

- Draft a "Clean Bill Act." America must not allow important legislation to become convoluted by trite issues, earmarks and political pandering.

- End legislative "riders" whose provisions have little or nothing to do with the subject matter of the bill to which they are attached.
- Stop the practice of gutting bills—called reconciliation—after they have been passed, and inserting whatever Congress wants to add just to speed up the legislative process.
- Stop "trading Democracy."
- Issue an executive order to stop all waste, fraud and abuse in America. Fight greed and corruption with a special prosecutor and a special court. Arrest, imprison and confiscate *all* wealth and power of these criminals, including bankers, corporate and government leaders.
- Fully enforce 1970 RICO (Racketeer-Influenced Corrupt Organizations). Corruption convictions of guilty persons should result in confiscation of 100 percent of cash and assets of the accused.

To my fellow believers:

- Do not take—steal—what does not belong to you.
- Do not covet what others own or possess.
- "Among you there must not be even a hint of... greed, because [this is] improper for God's holy people" (Eph. 5:3).

- "For of this you can be sure: No...greedy person—such a man is an idolater—has any inheritance in the kingdom of Christ and of God" (v. 5).
- "Let no one deceive you with empty words, for because of such things God's wrath comes on those who are disobedient" (v. 6).
- Do not vote for greedy or corrupt candidates! Or, in God's words: "Do not be partners with them" (v. 7).

To my fellow citizens:

- Elect leaders—with virtue, self-reliance and love for country—and stop electing freedom-stealing progressives.
- Adopt a national attitude toward "earning" wealth and ownership, and refuse the attitude of right of entitlement.
- Read the Holy Bible to discover for yourself the biblical roots of our nation's foundation.
- Read the Declaration of Independence so that you will know exactly why America's forefathers removed the dictator's chains. (See Appendix B.)
- Read the U.S. Constitution and its amendments to learn how the president, Congress and judiciary are supposed to conduct business on

Capitol Hill. (See Appendix C.)
- Initiate a civilian greed and corruption sting to put an end to waste, fraud and abuse.

There is a gun pointed at the back of your head. The waste, fraud and abuse of public officials are holding citizens hostage and can no longer be accepted—especially if we expect America to pull out of her economic downturn and return to prosperity. I have heard it said that most politicians are nothing but pirates and thieves. This chapter offers indisputable proof.

Part of my job in the Army was to instruct fellow team members and police officers on how to take control of a hostage situation. At the beginning of my class, I always leaned forward and looked the guys dead in the eye: "If you are ever taken hostage, you have a 50/50 chance of being killed. Decide right here and now whether you are going to allow a dirty, low-down, no-good punk to gag you, tie your feet and hands and rob you of your future... or take him down."

I'm looking you dead in the eye, America. We must take control. We are in the Eleventh Hour....

If the more aged and experienced men who have filled the office of President of the United States even in the infancy of the Republic distrusted their ability to discharge the duties of that exalted station, what ought not to be the apprehensions of one so much younger and less endowed now that our domain extends from ocean to ocean, that our people have so greatly increased in numbers, and at a time when so great diversity of opinion prevails in regard to the principles and policy which should characterize the administration of our Government?...

In assuming responsibilities so vast I fervently invoke the aid of that Almighty Ruler of the Universe in whose hands are the destinies of nations and of men to guard this Heaven-favored land against the mischief's which without His guidance might arise from an unwise public policy. With a firm reliance upon the wisdom of Omnipotence to sustain and direct me in the path of duty which I am appointed to pursue, I stand in the presence of this assembled multitude of my countrymen to take upon myself the solemn obligation "to the best of my ability to preserve, protect, and defend the Constitution of the United States." [1]

—President James Knox Polk
Inaugural Address
March 4, 1845

ELEVENTH HOUR

Then Jesus came to them and said, "All authority in heaven and on earth has been given to me. Therefore go and make disciples of all nations...teaching them to obey everything I have commanded you. And surely I will be with you always, to the very end of the age."

—Matthew 28:18-20

We must be willing, individually and as a Nation, to accept whatever sacrifices may be required of us. A people that values its privileges above its principles soon loses both.

—President Dwight David Eisenhower
First Inaugural Address, January 20, 1953

It was early evening at Fort Pickett, just after the flag had been lowered for the day. While performing my duties as the desk Sergeant—the most senior military police officer on the base at this hour—I received a radio call from PFC Jenkins.

"I'm stopping a vehicle for speeding, Sergeant. He's a possible double nickel," or 10-55, which is military police ten code for "drunk driving."

Protocol required that any units available to assist in this kind of incident be summoned to the location for backup. One never knew when an intoxicated person could become combative.

Less than five minutes later, I received another call from the Private. "10-22…disregard my last traffic stop. I'm returning to the station."

I immediately spun around to the microphone, slapped on the switch and barked, "This had better be good!" At the same time, I was thinking to myself, *What could have happened to cause a military policeman to abandon his sworn duties? No police officer in his right mind would let a suspected drunk, drive off to threaten the safety of others on the road.*

What I heard next was a voice I didn't recognize. "Don't worry, Benesch. It's good."

"Who is this?" I replied.

"Major Brackett, the field officer of the day (FOD), and I have the situation under control. I told the MP to let the driver go."

After hours, FODs performed the duties of the post commander. At this moment, the Major was the acting post commander, with the authority designated to him. But his jurisdiction did not extend to my position, which gave me the sole responsibility for all the military police officers on the base—and I had some business to settle with the Private who had released a possible DUI.

"Sir, proceed immediately to the Provost Marshall's

office," I directed him to my location.

On my door was a sign reading, "Desk Sergeant Only. No Others Allowed." Inside that room were military police firearms—M-16 rifles, 12-gauge shotguns, 38s, 9 mms, 45s and riot control equipment. It was a regular arsenal, and I was responsible for guarding the weapons, but most importantly, the lives of the men under my command.

It wasn't long before the Private making the traffic stop walked through that door, his head hung low. He was followed by the FOD, Major Brackett. Tall and slender, with a commanding presence, the Major was well-spoken and spit-shined. He burst into my office with all the bravado of a man who thinks he owns the world. By this time, I had received a report via radio that he had been drinking on duty at the officers' club with an old buddy— and it was his friend's traffic arrest he had excused.

"OK, let's play Army," Major Brackett began in a condescending tone. "I'll be the acting post commander, and you be the Sergeant. *I* give the orders."

"No, *sir!*" I objected. "You will be the drunk FOD on duty who is obstructing justice and acting in a manner unbecoming an officer and a gentleman."

He began to argue with me, and I replied with the standard response we give to all who outrank us. "Sir, do not confuse your rank with my authority. You are under arrest. You have the right to remain silent…"

Like many drunks, he became belligerent—cursing

and gesturing—then attempted to challenge me physically by poking his forefinger into my chest. At that point, I grabbed his wrist, twisting it in an Aikido maneuver, and forced him down, introducing his face to the tile floor.

Before the Major was cuffed and escorted to the secure base "hotel"—detention—I employed the customary military police measures for prisoner protection: removing any sharp objects such as insignia, belt, pens, right down to his shoelaces. In the next few minutes, he was incarcerated in an 8 x 8 x 7 steel cage appropriate for the common criminal he had chosen to become. He didn't remain with us long, though, before the post commander released him on his own recognizance.

The next day, I was summoned to the post commander's office where the Commander, the Sergeant Major and the Provost Marshal congratulated me. "Well done, Benesch. You handled yourself professionally. Uh…Major Brackett has asked us to convey his apologies and his sincere regret over last evening's events."

There was another pause before the Provost Marshal continued, "Would you be willing to withdraw the charges in view of the fact that the Major has served our country for twenty-four years?"

Without a moment's hesitation, I responded, "Absolutely, sir…if the Major resigns his commission with the U.S. Army and retires, effective immediately."

Within thirty days, the Major had retreated to what we called "Fort Living Room"—home. He never again overreached his authority or abused his power—at least not while wearing the distinguished uniform of the United States Army—or brought harm to my brotherhood and the citizens we were sworn to protect.

I was not going to allow another person to die on my watch while following arrogant, self-aggrandizing leadership. Once was enough. The law is the law. If we are going to protect this nation, we must be willing to apprehend all perpetrators, no matter their rank, public position or church status.

We must use the authority that is not only our right, but our duty[3]—both as citizens of the United States and, if we are believers, as citizens of the kingdom of God!

Abuse of Power

Some call abuse of power "good politics." I say, no way. Wrong is wrong, no matter how well-intentioned the wrongdoer may be. I can no longer watch atrocities being committed and say nothing while so many defend abusive public officials and their blatant disregard for the Constitution and the laws of this country. Nor will I stand by and allow any individual to call it "good politics" or "the way things are."

My neighbor calls this kind of logic "realism." Just the other day, he and I were discussing political issues and I mentioned my view on fidelity. "Public officials who would cheat on their wives would most definitely cheat on their country."

"Oh, Jim, I'm a realist," the neighbor replied. "We can't go that far."

"Oh, really? Realism sounds a lot like communism or progressivism to me," I countered. "At the very minimum, realism seems to be despotism, just hiding behind a more acceptable term."

I have watched these realists abuse every law possible because they lack the will, strength and righteousness to correct wrongdoing. It seems that for many people, just going along with the crowd is easier and makes better sense. I love my neighbor, but I am not going along with him on this.

Allow me to give another personal example of confronting the abuse of power and authority. Many years ago, as a young businessman and president of a small construction company, I, along with the corporation I worked for, was served papers by a sheriff's deputy. An employee claimed that he was hurt on the job. In his complaint to the court, he alleged that he had fallen off some scaffolding, injuring his foot. The language used by the lawyer, however, practically accused me of pushing him off the scaffolding myself! Since I was not present at the time, I wondered how I could have been personally responsible. The truth didn't stop his lawyer from digging into every pocket he could find.

I didn't answer the complaint, and the accuser's

lawyer filed for relief through a legal maneuver called a default judgment—a judicial tradition whereby the court grants legal access to a defendant's bank account if they fail to correctly follow procedure. Although this is one of many tricks available to lawyers, default judgments are unconstitutional; the Seventh Amendment protects citizens: "In suits at common law—a system of laws originated and developed in England—where the value in controversy shall exceed twenty dollars, the right of trial by jury shall be preserved."[4] That means that every dispute where the amount in question exceeds twenty dollars must be tried by a jury.

When I received notice that the accuser's lawyer was seeking to violate my constitutional rights, I swung into action and showed up in court with a motion to dismiss the accuser's motion. Courts don't like to listen to us common citizens, though. Apparently, if people lack a law degree, many courts and other lawyers don't take them seriously or may even treat them with disrespect.

When my case was called, the judge shrugged me off, lecturing me on how I had violated his court's "civil rules of procedure" or what my neighbor calls "reality." The judge, quite rude and condescending, seemed to be looking to find me guilty, trial or not. I stood by and took his berating. Judging from the smug expressions on the attorneys' faces, they were getting a kick out of watching me get stomped.

When the judge had finished assassinating my

character and demeaning my education and my rights, I calmly asked, "Is that all, Your Honor?" Judges enjoy their position, you know, so I stroked his ego, all the while thinking to myself, *Hmmm…another Major Brackett. When will I ever see the last of these abusers of authority?*

With that, I focused on the task at hand and began to defend my motion to dismiss the accuser's. I had a lot riding on this court's opinion.

"You violated our rules," the judge interrupted again.

"But your rules violate the supreme law of the land, the very foundation from which you derive your rules, power and authority. I will not stand for your disregard of the Constitution, Your Honor!"

"Bu-but, young man…"

At this point I had had enough of this public official's abuse. "Sir! Would you like for me to read the Constitution to you? If you rule against me, you will be violating my civil and constitutional rights, and I will go right over to the Tennessee Supreme Court and file judicial misconduct charges to see you de-robed and disbarred!"

At that moment, the attorney for the plaintiff leaped to the judge's defense and went off into a diatribe. The courtroom took on the aura of a pack of thieves or a den of wolves—I could almost see their fangs—but I held my ground. "I object, Your Honor! I am in disbelief that this court would allow the trampling of individual rights, liberties and justice, just because you are all members of the same club!"

Surprisingly the judge agreed with me. "The right of a trial by jury shall be preserved. Therefore, there can be no default judgment. I rule in favor of the defendant's motion. Court adjourned."

The observers appeared astonished, even mesmerized. They were staring at me as if they had never witnessed the administration of justice before. Maybe they hadn't. Maybe they haven't seen it since. Fighting for what is right is a lot more difficult than one would think. I believe that we expect people to do the right thing. When they don't, most just chalk it up to "reality." I call it cowardice. We must take control to ensure that good prevails over evil and that justice trumps injustice.

Other examples of abuse include random DUI and roadside drug checks…and police officers who stop drivers for speeding, then ask to search their vehicles. This kind of conduct is a blatant violation of the U.S. Constitution's Fourth Amendment that states: "The right of the people to be secure in their persons, houses, papers, and effects, against unreasonable searches and seizures, shall not be violated, and no warrants shall issue, but upon probable cause, supported by oath or affirmation, and particularly describing the place to be searched, and the persons or things to be seized."[5]

Law enforcement officials must describe the places to be searched and state to a court, the reason for the search. Instead, I know many police officers who use trickery and in the process violate the Constitution.

Contrary to law enforcement's opinion civil rights violations do not occur when a court declares a constitutional violation; no, they occur the very moment a public official steps across the line of constitutional protection. In addition, requests for searches must be supported by hard evidence—what the law regards as reasonable/probable cause and/or eyewitness testimony. "Mere suspicion or belief, unsupported by facts or circumstances, is insufficient" to be considered probable/reasonable cause.[6]

But the abuse doesn't stop there. We have already discussed many issues where public officials are disobeying the law. The aliendemic, public corruption and a whole host of other constitutional infringements are against the law of the land. We are slowly being boiled to death.

Take the "Don't Ask, Don't Tell" issue. Current military law forbids, and even requires the discharge of known homosexual service members.[7] Personally, I would prefer that military law be restored to pre-Clinton era policy where zero-tolerance prevailed, but I'll settle for "Don't Ask, Don't Tell." I know that many would like to see this policy overturned and homosexuals allowed to openly flaunt their sexual preferences, but the "reality" is that the majority of American citizens oppose this movement. Military law is on our side, not theirs. However, the law isn't stopping some vigilantes, or what I like to call "judicial terrorists," from degrading our nation through willful and wanton disregard for the law of the land.

In March 2010, Army Lieutenant General Benjamin Mixon wrote a letter to "Stars and Stripes," a military publication, urging soldiers to oppose the proposed changes to President Clinton's homosexual military ruling. The general was right in instructing his soldiers to stand firm in the face of rule-breakers. General Mixon is only enforcing military law. Isn't that exactly what we demand of those who have been charged with defending our nation—to enforce the rules, as is, no questions?

Now General Mixon is under attack by the bullying tactics of the pro-homosexual movement and Army Secretary John McHugh—former Republican congressman—along with a band of vigilantes known, in this case, as senior Defense Department officials.[8]

Even though open homosexuality is outlawed in America's military, senior public officials are knowingly making a mockery of the law, just as Major Brackett did. What I don't understand is why General Mixon has not arrested the Army Secretary, as well as any other member of the Defense Department, for obstruction of justice, abuse of power, misrepresentation of authority and conduct unbecoming officers and gentlemen. As in my case, he currently has the law on his side, no matter how that law may change in the future. Further, it is the general's duty to arrest the Secretary of the Army. In fact, the general's current action—or what I consider inaction—is dereliction of duty, not good politics, sir!

This homosexual movement has momentum on its side, but courageous people must stand in the gap to protect our children from falling prey to what is coming next—legalized same-sex marriage.

Same-Sex "Marriage"…or Medical Mayhem?

If Americans continue to stand by and do nothing to curb the same-sex marriage momentum, our children will be raised in a world where, sooner or later, anything goes. That includes gross sexual immorality, specifically same-sex marriage. If this movement isn't crushed soon, I can see a future with multiple—three or more—legal spouses. In fact, I have heard that married couples already swap partners so as to taste the double dealings of diversity.

What concerns me most about the homosexual agenda is not what can happen to Jim Benesch, but what will happen to the billions of children who are being raised in a world that seems to be shifting its moral position to accommodate this new wave of "equality." I am concerned that our children are attending public schools that are teaching what is labeled as "sexual neutrality." I am appalled that our children must obey leaders who have sold their souls to the devil and are glad to hand the future of this nation over to him as well. Our children are not only exposed to evil, but they are being forced to learn about sexual perversion and encouraged to participate in homosexual experimentation, just so they can be accepted.

The hard, cold "reality" is that children will do what they must to conform and co-exist. Just look at the fact that most abused children don't see their abusers as criminals. Children are adaptable and will adjust, for the most part, to their circumstance—even going so far as to view abuse as a twisted symbol of love. Where do we stop? If it were not for our laws, there would be no limits and absolutely no safety and security to speak of. I believe that without laws, America would resemble the outlaw territory of northern Mexico. Oh, wait! Did I discuss that in the chapter entitled "Aliendemic"?

Get it? Do you understand that the homosexual agenda isn't just about us, but it is targeting our children, grandchildren and great-grandchildren? As adults and as parents, we can withstand social pressures, defend ourselves from homosexual advances and resist forced acceptance of their agenda.

Please understand that I don't write to ridicule. I write to express my beliefs, to correct those who might be sitting on the fence of indecision and to warn my fellow believers who have accepted this behavior. For believers, may I remind you that we must not even eat with christians who have accepted sexual immorality as "realistic"[9] or even worse, have sent their children out into an evil world with no protection at all.

Allow me to explain further about the innocence

and impressionability of our children and why I believe we must head off the homosexual agenda at the pass. In the recent Wisconsin Federal Court decision, which determined the "National Day of Prayer" to be unconstitutional, Judge Crabb—who presides over the court where this case was filed—stated on page 40 of her opinion that "the Supreme Court emphasize the 'impressionable' nature of children." Further, as the Court has pointed out: "Adolescents are often susceptible to pressure from their peers towards conformity, and… influence is strongest in matters of social convention."[10]

The impressionability of our children is so concerning to the courts of the United States that they are using this argument to prevent religion from influencing our children, yet encouraging homosexuality and same-sex marriage by the same means. To object to influencing children with regard to religion only to force homosexual conformity and perverted sexual conduct is hypocrisy at its most extreme. These progressives consider themselves to be on the moral high ground and dare to call religious groups "bullies and intimidators"![11]

I have a family friend who is a Republican legislator serving as a representative for the state of Massachusetts. He considers himself "a successful arbitrator," a virtual bridge between two opposing sides—progressive globalism. He is eloquent, likable, well-educated, and, in my opinion, a christian with a lower-case "c."

He voted in favor of same-sex marriage and

convinced several fellow Republicans to do the same. This esteemed "representative" of America's moral values has sacrificed our convictions and forced believers to be governed by an evil agenda. He has jeopardized the souls of those who choose this world over the kingdom of God by exploiting their innocence and convincing others that this is "reality." Why has he sold out his beliefs? My Republican friend has successfully pushed hard for same-sex marriage just so his community could have a new fire truck. That's right—a fire truck!

National leaders, including President Barack Obama and Secretary McHugh, are leading the sexually immoral charge against America's innocents—our children—who as young as kindergarten age, are being taught that the same-sex agenda is the new norm. The educational agenda for 2011 promotes same-sex relationships, and hate crime laws—H.R.3017— make you a criminal if you try to speak out against it.[12]

The public school system is stealing the innocence of our children and believers are doing little to nothing to stop this harm. We need to take notice that there will come a time that we must answer for lethargy. "If anyone causes one of these little ones who believe in me to sin, it would be better for him to have a large millstone hung around his neck and to be drowned in the depths of the sea. Woe to the world because of the things that cause people to sin!" (Matt 18: 6-7).

Our very future as a civilization is being threatened

as families are now forced to expose their children and themselves to diseases that are completely preventable. Not only are the diseases I am about to describe preventable, but the medical problems listed below—only a very few of the complete list—are brought about by blatant disregard for our Highest Authority, who clearly states: "Do not lie with a man as one lies with a woman; that is detestable" (Lev. 18:22). Yet individuals deliberately choose to engage in homosexuality.

What does the Creator have to say about this behavior? "Therefore God gave them over in the sinful desires of their hearts to sexual impurity for the degrading of their bodies with one another. They exchanged the truth of God for a lie, and worshiped and served created things rather than the Creator— who is forever praised. Amen. Because of this, God gave them over to shameful lusts. Even their women exchanged natural relations for unnatural ones. In the same way the men also abandoned natural relations with women and were inflamed with lust for one another. Men committed indecent acts with other men, and **received in themselves the due penalty for their perversion**" (Rom. 1:24-27). Among those "due penalties for their perversion" might well be the following:

- Anal Cancer—a disease in which malignant cancer cells invade the tissues of the anus, which is the end of the large intestine, below the rectum, through which solid waste leaves the body.

- Chlamydia Trachomatis—a bacterium that causes a disease called trachoma that results in blindness.

- Cryptosporidium—an infection of the small intestine that is caused by the parasite cryptosporidium. The main symptom is diarrhea and is associated with ingesting fecal matter.

- Herpes Simplex Virus—blisters or ulcers, usually painful. More than 45 million people nationwide are infected with genital herpes. **There is no known cure.**

- Human Immunodeficiency Virus HIV/Acquired Immunodeficiency Syndrome AIDS—an acute infection caused by the human immunodeficiency virus (HIV), a virus that gradually destroys the immune system and in many cases leads to immune system disorders that often cause death. Can take as long as six months to be identified by sexually transmitted infections (STI) tests. **There is no known cure**. According to the Center for Disease Control Prevention (CDCP), 1.1 million people in the United States are living with diagnosed or undiagnosed AIDS. The cost per patient each year averages $25,200 and will total $600,000 before the patient dies of the disease.[13]

- Human Papilloma Virus (HPV)—considered the most common STI. It is not fully known whether HPV ever clears the body and can lead to warts, lesions and cancer.

- Gonorrhea—infection caused by Bacterium Neisseria that can lead to many complications, including inflammation of heart valves, arthritis and the eyes.

- Viral Hepatitis Types B & C—liver inflammation caused by viruses.

- Syphilis—a sexually transmitted disease caused by Treponema pallidum, a microscopic organism called a spirochete. This worm-like, spiral-shaped organism infects people by burrowing into moist mucus membranes. Can damage major organs like the heart, brain and can also cause death.[14]

"Sexual transmission of some of these diseases is so rare in the exclusively heterosexual population as to be virtually unknown.... King County, Washington (Seattle), reported that 85 percent of syphilis cases were among self-identified homosexual practitioners. And syphilis among homosexual men is now at epidemic levels in San Francisco."[15] That's Nancy Pelosi's congressional district; she's the third person in line for the Oval Office.

The cost of these diseases is staggering, too, and is limiting the money available to fight illnesses that affect the entire population, no matter their sexual persuasion. Now that's diversity! Take Chlamydia Trachomatis, for instance, a bacterium that causes a disease called trachoma resulting in blindness so frequently, it places a $25 billion-per-year burden on world health funding. Trachoma affects approximately 500 million people worldwide, primarily those found in rural communities, the developing world and among people who indulge in "unsafe sexual practices"—including homosexuals. Currently, 6-9 million people worldwide have suffered partial or complete blindness from trachoma.[16]

The homosexual movement is requiring a sweeping health care bill, which is even now in progress, to cover the cost of these self-inflicted abominations brought about by the lack of self-control and lack of respect for the human body.[17] In other words, 97-99 percent of the entire nation—the heterosexual community—is being forced to pay the bill that—homosexual behavior—1-3 percent lay at our feet. Think how many hundreds of billions of dollars could be saved annually if our public officials would stop aiding homosexuality. In fact, this author believes officials are actually promoting a pandemic!

Prior to the Health Information Protection Act of 2003 (HIPA), sexually transmitted diseases were reported by medical personnel to protect the community from an outbreak of disease. Now, in an effort to protect homosexuals, the general public faces threats—sexually-transmitted diseases—it no longer is allowed to identify. What was once considered legally responsible and protective behavior by our medical doctors is now labeled criminal conduct.

Yet, if we don't tolerate the government's be-havior, they will threaten to sue us for everything we've got, fine us, take our families away and imprison us. Have you ever stopped to think that this is exactly why we believers haven't done anything to stop it—because we have put our earthly treasures above truth and righteousness?

Homosexuality brings about the wrath of the One who gives life…and can take it away. Homosexuality is not a lifestyle, it is a death style, both medically and spiritually. We had better stand up against this insidious behavior that is eating at the heart of America, or be handed over to depravity and destruction—eternally!

There is only one thing I can think of that is more disturbing to me than teaching our children sexual immorality, and that is robbing them of life before they are even born.

Abortion—License to Kill

In the past thirty-two years, the so-called "humanitarian" citizens of the world have murdered 1.5 billion babies— one-fourth of the earth's population, not including deaths caused by war, disease and natural disasters. In America, abortions account for 1.35 million deaths per year—one child killed every twenty seconds since 1973, when the Roe v. Wade Supreme Court decision was handed down. Since then, this "peaceful" nation has killed 50 million of the yet unborn—more than heart disease, cancer and lung disorders combined, or one of every six

Americans. In addition, we have assisted other nations by funding worldwide abortion activity.[18]

If someone murders an abortionist, that person receives life in prison, but the abortionist doesn't even receive a slap on the wrist…because he (or she) has a license to kill.

As a major thrust of this book suggests, we are a progressive nation moving toward communism. I fear that if we achieve that state, our Stalinist tactics will elevate our abortion rate to the same level as Russia or perhaps even Red China. Russia accounts for 6.8 million abortions annually; China is responsible for over 10 million. Think about it: Russia and China—these two countries alone—obliterate the entire population of the state of Florida once a year.[19]

After reading these statistics, are you as outraged as I am? Maybe you're one who believes we need abortion to control the population or that abortion is a right or a privilege granted medical doctors to induce or force labor at a mother's choosing. Did you know that many abortions have resulted in live births? I'm not talking about some blob of tissue. I'm not talking about a "choice," or some other progressive label. I'm talking about living, breathing human beings with the potential for greatness. I'm talking about creation.[20]

Are you aware of the medical protocol for those instances when an abortion goes "awry"? They wrap the baby in a sheet and hide it in a janitor's closet or some other secluded area until the baby, tortured by suffocation, dies—a process that requires from 45 minutes to a full eight hours. I can't even imagine the monster who could do such a thing! Would you believe that the institutions that perform such abortions do not feed, nurture or in any way assist in saving life? How can that be? The doctors' explanation: "National guidelines...babies born before 22 weeks should not be given medical treatment."[21]

Aren't doctors sworn to protect life, to uphold it, to resuscitate it, to do everything in their power to prolong it? In any other situation—such as finding a baby in a trash can, for example—the Good Samaritan law requires that any citizen observing a person needing emergency medical care must, at the very minimum, stop and call for help. In the event that the citizen has medical training, he or she must render any and all life-saving assistance possible—except when under the "protective" umbrella of an abortion clinic, that is.[22]

Don't be misled by the progressives, the conclusion of "a peculiar mind." Abortion is a miscarriage of justice, an ending of life, a failure of society, the termination of civilization.

Pro-life vs Pro-choice

For pro-choice advocates to say that genocide is wrong and yet go hand in hand with abortion, signing the death warrants of the most innocent and vulnerable, defies all logic. To add insult to injury, those who, like me, oppose abortion are forced by pro-abortion public officials to pay for this unconscionable practice—either totally or partially. Although I, and many others like me, strictly disagree with the pro-choice agenda and do not in any way participate in abortion, we are oppressed by a tyrannical government that doesn't care about our beliefs—religious or not.

Taxes are one thing, but to mandate payment for the wretched conduct of others by those who are not in favor...well, I can't think of a better example to prove my point about the direction of this nation. What happened to "life," in "life, liberty, and the pursuit of happiness"?[23] The forefathers established a government that is supposed to protect life and property, but it appears that today's progressives are bent on destroying life, seizing private property and snatching happiness. I can think of no greater example of stealing happiness than to force life-loving Americans to pay for death.

The abortion agenda all too plainly demonstrates that most public officials currently leading this nation don't care about life. They only use it as a stick or a carrot, depending upon which way the cultural winds of America happen to be blowing.

After all the years of debate, what finally settled the issue of pro-life vs. pro-choice for me? Until I read the following Scripture, I was a fence-sitter, sitting idly by like so many others, watching the weeds of "progress" choking out life. I had questions because I hadn't heard the truth. But now my questions as to when life begins have been answered, and I am eager to share the truth with you.

In the book of Psalms, inspired by the Creator of the universe, David wrote: "For you created my inmost being; you knit me together in my mother's womb. I praise you because I am fearfully and wonderfully made; your works are wonderful, I know that full well. My frame was not hidden from you when I was made in the secret place. When I was woven together in the depths of the earth, your eyes saw my unformed body. All the days ordained for me were written in your book before one of them came to be" (Psalms 139:13-16).

Now, before you write me off as a religious fanatic, let me say that I know about the "voices of reason," because at one time, I was one of them. Now I find myself speaking on behalf of Divine Providence instead of a political party or the feminist movement. What I have just shared is the reason I am an advocate for the Framers instead of the progressives. Certainly, people have been given free will to pick and choose. Choice is God-given. We have the right to choose, but we must live with the consequences of our choices, for He also commands, "This day I call heaven and earth as witnesses against you that I have set before you life and death, blessings and curses. Now choose life, so that you and your children may live and that you may love the LORD your God, listen to his voice, and hold fast to him. For the Lord is your life." (Deut. 30:19-20).

Power vs. Authority

In the early 70s, the Supreme Court determined that the choice between life and death is a woman's individual right. For many, killing the yet unborn is power that derives its authority from the United States Constitution. This "power" to determine whether a baby shall live or die can cause a "God syndrome"—a kind of false sense of empowerment that makes some women feel strong and independent.

These believe that power and authority are one and the same. Many dictionary definitions agree with this conclusion, citing that power and authority are interchangeable. I submit to you that they are not. I don't believe power and authority could be synonymous because people may possess the ability—the brute strength—to forcibly impose their will upon others, but may lack the authority to do so. To impose one's will over another is abusive and often leads individuals to be charged as criminals.

Earlier, I explained that taxaquences were the ultimate power, and now I am saying that power is ultimate control. When a person or other entity has power and lacks virtue, misuse can occur—resulting in oppression, even when authority is granted.

Authority is the charge that grants permission or sets precedence. Administrative agencies and people may possess the authority to effect changes in policy, but at the same time lack the power to enforce them because an opposing force may be greater or the standing rule of law may forbid such orders. Officials who pervert justice by stepping outside of their authority promote tyranny.

Constitutional authority grants permission to individuals, courts, Congress and the President of the United States of America. Constitutional authority, combined with power, can be an extremely beneficial force, but corrupted or irresponsibly enforced, can lead to tyranny and oppression.

The Eighteenth Amendment, ratified January 16, 1919, prohibited the manufacture and sale of intoxicating liquors, as well as importing or exporting such products. The amendment was called "Prohibition."[24] Prohibition had behind it the full weight and authority of the U.S. Constitution, but Congress was irresponsible and lacked the power to enforce it. In fact, the Eighteenth Amendment is still blamed for the outbreak of racketeering and organized crime during the era called the "Roaring Twenties."[25]

Fifteen years later, on December 5, 1933, Congress repealed Prohibition by ratifying the Twenty-first Amendment. Power and authority are not the same, but I will agree that without one, you can't peacefully enjoy the other. In the same way that America dealt with Prohibition, she must constitutionally address the issues I have raised, or I fear we could see another outbreak of violence, civil insurrection or even a revolution.[26]

Citizens Must Vote Righteousness

When I speak to groups of people, many stop me and ask, "How do you know for whom to vote?" Easy.

Look at the party platforms. Study voting records. Listen to what candidates and leaders are saying and writing. Question them. Do they promise to follow the Lord or their party? Do they accurately interpret the Constitution, or do your leaders blame "activist judges" instead of their own shortcomings? Do the behaviors of your representatives line up with the Word of God, or do they serve special interests? Do your government officials try to please everybody all of the time, or do they side with righteousness? When the community is in need, are they filling sand bags, assisting with evacuations or running for high ground, crossing their fingers and complaining? Are candidates investing their financial war chests and risking their political careers to right injustices, or are they just saving up for their personal retirement?

Oh, don't get me wrong, I know why most people follow the world and not the Word. They want to blame something or someone else for their disobedience. When their walk on earth is over, most people want to blame those in authority, the ones they claim God sent.

This pass-the-buck mentality is nothing new. When Adam and Eve ate of the fruit of the forbidden tree, and God asked Adam why he disobeyed—Adam's reply was the same as that often used by today's lethargic citizen: "'It's the [other party] you put here with me—[they] gave me some fruit from the [forbidden] tree, and I ate it.' Then the LORD God said ... 'What is this you have done?'... 'The [elites/media/government] deceived me and I ate'".[27]

How can we take responsibility for the crisis that our inaction has caused? We must stand for leadership that will repair the damage our impurity, abortion, same-sex marriage and sexual immorality are bringing upon this nation.

The National Day of Prayer court case has disclosed a very important piece of information about the depth of godly character in America's public officials. In an Amicus Brief—friend of the court brief—filed by the American Center for Law and Justice, only thirty-one members of Congress filed in defense of the National Day of Prayer. According to my calculations, that is less than 6 percent of Congress. To my fellow Tennesseans, none of your U.S. Congressmen or Senators were listed. Only former Tennessee Volunteer, SEC Quarterback Heath Shuler ponyed up!

The following is a list of those who stood for righteousness: J. Randy Forbes, Robert B. Aderholt, Michele Bachmann, Roscoe G. Bartlett, John A. Boehner, John Boozman, Eric Cantor, K. Michael Conaway, Mary Fallin, Virginia Foxx, Trent Franks, Scott Garrett, Louie Gohmert, Wally Herger, Peter Hoekstra, Walter B. Jones, Jim Jordan, Doug LamVirgiborn, Thaddeus G. McCotter,

Patrick T. McHenry, Mike McIntyre, Jeff Miller, Sue Wilkins Myrick, Randy Neugebauer, Pete Olson, Mike Pence, Joseph R. Pitts, Heath Shuler, Adrian Smith, Lamar Smith, and Joe Wilson.[28]

If you are still not sure whom to trust to ensure that your children are allowed to receive their immortal inheritance, I can tell you: Entrust this nation only to representatives who have proven their fidelity to God, to their spouses, to their families and to the United States of America.

Fidelity

If our leaders acknowledged God and loved this country, there would be no poverty, no homelessness, no illegal drugs, no unfair wages, no job discrimination and no bank bailouts. No big corporate—what the forefathers called monopoly—bailouts, no insurance company bailouts, no pandering, no sixty-year war with North Korea. No $13 trillion going on $14 trillion federal debt, no greed, no corruption, no unemployment. No despotism—anarchy, communism, progressivism, etc. No abortion, no same-sex marriage, no congressmen sleeping with their "pages," aides or secretaries. No CEOs, corporate executives or directors making hundreds of millions per year, no out-of-control credit expansion or debt piled upon debt backing debt, issuing debt, debt, debt. Have I mentioned debt yet?

Leaders who love their constituents lead by example and treat others as they would have others treat them. Love of country is not a phrase. Rather, love of country is an action of the mind, body and spirit. Love is fidelity. It is patriotism that burns in the heart!

Fidelity is the strict observance of promises, duties, allegiance, loyalty and conjugal faithfulness. Fidelity is strict adherence to the principles of love. Fidelity doesn't just mean "I won't cheat on you, honey." Fidelity defines a person's trustworthiness and is not relegated to nuptials alone.[29]

If your government representatives are sleeping around with people other than their spouses, they are not promise-keepers, but promise-breakers. They are men and women who do not love anyone more than they love themselves. If they can't keep their promise to their spouse, how can they be trusted to keep an oath to "preserve, protect and defend the Constitution of the United States"?

For me, there are no levels of betrayal. All betrayal and infidelity violate the strict observance of promises, duties, allegiance, loyalty and faithfulness.

Fidelity requires that we: "Be imitators of God, therefore as dearly loved children and live a life of love, just as Christ loved us and gave himself up for us as a fragrant offering and sacrifice to God. But among you there must not be even a hint of sexual immorality, or of any kind of impurity, or of greed, because these are improper for God's holy people. Nor should there be obscenity, foolish talk, or coarse joking, which are out of place, but rather thanksgiving. For of this you can be sure: No immoral, impure or greedy person—such a man is an idolater—has any inheritance in the kingdom of Christ and of God. Let no one deceive you with empty words, for because of such things God's wrath comes on those who are disobedient. Therefore do not be partners with them" (Eph. 5:1-7). Keep your fidelity true and pure, for there is no future for a nation that is deceived or partners with disobedience.

Benesch Bullets

To the leadership of the United States:

- Cease all same-sex marriage discussions. Consider an amendment to define marriage—between one man and one woman.
- Restore military policies regarding homosexuality—prior to Bill Clinton.
- Quit agitating other nations by disregarding their laws and offending their cultural regulations regarding relationships and sexuality.
- Restore States' Rights by repealing Section 1 and Section 4 of the Fourteenth Amendment. This will limit federal authority.

- Restore States' Representation by repealing the Seventeenth Amendment. This will limit federal authority.
- Issue a moratorium on abortion. Consider an amendment to define life at conception.
- Respect, honor, protect and serve the United States Constitution, not a political platform or the progressive "new world order" ideology.

To my fellow believers:

- Expel leadership or members of the church who disobey or disregard the Word. "I am writing you that you must not associate with anyone who calls himself a brother but is sexually immoral or greedy, an idolater or a slanderer, a drunkard or a swindler. With such a [human] do not even eat" (1 Cor. 5:11).
- "Expel the wicked man from among you.... Are you not to judge those inside [the church]?" (1 Cor. 5:13, 12).
- Fulfill the Great Commission. (See Matt. 28:18-20.) Did you know that the Highest Authority is not the U.S. government and that *you* have been given responsibility to ensure that America is a reflection of the Creator's vision for the nations?
- Elect godly representatives and stop electing

officials who do not follow the teachings of Almighty God.

- Be imitators of God. Turn away from the ways of the world and, by example, teach your fellow man the purity of a believer. (See Ephesians 5:1-7.)

To my fellow citizens:

- Peaceably assemble and exercise your First Amendment rights. Petition government for redress to end government-subsidized abortion, government sexual diversification education and same-sex marriage.
- Read the Holy Bible to learn about creation, love, community, debt, greed, corruption, sexual immorality and the nation as America's Framers intended it to be.
- Elect representatives who will enact this Marriage Amendment defining marriage as: The government-sanctioned union between one consenting male, who at the time of marriage has reached the age of majority, and one consenting female, who at the time of marriage has reached the age of majority.
- Elect representatives who will ban taxpayer-funded abortion.

As citizens of these United States, we possess all authority under the Constitution. Our power and authority are reserved inviolate at the polls. By amendment, we must clarify the Constitution by forcing our public officials to take decision-making away from special interests and the courts and put an end to "judicial terrorism."

We must not waver in the face of danger and adversity, but we must be resolved, vigilant and steadfast in our commitments and dedication to the Lord and the Framers. Then, and only then, will we serve one another for the true greater good of America and the world.

CONCLUSION

I sit here weeping as I write these closing words just as I did when I held a dying patriot in my arms that night at Fort Pickett. Later that evening I found his murderer sitting in his barracks, still covered in blood. My men and I approached, marching with deliberation toward the perpetrator. Halting in front of him, he spoke before we could say a word. "I was wondering when you guys were going to get here." He was just waiting on us to arrest him.

Our investigation revealed that he and his accomplices had every intention of killing someone that evening. In the absence of guardians, they were able to pull it off. As this book has established, our leaders are guilty of everything from neglect to corruption to murder. They, too, are wondering why we haven't come to arrest them yet. Well, why haven't we?

I have learned the truth. We have been divided by party because public officials and their confidants have "become potent engines by which cunning, ambitious, and unprincipled men *and women* will be enabled to subvert the power of the people, and usurp for themselves the reins of government."[1]

They have caused the country to be split right down the middle—Republican vs. Democrat, CEO vs. working man or woman, African-American vs. Anglo-American, welfare recipient vs. taxpayer. The greater truth is that the largest majority of the nation are Christians who profess to embrace the principles of right living. Respectfully, I urge you: Don't listen to the president, the media, or any political party who would have you believe that America is no longer a Christian nation and that Christianity has no part in politics.

May I remind you that your morals,
your values and your beliefs are your politics,
and it is these—as the evidence of faith in Jesus Christ—that will
determine your eternal destiny.

One can no longer be a rank-and-file Republican or a rank-and-file Democrat. Why? Because the progressive policies of both parties require you to violate God's immutable laws. This nation is making my children and my grandchildren participate in acts that will seal their mortal fate and steal their immortality. Our children and our children's children cannot learn about God's ways if we continue to put public officials in office who are determined to take Him out of our lives.

I am calling for the *godly*—of all parties and persuasions—to stand up and step out from among the *ungodly.* You're either *for* God or you're *against* Him. You either follow His commandments or you don't. It's that simple. Upon our obedience to His principles—the Creator's Code—rests our foundation for time and for eternity.

George Washington, who I believe was the "Greatest Patriot" concluded: "Of all the dispositions and habits which lead to political prosperity, religion and morality are indispensible supports…. Let it simply be asked, where is the security for property, for reputation, for life, if the sense of religious obligation desert the oaths which are the instruments of investigation in courts of justice? Reason and experience both forbid us to expect that national morality can prevail in exclusion of religious principle…. It is substantially true that virtue or morality is a necessary spring of popular government."[2]

Herein I have stated my case. Will you return this book to the shelves of political and moral inactivity, or will you help stop the onslaught of global progressivism and restore to this nation God's politics of immortality?

NOTES

Introduction

1.   George Washington, "Washington's Farewell Address, 1796," *The Avalon Project: Documents in Law, History and Diplomacy,* Yale Law School, 2008, http://avalon.law.yale.edu/18th_century/washing.asp, par. 30.

Chapter 1

1.   Washington, "Farewell Address, " par. 30.
2.   Herbert Hoover, "History & Quotes: Classic Quotes by H.H. (1874-1964) Thirty-First U.S. President," ArcaMax Publishing, 2010, www. arcamax.com/quotes/s-30017-665221.
3.   Roget's II, *The New Thesaurus,* 3rd ed. by the Editors of The American Heritage Dictionaries, (Boston: Houghton Mifflin Company, 1995), s.v. "progressivism."
4.   See Hosea 4:6.
5.   Michael Hodges, *Grandfather Economic Report Series,* 1997-2010, http://grandfather-economic-report.com/debt-nat.htm(accessed   April 2009), summary section.
6. U.S. Department of the Treasury: Bureau of the Public Debt, *Treasury Direct: The Debt to the Penny and Who Holds It,* www.treasurydirect. gov/NP/BPDLogin?application=np (accessed 24 June 2009).
7.   Ed Hall, "U.S. National Debt Clock," *U.S. Department of the Treasury Figures,* www.brillig.com/debt_clock/ (accessed 26 Jun 2009).
8.   Hodges, *Grandfather Economic Report,* par. 2.
9.   Ibid.
10. *Roget's II,* s.v. "debt."
11. Peter G. Peterson Foundation,   I.O.U.S.A.: *The Movie,* 2010, www.iousathemovie.com/, at 10 min. 37 sec.

Chapter 2

1. Thomas Jefferson, "Letter to Samuel Kercheval (June 12,

1816)," TeachingAmericanHistory.org, Center for Public Affairs, Ashland University, 2006-2008, http://teachingamericanhistory. org/library/index. asp?document=459.

2. Office of the Press Secretary of the White House, President Barack Obama, Remarks by the President, Q&A session at closing of Fiscal Responsibility Summit (February 23, 2009), www.whitehouse.gov/ the_press_office/Remarks-by-the-President-in-QandA-session-at-closing-of-Fiscal-Responsibility-Summ, last paragraphs.

3. Peterson Foundation, I.O.U.S.A., at 4 minutes 08 seconds.

4. *Roget's II*, s.v. "tyranny."

5. Joan Reinold, "History of National Debt," eHow: *How To Do Just About Everything*, 1999-2009, www.ehow.com/about_4587454_history-national-debt.html?ref=Track2&utm_source=ask.

6. Ibid.

7. Andrew Jackson, "Farewell Address (March 4, 1837)," *Miller Center of Public Affairs*, University of Virginia, 2010, http://millercenter. org/scripps/archive/speeches/detail/3644, par 8

8. "U.S. Federal Debt as Percentage of GDP," U.S. Government Spending, 2010, www.usgovernmentspending.com/federal_debt_chart. html.

9. Ibid.

10. Peterson, I.O.U.S.A, at 6 min. 20 sec.

11. The Briefing Room of the White House, President Barack Obama, *Remarks by the President on the Fiscal Year 2010 Budget (February 26, 2009)*, www.whitehouse.gov/the_press_office/Remarks-by-the-President-on-the-Fiscal-Year-2010-Budget/, par. 15.

12. See Deuteronomy 15:1-3.

Chapter 3

1. Thomas Jefferson, "Letter to William Smith, Paris (November 13, 1787)," Thomas Jefferson, United States Library of Congress, 2000, www.loc.gov/exhibits/jefferson/105.html.

2. Richard M. Nixon, "Checkers Speech (September 23, 1952)," *American Experience Series: The Presidents*, National Endowment for the Humanities and the Corporation for Public Broadcasting, 1995-2010, www. pbs.org/wgbh/amex/presidents/37_nixon/psources/ps_checkers.html.

3. Multiple authors, *The 9/11 Commission Report: Final Report of the National Commission on Terrorist Attacks upon the United States*, 1st ed. (New York: W.W. Norton & Company, Ltd., 2004), 77.

4. Jeff Stein, "FBI Prevents Agents from Telling 'Truth' about 9/11 on PBS, October 1, 2008," CQ Politics, 2010, www.blogs.cqpolitics.

com/spytalk/2008/10/fbi-prevents-agents-from-telli.html.

5. "Gates Announces Review of Fort Hood Shootings: Secretary of Defense Wants Thorough Probe of Massacre at Army Base—Gates Refuses To Comment on Whether Rampage Was Terrorist Attack, November 19, 2009," *U.S. & World News*, WWCO, CBS Broadcasting, Inc., MMX, http://wcco.com/national/fort.hood.review.2.1322539.html.

6. Scott Shane, "U.S. Approves Targeted Killing of American Cleric [Anwar al-Awlaki], April 6, 2010," *New York Times World News: Middle East*, 2010, www.nytimes.com/2010/04/07/world/middleeast/07yemen.html.

7. David Wood, "Defense Secretary Robert Gates Pledges Full Disclosure of Fort Hood Shooting Probes, November 19, 2009," *Politics Daily*, 2010, Aol News, www.politicsdaily.com/2009/11/19/defense-secretary-robert-gates-pledges-full-disclosure-of-fort-h/.

8. "(U//FOUO) Rightwing Extremism: Current Economic and Political Climate Fueling Resurgence in Radicalization and Recruitment (April 7, 2009)," *Unclassified: Office of Intelligence and Analysis Assessment*, U.S. Department of Homeland Security. www.fas.org/irp/eprint/rightwing.pdf, 4–7.

9. *Wikipedia*, s.v. "Diplomacy," www.en.wikipedia.org/wiki/Diplomacy.

10. James Madison, "The Federalist No. 10, The Utility of the Union as a Safeguard Against Domestic Faction and Insurrection continue (November 22, 1787)," *Daily Advertiser*, 1994-2010, The Constitution Society, www.constitution.org/fed/federal10.htm.

11. *Merriam-Webster Online*, s.v. "politics," www.merriam-webster.com/dictionary/politics.

Chapter 4

1. John Adams, "Proclamation of Day of Fasting, Humiliation and Prayer (March 23, 1798)," Miller Center of Public Affairs, University of Virginia, 2010, http://millercenter.org/scripps/archive/speeches/detail/3942.

2. Office of the Press Secretary of the White House, George W. Bush, "Farewell Address to the Nation (January 15, 2009)," http://georgewbush-whitehouse.archives.gov/news/releases/2009/01/20090115-17.html, par. 16.

3. *Wikipedia*, s.v. "CityCenter," http://en.wikipedia.org/wiki/Citycenter.

4. U.S. Census Bureau, Median and Average Sales Prices of New Homes Sold in United States: Annual Data for 2009, http://www.census.

gov/const/uspriceann.pdf.

5. *Wikipedia*, s.v. "CityCenter."

6. "Do You Think UAW Workers Make $70 an Hour? UPDATED (November 18, 2008)," *Daily KOS*, Kos Media, LLC., http://www.dailykos.com/story/2008/11/19/04636/389/733/663386.

7. *Wikipedia*, s.v. "Dubai World," http://www.en.wikipedia.org/wiki/Dubai_World.

8. U.S. Government Accountability Office, *A Look at Our Future When Baby Boomers Retire: 2005 White House Conference On Aging, (December 12, 2005)*, www.gao.gov/cghome/2005/whitehousewalker1205/walker_whitehouse1212.pdf, 17.

9. *Wikipedia*, s.v. "Argentina," http://en.wikipedia.org/wiki/Argentina.

10. *Wikipedia*, s.v. "Milton Friedman," http://en.wikipedia.org/wiki/Milton_Friedman.

11. *Roget's II*, s.v. "economy."

12. *Wikipedia*, s.v. "FreeEnterprise/Capitalism," www.en.wikipedia.org/wiki/Free_enterprise.

13. *Roget's II*, s.v. "currency."

14. "Inflation Calculator: Money's Real Worth Over Time," Coin News.net: Numismatic Articles, Videos & Coin Collector Services, 2009, http://www.coinnews.net/tools/cpi-inflation-calculator/.

15. *Merriam-Webster Online*, s.v. "inflation," www.merriam-webster.com/dictionary/inflation.

16. *Roget's II*, s.v. "supply."

17. *Roget's II*, s.v. "demand."

18. *Wikipedia*, s.v. "Deflation," http://en.wikipedia.org/wiki/Deflation.

Chapter 5

1. James Madison, "Proclamation on Day of Public Humiliation and Prayer (July 23, 1813)," *Miller Center of Public Affairs*, University of Virginia, 2010, http://millercenter.org/scripps/archive/speeches/detail/3622.

2. Franklin Delano Roosevelt, "Fireside Chat 22: On Inflation and Food Prices (September 7, 1942)," *Miller Center of Public Affairs*, University of Virginia, 2010, http://millercenter.org/scripps/archive/speeches/detail/3328.

3. Niall Ferguson, *The Ascent of Money: A Financial History of the World* (New York: The Penguin Press, 2008), 21.

4. Ludwig Von Mises, *Omnipotent Government: The Rise of the Total*

State and Total War (New Haven: Yale University, 1944), 251. Also available online, http://mises.org/etexts/mises/og.asp, pdf.

5. *Merriam-Webster Online*, s.v. "agrarian," www.merriam-webster.com/dictionary/agrarian.

6. *The Free Dictionary* by Farlex, s.v. "deed of trust," http://legal-dictionary.thefreedictionary.com/Deed+of+Trust.

7. John Leland, "Sheriff in Chicago Ends Evictions in Foreclosures (October 8, 2008)," *The New York Times U.S. News*, 2008, www.nytimes.com/2008/10/09/us/09chicago.html?_r=1.

8. Ferguson, *The Ascent of Money*, 4-5.

9. Charles R. Grosvenor, Jr., "Savings and Loan Scandal," *In The 80s World News*, 1995-2010, http://www.inthe80s.com/sandl.shtml.

10. Ferguson, *The Ascent of Money*, 4-5.

11. Ibid., 228.

Chapter 6

1. James Monroe, "Eighth Annual Message (December 7, 18240)," *Miller Center of Public Affairs*, University of Virginia, 2010, http://millercenter.org/scripps/archive/speeches/detail/3606, par. 6.

2. Dwight David Eisenhower, "Eisenhower Doctrine (January 5, 1957)," *Miller Centerof Public Affairs*, University of Virginia, 2010, http://millercenter.org/scripps/archive/speeches/detail/3360.

3. Chris Buckley, "China PLA Officer Urges Challenging U.S. Dominance (March 1, 2010)." *Reuters*, 2010, www.reuters.com/article/idUSTRE6201CC20100301.

4. See Malachi 3:10-12.

5. See Deuteronomy 14:29; 26:12; 2 Chronicles 31:2-19.

6 Social Security Administration, *Social Security Programs Throughout the World: Asia and the Pacific, SSA Publication No. 13-11802, 2006*, Released: March 2007, www.ssa.gov/policy/docs/progdesc/ssptw/2006-2007/asia/ssptw06asia.pdf.

7. "Web of Deceit: Profile of a Con Artist (July 1, 2004)," *Macuser: Features*, www.macuser.co.uk/features/60007/web-of-deceit/page7.html.

8. U.S. Department of Justice: Federal Bureau of Investigation, *Common Fraud Schemes: What Is a Ponzi Scheme?*, www.fbi.gov/majcases/fraud/fraudschemes.htm, sec. 9 par. 1.

9. U.S. Department of Justice, *Litigation Release No. 20889 (February 9, 2009), Securities and Exchange Commission v. Bernard L. Madoff & Bernard L. Madoff Securities LLC, (S.D.N.Y. Civ. 08 CV 10971 (LLS)*, www.sec.gov/litigation/litre leases/2009/lr20889.htm.

10. United States Securities and Exchange Commission, *U.S.*

District Court for the Northern District of Texas Dallas Division, Securities and Exchange Commission v. R. Allen Stanford, James M. Davis, et al., Second Amended Complaint Case No.: 3:09-cv-0298-N, www.sec.gov/litigation/ complaints/2009/stanford-second-amended- 061909.pdf.

11. *Merriam-Webster Online,* s.v. "junket," http://www.merriam-webster.com/dictionary/junket.

12. U.S. Dept. of Justice: FBI, *Common Fraud Schemes,* sec. 9 par. 3.

13. "Getting foodstamps. It's Your Right," www.gettingfoodstamps. org.

14. Jerome R. Corsi and Kenneth Blackwell, "Democrats' War on Poverty Has Failed (September 6, 2006), *Human Events: Leading Conservative Media Since 1944,* 2010, www.humanevents.com/article.php?id=16860.

15. Robert Rector, "The Poverty Paradox: How America Spent $5 Trillion on the War on Poverty without Reducing the Poverty R a t e (September 22, 1993)," *The Heritage Foundation,* 2010, www.heritage.org/ Research/Reports/1993/09/The-Poverty-Paradox-How-America-Spent-5-Trillion-on-the-War-on-Poverty-without-Reducing-the-Poverty-Rate.

16. "Entitlements/Welfare Cost $129 Billion Monthly," *Control Congress,* 2008, http://controlcongress.com/uncategorized/ entitlementswelfare-cost-130billion-monthly.

17. *Merriam-Webster Online,* s.v. "communism," http://www. merriam-webster.com/dictionary/communism.

Chapter 7

1. John Quincy Adams, "Fourth Annual Message (December 2, 1828)," *Miller Center of Public Affairs,* University of Virginia, 2010, http:// millercenter.org/scripps/archive/speeches/detail/3517.

2. Jimmy Carter, "Debate with President Gerald Ford (Domestic Issues) (September 23, 1976)," *Miller Center of Public Affairs,* University of Virginia, 2010, http://millercenter.org/scripps/archive/speeches/ detail/5546.

3. Neal Boortz and John Linder, *The Fair Tax Book: Saying Goodbye to the Income Tax and the IRS* (New York: Harper Collins Publishers, Inc., 2005), 53-54.

4. Jack Guttentag, "Monthly Payment Calculator: Fixed-Rate Level-Payment Mortgages," *The Mortgage Professor's Web Site,* 2010, www. mtgprofessor.com/Calculators/Calculator7a.html.

5. U.S. Department of the Treasury Internal Revenue Service, *2009 Tax Table,* http://www.irs.gov/pub/irs-pdf/i1040tt.pdf, 101.

6. Christopher Chantrill, "U.S. Federal, State and Local Government Revenue: Fiscal Year 2008 in $ Billion," USGovernmentRevenue.com,

http://www.usgovernmentrevenue.com/yearrev2008_0.html.

7. Ibid.

8. Ibid.

9. Jefferson, "Letter to Kercheval," par. 7.

10. Adams, "Fourth Annual Message," par. 23.

11. U.S. Department of the Treasury Internal Revenue Service, *Publication 557: Tax-Exempt Status for Your Organization, Rev. June 2008,* 2010, www.irs.ustreas.gov/pub/irs-pdf/p557.pdf, 19.

12. *City Council Meeting Minutes, Columbia, Tennessee (June 4, 2009),*http://www.columbiatn.com/ccMinutes/PriorMinutes/2009/ccminutes6-4-09.pdf, 9.

13. "U.S. Income Taxpayers: 109,623,622; U.S. Retirees: 37,699,660; U.S. Population: 308,887,824 (March 17, 2010, 10:12pm, est)," *U.S. Debt Clock.org.*www.usdebtclock.org/.

14. Ibid.

15. P. H.Bellas, Little Bits of History, Foundations of Our Liberties, The Declaration of Independence, The Constitution, The Bill of Rights (Baltimore: K.C. Caldwell, Inc., 2003), 39.

16. Ibid., 60.

17. John F. Kennedy, "Inaugural Address (January 20, 1961)," *Miller Center of Public Affairs*, University of Virginia, 2010, http://millercenter.org/scripps/archive/speeches/detail/3365.

Chapter 8

1. Abraham Lincoln, "First Annual Message (December 3, 1861)," *Miller Center of Public Affairs,* University of Virginia, 2010, http://millercenter.org/scripps/archive/speeches/detail/3736.

2. Harry S. Truman, "On the Veto of the Taft-Hartley Bill (June 20, 1947)," *Miller Center of Public Affairs,* University of Virginia, 2010, http://millercenter.org/scripps/archive/speeches/detail/3344.

3. United States Department of Labor: Bureau of Labor Statistics, *The Employment Situation: December 2009,* 5.

4. "U.S. Actual Unemployed: 26,296,971 (March 24, 2010, 10:41am, est)," *U.S. Debt Clock.org.* http://www.usdebtclock.org/.

5. United States Department of Labor: Bureau of Labor Statistics. *The Employment Situation: December 2009,* 5.

6. Office of the Press Secretary of the White House, President George W. Bush, *Remarks by the President in Address to the United Nations General Assembly (September 12, 2002),* http://georgewbush-whitehouse.archives.gov/news/releases/2002/09/20020912-1.html,par. 26.

7. Colin Powell, "War in Iraq: Transcript of Powell's U.N.

presentation (February 5, 2003)," CNN.com/U.S, www.cnn.com/2003/US/02/05/sprj.irq.powell.transcript/, part 5, par. 21; part 6, par. 38, 39.

8. "President Obama to Oprah: I Give Myself a Solid B+ (Video)," *The Huffington Post*, December 13, 2009, www.huffingtonpost.com/2009/12/13/president-obama-to-oprah_n_390584.html, par. 2.

9. Franklin D. Roosevelt, "Fireside Chat 4: On Economic Progress (October 22, 1933)," *Miller Center of Public Affairs*, University of Virginia, 2010, http://millercenter.org/scripps/archive/speeches/detail/3301.

10. Montana Department of Corrections. Legislative Audit Division. *Two Rivers Regional Detention Facility in Hardin, Montana Legislature Memorandum (November 27, 2007) to Scott A. Seacat, Legislative Auditor,* from Steve Erb, Senior Performance Auditor, www.cor.mt.gov/content/Resources/CorAdvCouncil/Archive/February2008/AuditorReport.pdf.

11. United States Department of Labor: Bureau of Labor Statistics. *The Employment Situation: December 2009*, 3.

12. Robert Creamer, "An Obama Administration Must Deal with the Underlying Cause of Our Economic Meltdown: The Increasing Concentration of Wealth," *The Huffington Post*, October 9, 2008, www.huffingtonpost.com/robert-creamer/an-obama-administration-m_b_133248.html.

13. President Obama, *The Huffington Post*, par. 5.

14. "Tennessee to Send Out 853 Layoff Notices This Week (March 24, 2010)," WKRN.com.2000-2010, www.wkrn.com/global/story.asp?s=12195762.

15. *Roget's II,* s.v. "durable."

16. Samuelson, Paul A. with assistance of William Samuelson, *Economics*, 11th ed. (New York: McGraw-Hill Cook, 1980), 242.

17. Adams, "Fourth Annual Message," par. 19.

18. U.S. Department of Labor: Bureau of Labor Statistics. The Employment Situation: December 2009, 5.

19. City of Nashville [Tennessee] Mayor's Office, *Music City Center Presentation to the Council: Remarks by Mayor Karl Dean (April 13, 2009)*, www.nashville.gov/mayor/news/2009/pr/0413.asp.

20. "Convention Center Tops Metro Agenda (January 19, 2009)," *Music City Center*, 2010, www.musiccitycenter.net/news.php?article_id=40.

21. U.S. Small Business Administration, Office of Advocacy, *Frequently Asked Questions: How important are small businesses to the U.S. economy?* http://web.sba.gov/faqs/faqindex.cfm?areaID=24.

22. United States Department of Labor: Bureau of Labor Statistics, *The Employment Situation: December 2009*, 3.

Chapter 9

1.   Theodore Roosevelt, "Quotes from a letter to the American Defense Society (January 3,1919)," *Free Republic, LLC,* 2000-2008, www. freerepublic.com/focus/f-news/1608833/posts, par. 2.

2.   Ronald Reagan, "'Evil Empire' Speech (March 8, 1983)," *Miller Center of Public Affairs,* University of Virginia, 2010, http://millercenter. org/scripps/archive/speeches/detail/3409, par. 34.

3.   Fact Monster: *The Columbia Electronic Encyclopedia,* 6th ed., s.v. "History of Bohemia," www.factmonster.com/ce6/world/A0856951. html.

4.   *Merriam-Webster Online,* s.v. "Bohemian," www.merriam-webster.com/dictionary/bohemian.

5.   U.S. Department of the Interior: National Park Service, *Statue of Liberty, National Monument Bedloe's Island, New York,* www.nps.gov/history/ history/online_books/hh/11/hh11a.htm, par. 4.

6.   U.S. Citizenship & Immigration Services, *General Path to Citizenship,* www.uscis.gov/portal/siteuscismenuitemeb1d4c2a3e5b9ac892 43c6a7543f6d1a?vgnextoid=86bd6811264a3210VgnVCM100000b92ca60 aRCRD&vgnextchannel=86bd6811264a3210VgnVCM100000b92ca60aR CRD.

7.   Tamie Dehler, "Genealogy: Many Americans are Descended from Germans (March 1, 2008)," Tribstar.com, http://tribstar.com/ history/x1155739176/Genealogy-Many-Americans-are-descended-from-Germans, par. 6.

8.   United States Department of Justice, Civil Rights Division, *Presidential Executive Order 13166 by President Bill Clinton, August 11, 2000,* http://www.justice.gov/crt/ cor/Pubs/eolep.php.

9.   *Translation Services USA,* Translation from English to Czech, 2010, http://www.translation-services-usa.com/czech.php.

10. *Immigration Reform & Control Act of 1986,* http://www.oig.lsc. gov/legis/irca86.htm.Global Security.org; U.S. Casualties In Iraq, 2000-2010, GlobalSecurity.org. All rights reserved, http://www.globalsecurity. org/military/ops/iraq_casualties.htm.

11. OneNewsNow.com, February 22, 2007 by Jim Brown, 2007, The Mexican Invasion and Occupation: Who Pays? Another Form of Corp Welfare, http://www.mexicanoccupation.blogspot.com/2010/04/how-many-americans-murdered-by-illegals.html.

Chapter 10

1. Jackson, "Farewell Address," par. 3, 8, 29.

2. James E. Benesch, *Speech to Maury County Rotary Club*, February 6, 2009.

3. United States General Accounting Office, *Fraud, Waste, and Abuse: The Cost of Mismanagement, B-280800 (September 14, 1998),* http://archive.gao.gov/paprpdf2/161139.pdf, 2-20.

4. U.S. Department of Transportation: Office of the Secretary of Transportation, *Report on DOT's Suspension and Debarment Program Does Not Safeguard Against Awards to Improper Parties, Report Number ZA2010034 (January 7, 2010),* www.oig.dot.gov/sites/dot/files/Suspension_and_Debarment_1.7.10_0.pdf,2.

5. Don Wise, "African Orphan Development Authority: Self-Sustainability, Large-Population, Humanitarian and Large-Scale Economic Project " (working paper, 2007-2010).

6. Anup Shah, "Poverty Facts and Stats," *Global Issues: Social, Political, Economic and Environmental Issues that Affect Us All,* 1998-2010, www.globalissues.org/article/26/poverty-facts-and- stats.

7. Jack Liu and Kerry D'Agastino, "Facts on World Hunger and Poverty," End Poverty Campaign: Hearts & Minds, 1997-2010, www.heartsandminds.org/poverty/hungerfacts.htm.

8. James Madison, "Famous Quotations on Banking by Presidents," The Money Master.com, www.themoneymasters.com/the-money-masters/famous-quotations-on-banking/, quote 4.

9. James Madison, "The Federalist No. 10: The Utility of the Union as a Safeguard Against Domestic Faction and Insurrection (continued) (November 22, 1787), *Daily Advertiser,* 1994-2010, www.constitution.org/fed/federa10.htm.

10. James Madison, "The Federalist No. 57: The Alleged Tendency of the New Plan to Elevate the Few at the Expense ofthe Many Considered in Connection with Representation (February 19, 1788)," *New York Packet,* 1994-2010,The Constitution Society, www.constitution.org/fed/federa57.htm, par. 3.

11. Bellas, *Little Bits of History,* 21.

12. Madison, "The Federalist No. 57," par. 3.

13. Amy Borros, "Exposing Execs' 'Stealth' Compensation (September 26, 2004)," *BusinessWeek,* www.businessweek.com/bwdaily/dnflash/sep2004/nf20040924_8648_db016.htm, par.1-3.

14. Geraldine Fabrikant, "G.E. Expenses for Ex-Chief Cited in Divorce Papers (September 6, 2002)," *New York Times: Business,* www.nytimes.com/2002/09/06/business/06CHIE.html, par. 3, 11, 12.

15. Jaime Holguin, "GE: SEC Probing Welch's Compensation (September 16, 2002)," *CBS News: U.S.,* www.cbsnews.com/stories/2002/09/16/national/main522126.shtml,par.8.

16. T.D. Ameritrade, General Electric Co, NYSE Symbol: GE, 2010 T. D. Ameritrade, Tuesday, May 11, 2010, monthly chart from June 1, 2000 – May 11, 2010, http://www.research.ameritrade.com/wws/stocks/charts/charts.asp?display=popup.

17. Merrill Lynch CEO Thain Spent $1.22 Million on Office (January 22,2009)," *CNBC: U.S. News,* www.cnbc.com/id/28793892/Merrill_Lynch_CEO_Thain_Spent_1_22_Million_On_Office, par. 1, 3.

18. "Goldman Sachs Group Inc.: Executive Salaries, Bonuses, and Stock Options and other Compensation for 2007," CompanyPay. com, 2010, CompanyPay.com all rights reserved., www.companypay. com/executive.com/executive/compensation/goldman-sachs-group-inc. asp?yr=2008.

19. "Occidental-Petroleum Corp.: Executive Salaries, Bonuses, Stock Options and other Compensation for 2007, CompanyPay.com, 2010, www.companypay.com/executive/compensation/occidental-petroleum-corp.asp?yr=2008.

20. David Goldman, "The top 10 highest paid CEOs are… (August 14, 2009)," CNN Money.com, http://money.cnn.com/2009/08/14/news/companies/highest_paid_ceos/.

21. Wise, "African Orphan Development Authority."

22. Marko Tervio, "The Difference That CEOs Make: An Assignment Model Approach," *American Economic Review 98,* no. 3 (2008): 1, www.aeaweb.org/articles.php?doi=10.1257/aer.98.3.642.

23. "Blackstone Chief Tops Pay Ranking (August 13, 2009)," *New York Times: Dealbook,* http://dealbook.blogs.nytimes.com/2009/08/13/schwarzman-tops-list-of-highest-paid-chiefs/.

24. Michael B. Metzger, Jane P. Mallor, A. James Barnes, Thomas Bowers and Michael J. *Phillips, Business Law And The Regulatory Environment, Concepts and Cases,* Lusk Series, 6th ed., Irwin, (Homewood, Illinois: Irwin, 1986), 1355-1359.

25. Thomas Jefferson, "Quotation #37700," The Quotations Page,1994-2007, www.quotationspage.com/quote/37700.html. (Note to reader: There is a question as to whether or not this quote can be attributed to Thomas Jefferson.)

26. U.S. District Court, Northern District of Illinois, Eastern Division, United States of America vs. John Harris, No. 08-CR 888-5 Judge James B. Zagel, http://blogs.suntimes.com/blago/harrisplea.pdf, 2-25.

27. Amir Efrati and Robert Frank, "Madoff's Wife Cedes Asset Claim, Swindler Husband Plays Fate Like His Fraud Ahead of Monday's

Sentencing" (June 28, 2009)," *The Wall Street Journal*/Law, http://online.wsj.com/article/SB124612092335264949.html.

28. Kathy Kiely, "Ted Kennedy: A Lifetime of Public Service (August 27, 2009)," *USA Today:Washington*, www.usatoday.com/news/washington/2009-08-26-ted-kennedy-obit_N.htm, par. 34.

29. "Corruption Named as Key Issue by Voters in Exit Polls (November 8, 2006)," CNN.com Politics: America Votes 2006, http://www.cnn.com/2006/POLITICS/11/07/ election.exitpolls/index.html, par. 2.

30. "The Cost of Crime: It Just Doesn't Pay!, New Crime Study Pegs Cost At $1.7 Trillion Annually," *Davidson News & Events*, Davidson College, NC, 2006, www2.davidson.edu/news/news_archives/archives99/9910_anderson.html.

Chapter 11

1. James K. Polk, "Inaugural Address (March 4, 1845)," *Miller Center of Public Affairs*, University of Virginia, 2010, www.millercenter.org/scripps/archive/speeches/detail/3550, par. 2-3.

2. Dwight David Eisenhower, "First Inaugural Address (January 20, 1953)," *Miller Center of Public Affairs*, University of Virginia, 2010 www.millercenter.org/scripps/archive/speeches/detail/3356, par. 46.

3. Bellas, *Little Bits of History*, 19-21.

4. Ibid., 54.

5. Ibid., 53.

6. Henry Campbell Black, M. A., *Black's Law Dictionary*, 5th ed., (St. Paul, Minn: West Publishing Co., 1979), 1081.

7. Sharon Weinberger, "Army Secretary Says He's Met With Gay Soldiers, March 31, 2010)," *AOL News: Nation*, www.aolnews.com/nation/article/army-secretary-john-mchugh-says-hes-met-with-gay-soldiers/19421541, par. 5.

8. Ibid., par. 9.

9. See 1 Corinthians 5:11.

10. U.S. District Court: Western District of Wisconsin, *Freedom From Religion Foundation, Inc., Anne Nicole Gaylor, Annie Laurie Gaylor, Dan Barker, Paul Gaylor, Phyllis Rose and Jill Dean, Plaintiffs v. President Barack Obama and White House Press Secretary Robert L. Gibbs, Defendants Opinion and Order,* 08-cv-588-bbc, (April 15, 2010), www.wiwd.uscourts.gov/assets/pdf/FFRF_v_obama_ORDER.pdf, 40.

11. Ibid., 41.

12. U.S. Senate, 111th Congress (2009-2010) 1st Session, H.R. 3017: A Bill to Prohibit Employment Discrimination on the Basis of

Sexual Orientation or Gender Identity, (June 24, 2009), http://frwebgate. access.gpo.gov/cgi-bin/getdoc.cgi?dbname=111_cong_bills&docid=f: h3017ih.txt.pdf, 2, 3.

13. "HIV Patients Will Spend $600K for Lifetime Care; Those Diagnosed with AIDS Expected to Live Average of 24 Years, Study Says (November 10, 2006)," *msnbc: Health*,/www.msnbc.msn.com/ id/15655257/.

14. John R. Diggs, Jr., M.D., "The Health Risks of Gay Sex," *Corporate Resource Council*, 2002, www.corporateresourcecouncil.org/white_ papers/Health_Risks.pdf, 3.

15. Ibid., 3.

16. U.S. Department of Health and Human Services: Center for Disease Control and Prevention, Sexually Transmitted Diseases: Chlamydia—CDC Factsheet, www.medterms.com/script/main/ art. asp?articlekey=14966.

17. The Holy Bible, English Standard Version, Abomination, Leviticus 18:22, 2001 by Crossway Bibles, a publishing ministry of Good News Publishers. All rights reserved, http://www.gnpch.org/esv/search/ ?passage=Leviticus+18%.

18. "Let's Kiss the Bloodiest Century in History Goodbye," *The Movement For A Better America*, 2010, www.movementforabetter america. org/campaign2010.html., par., 7.

19. Ibid., par. 9.

20. "Jill Stanek Bio," Jill Stanek.com, www.jillstanek.com/jill-stanek.html, par. 2.

21. Vanessa Allen and Andrew Levy, " 'Doctors Told Me It Was Against the Rules to Save My Premature Baby' (September 10, 2009)," MailOnline, www.dailymail.com.uk/news/article-1211950/Premature-baby-left-die-doctors-mother-gives-birth-just-days-22-week-care-limit. html.

22. *USLegal Definitions*, s.v. "Good Samaritans Law & Legal Definition," 2001-2010 USLegal, Inc., www.definitions.uslegal.com/g/ good-samaritans/.

23. Bellas, *Little Bits of History*, 19.

24. *Black's Law Dictionary*, 5th ed., s.v. "Probition."

25. Edward A. Taggert, "Prohibition! The Failure of the 'Noble Experiment' in Reading & Berks County (1920-1933)," *The Historical Society of Berks County (PA)*, 2010, www.berkshistory.org/articles/prohibition.html, par. 1.

26. *Black's Law Dictionary*, 5th ed., s.v. "Revolution."

27. See Genesis 3:11-13.

28. U.S. District Court: Western District Of Wisconsin, *Freedom*

From Religion Foundation, Inc., et al., v. President Barack Obama et al.: Amici Curiae Brief of the American Center for Law and Justice (March 19, 2009), 1. http://www.aclj.org/media/pdf/ACLJAmicibrief-Final.pdf.

29. *The Free Dictionary*, s.v. "fidelity," www.thefreedictionary.com/fidelity.

Conclusion

1. Washington, "Farewell Address," par. 18.
2. Ibid., par. 28.

Appendix A
United States Allies

Albania*	Jamaica
American Samoa	Japan
Australia	Jordan
Bahamas	Kyrgyzstan
Bahrain	Kosovo
Belgium*	Kuwait
Brazil	Laos
Bulgaria*	Latvia*
Canada*	Lithuania*
Chile	Luxembourg*
Colombia	Mexico
Costa Rica	Netherlands*
Croatia*	New Zealand
Czech Republic*	Norway*
Denmark*	Panama
Dominican Republic	Philippines
Estonia*	Poland*
Ethiopia	Portugal*
France*	Romania*
Georgia	Singapore
Germany*	Slovakia*
Great Britain	Slovenia*
Greece*	Spain*
Greenland	South Korea
Guam	Taiwan
Hungary*	Turkey*
Iceland*	Netherlands
Israel	United Kingdom*
Italy*	Ukraine

* Indicates that this ally is also a North Atlantic
  Treaty Organization (NATO) member

Appendix B

The Declaration of Independence:

A Transcription

IN CONGRESS, July 4, 1776.

The unanimous Declaration of the thirteen united States of America,

When in the Course of human events, it becomes necessary for one people to dissolve the political bands which have connected them with another, and to assume among the powers of the earth, the separate and equal station to which the Laws of Nature and of Nature's God entitle them, a decent respect to the opinions of mankind requires that they should declare the causes which impel them to the separation.

We hold these truths to be self-evident, that all men are created equal, that they are endowed by their Creator with certain unalienable Rights, that among these are Life, Liberty and the pursuit of Happiness.--That to secure these rights, Governments are instituted among Men, deriving their just powers from the consent of the governed, —That whenever any Form of Government becomes destructive of these ends, it is the Right of the People to alter or to abolish it, and to institute new Government, laying its foundation on such principles and organizing its powers in such form, as to them shall seem most likely to effect their Safety and Happiness. Prudence, indeed, will dictate that Governments long established should not be changed for light and transient causes; and accordingly all experience hath shewn, that mankind are more disposed to suffer, while evils are sufferable, than to right themselves by abolishing the forms to which they are accustomed. But when a long train of abuses and usurpations, pursuing invariably the same Object evinces a design to reduce them under absolute Despotism, it is their right, it is their duty, to throw off such Government, and to provide new Guards for their future security.--Such has been the patient sufferance of these Colonies; and such is now the necessity which constrains them to alter their former Systems of Government. The history of the present King of Great Britain is a history of repeated injuries and usurpations, all having in direct object the establishment of an absolute Tyranny over these States. To prove this, let Facts be submitted to a candid world.

He has refused his Assent to Laws, the most wholesome and necessary for the public good. He has forbidden his Governors to pass Laws of immediate and pressing importance, unless suspended in their operation till his Assent should be obtained; and when so suspended, he has utterly neglected to attend to them. He has refused to pass other Laws for the accommodation of large districts of people, unless those people would relinquish the right of Representation in the Legislature, a right inestimable to them and formidable to tyrants only. He has called together legislative bodies at places unusual, uncomfortable, and distant from the depository of their public Records, for the sole purpose of fatiguing them into compliance with his measures. He has dissolved Representative Houses repeatedly, for opposing with manly firmness his invasions on the rights of the people. He has refused for a long time, after such dissolutions, to cause others to be elected; whereby the Legislative powers, incapable of Annihilation, have returned to the People at large for their exercise; the State remaining in the mean time exposed to all the dangers of invasion from without, and convulsions within. He has endeavoured to prevent the population of these States; for that purpose obstructing the Laws for Naturalization of Foreigners; refusing to pass others to encourage their migrations hither, and raising the conditions of new Appropriations of Lands. He has obstructed the Administration of Justice, by refusing his Assent to Laws for establishing Judiciary powers. He has made Judges dependent on his Will alone, for the tenure of their offices, and the amount and payment of their salaries. He has erected a multitude of New Offices, and sent hither swarms of Officers to harrass our people, and eat out their substance. He has kept among us, in times of peace, Standing Armies without the Consent of our legislatures. He has affected to render the Military independent of and superior to the Civil power. He has combined with others to subject us to a jurisdiction foreign to our constitution, and unacknowledged by our laws; giving his Assent to their Acts of pretended Legislation: For Quartering large bodies of armed troops among us: For protecting them, by a mock Trial, from punishment for any Murders which they should commit on the Inhabitants of these States: For cutting off our Trade with all parts of the world: For imposing Taxes on us without our Consent: For depriving us in many cases, of the benefits of Trial by Jury: For transporting us beyond Seas to be tried for pretended offences For abolishing the free System of English Laws in a neighbouring Province, establishing therein an Arbitrary government, and enlarging its Boundaries so as to render it at once an example and fit instrument for introducing the same absolute rule into these Colonies: For taking away our Charters, abolishing our most valuable Laws, and altering fundamentally the Forms of our Governments: For suspending our own Legislatures, and declaring themselves invested with power to legislate for us in all cases whatsoever. He has abdicated Government here, by declaring us out of his Protection and waging War against us. He has plundered our seas, ravaged our Coasts, burnt our towns, and destroyed the lives of our people. He is at this time transporting large Armies of foreign Mercenaries to compleat the works of death, desolation and tyranny, already begun with circumstances of Cruelty & perfidy scarcely paralleled in the most barbarous ages, and totally unworthy the Head of a civilized nation. He has constrained our fellow Citizens taken Captive on the high Seas to bear Arms against their Country, to become the executioners of their friends and Brethren, or to fall themselves by their Hands. He has excited domestic insurrections amongst us, and has endeavoured to bring on the inhabitants of our frontiers, the merciless Indian Savages, whose known rule of warfare, is an undistinguished destruction of all ages, sexes and conditions.

In every stage of these Oppressions We have Petitioned for Redress in the most humble terms: Our repeated Petitions have been answered only by repeated injury. A Prince whose character is thus marked by every act which may define a Tyrant, is unfit to be the ruler of a free people.

Nor have We been wanting in attentions to our Brittish brethren. We have warned them from time to time of attempts by their legislature to extend an unwarrantable jurisdiction over us. We have reminded them of the circumstances of our emigration and settlement here. We have appealed to their native justice and magnanimity, and we have conjured them by the ties of our common kindred to disavow these usurpations, which, would inevitably interrupt our connections and correspondence. They too have been deaf to the voice of justice and of consanguinity. We must, therefore, acquiesce in the necessity, which denounces our Separation, and hold them, as we hold the rest of mankind, Enemies in War, in Peace Friends.

We, therefore, the Representatives of the united States of America, in General Congress, Assembled, appealing to the Supreme Judge of the world for the rectitude of our intentions, do, in the Name, and by Authority of the good People of these Colonies, solemnly publish and declare, That these United Colonies are, and of Right ought to be Free and Independent States; that they are Absolved from all Allegiance to the British Crown, and that all political connection between them and the State of Great Britain, is and ought to be totally dissolved; and that as Free and Independent States, they have full Power to levy War, conclude Peace, contract Alliances, establish Commerce, and to do all other Acts and Things which Independent States may of right do. And for the support of this Declaration, with a firm reliance on the protection of divine Providence, we mutually pledge to each other our Lives, our Fortunes and our sacred Honor.

The 56 signatures on the Declaration appear in the positions indicated:

Column 1 **Georgia:** Button Gwinnett Lyman Hall George Walton

Column 2 **North Carolina:** William Hooper Joseph Hewes John Penn **South Carolina:** Edward Rutledge Thomas Heyward, Jr. Thomas Lynch, Jr. Arthur Middleton

Column 3 **Massachusetts:** John Hancock **Maryland:** Samuel Chase William Paca Thomas Stone Charles Carroll of Carrollton **Virginia:**George Wythe Richard Henry Lee Thomas Jefferson Benjamin Harrison Thomas Nelson, Jr. Francis Lightfoot Lee Carter Braxton

Column 4 **Pennsylvania:** Robert Morris Benjamin Rush Benjamin Franklin John Morton George Clymer James Smith George Taylor James Wilson George Ross **Delaware:** Caesar Rodney George Read Thomas McKean

Column 5 **New York:** William Floyd Philip Livingston Francis Lewis Lewis Morris **New Jersey:** Richard Stockton John Witherspoon Francis Hopkinson John Hart Abraham Clark

Column 6 **New Hampshire:** Josiah Bartlett William Whipple **Massachusetts:** Samuel Adams John Adams Robert Treat Paine Elbridge Gerry **Rhode Island:** Stephen Hopkins William Ellery **Connecticut:** Roger Sherman Samuel Huntington William Williams Oliver Wolcott **New Hampshire:** Matthew Thornton

Appendix C

The Constitution of the United States

Here is the complete text of the U.S. Constitution. The original spelling and capitalization have been retained.

We the People of the United States, in Order to form a more perfect Union, establish Justice, insure domestic Tranquility, provide for the common defence, promote the general Welfare, and secure the Blessings of Liberty to ourselves and our Posterity, do ordain and establish this Constitution for the United States of America.

Article I

Section 1. All legislative Powers herein granted shall be vested in a Congress of the United States, which shall consist of a Senate and House of Representatives.

Section 2. The House of Representatives shall be composed of Members chosen every second Year by the People of the several States, and the Electors in each State shall have the Qualifications requisite for Electors of the most numerous Branch of the State Legislature.

No Person shall be a Representative who shall not have attained to the age of twenty five Years, and been seven Years a Citizen of the United States, and who shall not, when elected, be an Inhabitant of that State in which he shall be chosen.

Representatives and direct Taxes shall be apportioned among the several States which may be included within this Union, according to their respective Numbers, which shall be determined by adding to the whole Number of free Persons, including those bound to Service for a Term of Years, and excluding Indians not taxed, three fifths of all other Persons. The actual Enumeration shall be made within three Years after the first Meeting of the Congress of the United States, and within every subsequent Term of ten Years, in such Manner as they shall by Law direct. The Number of Representatives shall not exceed one for every thirty Thousand, but each State shall have at Least one Representative; and until such enumeration shall be made, the State of New Hampshire shall be entitled to chuse three, Massachusetts eight, Rhode-Island and Providence Plantations one, Connecticut five, New-York six, New Jersey four, Pennsylvania eight, Delaware one, Maryland six, Virginia ten, North Carolina five, South Carolina five, and Georgia three.

When vacancies happen in the Representation from any State, the Executive Authority thereof shall issue Writs of Election to fill such Vacancies.

The House of Representatives shall chuse their Speaker and other Officers; and shall have the sole Power of Impeachment.

Section 3. The Senate of the United States shall be composed of two Senators from each State, chosen by the Legislature thereof, for six Years; and each Senator shall have one Vote.

Immediately after they shall be assembled in Consequence of the first Election, they shall be divided as equally as may be into three Classes. The Seats of the Senators of the first Class shall be vacated at the Expiration of the second Year, of the second Class at the Expiration of the fourth Year, and the third Class at the Expiration of the sixth Year, so that one third may be chosen every second Year; and if Vacancies happen by Resignation, or otherwise, during the Recess of the Legislature of any State, the Executive thereof may make temporary Appointments until the next Meeting of the Legislature, which shall then fill such Vacancies.

No Person shall be a Senator who shall not have attained to the Age of thirty Years, and been nine Years a Citizen of the United States and who shall not, when elected, be an Inhabitant of that State for which he shall be chosen.

The Vice President of the United States shall be President of the Senate, but shall have no Vote, unless they be equally divided.

The Senate shall chuse their other Officers, and also a President pro tempore, in the Absence of the Vice President, or when he shall exercise the Office of President of the United States.

The Senate shall have the sole Power to try all Impeachments. When sitting for that Purpose, they shall be on Oath or Affirmation. When the President of the United States is tried, the Chief Justice shall preside: And no Person shall be convicted without the Concurrence of two thirds of the Members present.

Judgment in Cases of Impeachment shall not extend further than to removal from Office, and disqualification to hold and enjoy any Office of Honor, Trust or Profit under the United States: but the Party convicted shall nevertheless be liable and subject to Indictment, Trial, Judgment and Punishment, according to Law.

Section 4. The Times, Places and Manner of holding Elections for Senators and Representatives, shall be prescribed in each State by the Legislature thereof; but the Congress may at any time by Law make or alter such Regulations, except as to the Places of chusing Senators.

The Congress shall assemble at least once in every Year, and such Meeting shall be on the first Monday in December, unless they shall by Law appoint a different Day.

Section 5. Each House shall be the Judge of the Elections, Returns and Qualifications of its own Members, and a Majority of each shall constitute a Quorum to do Business; but a smaller Number may adjourn from day to day, and may be authorized to compel the Attendance of absent Members, in such Manner, and under such Penalties as each House may provide.

Each House may determine the Rules of its Proceedings, punish its Members for disorderly Behaviour, and, with the Concurrence of two thirds, expel a Member.

Each House shall keep a Journal of its Proceedings, and from time to time publish the same, excepting such Parts as may in their Judgment require Secrecy; and the Yeas and Nays of the Members of either House on any question shall, at the Desire of one fifth of those Present, be entered on the Journal.

Neither House, during the Session of Congress, shall, without the Consent of the other, adjourn for more than three days, nor to any other Place than that in which the two Houses shall be sitting.

Section 6. The Senators and Representatives shall receive a Compensation for their Services, to be ascertained by Law, and paid out of the Treasury of the United States. They shall in all Cases, except Treason, Felony and Breach of the Peace, be privileged from Arrest during their Attendance at the Session of their respective Houses, and in going to and returning from the same; and for any Speech or Debate in either House, they shall not be questioned in any other Place.

No Senator or Representative shall, during the Time for which he was elected, be appointed to any civil Office under the Authority of the United States, which shall have been created, or the Emoluments whereof shall have been encreased during such time: and no Person holding any Office under the United States, shall be a Member of either House during his Continuance in Office.

Section 7. All Bills for raising Revenue shall originate in the House of Representatives; but the Senate may propose or concur with Amendments as on other Bills.

Every Bill which shall have passed the House of Representatives and the Senate, shall, before it become a Law, be presented to the President of the United States; if he approve he shall sign it, but if not he shall return it, with his Objections to that House in which it shall have originated, who shall enter the Objections at large on their Journal, and proceed to reconsider it. If after such Reconsideration two thirds of that House shall agree to pass the Bill, it shall be sent, together with the Objections, to the other House, by which it shall likewise be reconsidered, and if approved by two thirds of that House, it shall become a Law. But in all such Cases the Votes of both Houses shall be determined by Yeas and Nays, and the Names of the Persons voting for and against the Bill shall be entered on the Journal of each House respectively. If any Bill shall not be returned by the President within ten Days (Sundays excepted) after it shall have been presented to him, the Same shall be a Law, in like Manner as if he had signed it, unless the Congress by their Adjournment prevent its Return, in which Case it shall not be a Law.

Every Order, Resolution, or Vote to which the Concurrence of the Senate and House of Representatives may be necessary (except on a question of Adjournment) shall be presented to the President of the United States; and before the Same shall take Effect, shall be approved by him, or being disapproved by him, shall be repassed by two thirds of the Senate and House of Representatives, according to the Rules and Limitations prescribed in the Case of a Bill.

Section 8. The Congress shall have Power To lay and collect Taxes, Duties, Imposts and Excises, to pay the Debts and provide for the common Defence and general Welfare of the United States; but all Duties, Imposts and Excises shall be uniform throughout the United States;

To borrow Money on the credit of the United States;

To regulate Commerce with foreign Nations, and among the several States, and with the Indian Tribes;

To establish an uniform Rule of Naturalization, and uniform Laws on the subject of Bankruptcies throughout the United States;

To coin Money, regulate the Value thereof, and of foreign Coin, and fix the Standard of Weights and Measures;

To provide for the Punishment of counterfeiting the Securities and current Coin of the United States;

To establish Post Offices and post Roads;

To promote the Progress of Science and useful Arts, by securing for limited Times to Authors and Inventors the exclusive Right to their respective Writings and Discoveries;

To constitute Tribunals inferior to the supreme Court;

To define and punish Piracies and Felonies committed on the high Seas, and Offences against the Law of Nations;

To declare War, grant Letters of Marque and Reprisal, and make Rules concerning Captures on Land and Water;

To raise and support Armies, but no Appropriation of Money to that Use shall be for a longer Term than two Years;

To provide and maintain a Navy;

To make Rules for the Government and Regulation of the land and naval Forces;

To provide for calling forth the Militia to execute the Laws of the Union, suppress Insurrections and repel Invasions;

To provide for organizing, arming, and disciplining, the Militia, and for governing such Part of them as may be employed in the Service of the United States, reserving to the States respectively, the Appointment of the Officers, and the Authority of training the Militia according to the discipline prescribed by Congress;

To exercise exclusive Legislation in all Cases whatsoever, over such District (not exceeding ten Miles square) as may, by Cession of particular States, and the Acceptance of Congress, become the Seat of the Government of the United States, and to exercise like Authority over all Places purchased by the Consent of the Legislature of the State in which the Same shall be, for the Erection of Forts, Magazines, Arsenals, dock-Yards, and other needful Buildings;—And

To make all Laws which shall be necessary and proper for carrying into Execution the foregoing Powers, and all other Powers vested by this Constitution in the Government of the United States, or in any Department or Officer thereof.

Section 9. The Migration or Importation of such Persons as any of the States now existing shall think proper to admit, shall not be prohibited by the Congress prior to the Year one thousand eight hundred and eight, but a Tax or duty may be imposed on such Importation, not exceeding ten dollars for each Person.

The Privilege of the Writ of Habeas Corpus shall not be suspended, unless when in Cases of Rebellion or Invasion the public Safety may require it.

No Bill of Attainder or ex post facto Law shall be passed.

No Capitation, or other direct, Tax shall be laid, unless in Proportion to the Census or Enumeration herein before directed to be taken.

No Tax or Duty shall be laid on Articles exported from any State.

No Preference shall be given by any Regulation of Commerce or Revenue to the Ports of one State over those of another: nor shall Vessels bound to, or from, one State, be obliged to enter, clear or pay Duties in another.

No Money shall be drawn from the Treasury, but in Consequence of Appropriations made by Law; and a regular Statement and Account of Receipts and Expenditures of all public Money shall be published from time to time.

No Title of Nobility shall be granted by the United States: And no Person holding any Office of Profit or Trust under them, shall, without the Consent of the Congress, accept of any present, Emolument, Office, or Title, of any kind whatever, from any King, Prince, or foreign State.

Section 10. No State shall enter into any Treaty, Alliance, or Confederation; grant Letters of Marque and Reprisal; coin Money; emit Bills of Credit; make any Thing but gold and silver Coin a Tender in Payment of Debts; pass any Bill of Attainder, ex post facto Law, or Law impairing the Obligation of Contracts, or grant any Title of Nobility.

No State shall, without the Consent of the Congress, lay any Imposts or Duties on Imports or Exports, except what may be absolutely necessary for executing it's inspection Laws: and the net Produce of all Duties and Imposts, laid by any State on Imports or Exports, shall be for the Use of the Treasury of the United States; and all such Laws shall be subject to the Revision and Controul of the Congress.

No State shall, without the Consent of Congress, lay any Duty of Tonnage, keep Troops, or Ships of War in time of Peace, enter into any Agreement or Compact with another State, or with a foreign Power, or engage in War, unless actually invaded, or in such imminent Danger as will not admit of delay.

Article II

Section 1. The executive Power shall be vested in a President of the United States of America. He shall hold his Office during the Term of four Years, and, together with the Vice President, chosen for the same Term, be elected, as follows:

Each State shall appoint, in such Manner as the Legislature thereof may direct, a Number of Electors, equal to the whole Number of Senators and Representatives to which the State may be entitled in the Congress: but no Senator or Representative, or Person holding an Office of Trust or Profit under the United States, shall be appointed an Elector.

The Electors shall meet in their respective States, and vote by Ballot for two Persons, of whom one at least shall not be an Inhabitant of the same State with themselves. And they shall make a List of all the Persons voted for, and of the Number of Votes for each; which List they shall sign and certify, and transmit sealed to the Seat of the Government of the United States, directed to the President of the Senate. The President of the Senate shall, in the Presence of the Senate and House of Representatives, open all the Certificates, and the Votes shall then be counted. The Person having the greatest Number of Votes shall be the President, if such Number be a Majority of the whole Number of Electors appointed; and if there be more than one who have such Majority, and have an equal Number of Votes, then the House of Representatives shall immediately chuse by Ballot one of them for President; and if no Person have a Majority, then from the five highest on the List the said House shall in like Manner chuse the President. But in chusing the President, the Votes shall be taken by States, the Representation from each State having one Vote; A quorum for this Purpose shall consist of a Member or Members from two thirds of the States, and a Majority of all the States shall be necessary to a Choice. In every Case, after the Choice of the President, the Person having the greatest Number of Votes of the Electors shall be the Vice President. But if there should remain two or more who have equal Votes, the Senate shall chuse from them by Ballot the Vice President.

The Congress may determine the Time of chusing the Electors, and the Day on which they shall give their Votes; which Day shall be the same throughout the United States.

No Person except a natural born Citizen, or a Citizen of the United States, at the time of the Adoption of this Constitution, shall be eligible to the Office of

President; neither shall any Person be eligible to that Office who shall not have attained to the Age of thirty five Years, and been fourteen Years a Resident within the United States.

In Case of the Removal of the President from Office, or of his Death, Resignation, or Inability to discharge the Powers and Duties of the said Office, the Same shall devolve on the Vice President, and the Congress may by Law provide for the Case of Removal, Death, Resignation or Inability, both of the President and Vice President, declaring what Officer shall then act as President, and such Officer shall act accordingly, until the Disability be removed, or a President shall be elected.

The President shall, at stated Times, receive for his Services, a Compensation, which shall neither be encreased nor diminished during the Period for which he shall have been elected, and he shall not receive within that Period any other Emolument from the United States, or any of them.

Before he enter on the Execution of his Office, he shall take the following Oath or Affirmation:—"I do solemnly swear (or affirm) that I will faithfully execute the Office of President of the United States, and will to the best of my Ability, preserve, protect and defend the Constitution of the United States."

Section 2. The President shall be Commander in Chief of the Army and Navy of the United States, and of the Militia of the several States, when called into the actual Service of the United States; he may require the Opinion, in writing, of the principal Officer in each of the executive Departments, upon any Subject relating to the Duties of their respective Offices, and he shall have Power to grant Reprieves and Pardons for Offences against the United States, except in Cases of Impeachment.

He shall have Power, by and with the Advice and Consent of the Senate, to make Treaties, provided two thirds of the Senators present concur; and he shall nominate, and by and with the Advice and Consent of the Senate, shall appoint Ambassadors, other public Ministers and Consuls, Judges of the supreme Court, and all other Officers of the United States, whose Appointments are not herein otherwise provided for, and which shall be established by Law: but the Congress may by Law vest the Appointment of such inferior Officers, as they think proper, in the President alone, in the Courts of Law, or in the Heads of Departments.

The President shall have Power to fill up all Vacancies that may happen during the Recess of the Senate, by granting Commissions which shall expire at the End of their next Session.

Section 3. He shall from time to time give to the Congress Information of the State of the Union, and recommend to their Consideration such Measures as he shall judge necessary and expedient; he may, on extraordinary Occasions, convene both Houses, or either of them, and in Case of Disagreement between them, with Respect to the Time of Adjournment, he may adjourn them to such Time as he shall think proper; he shall receive Ambassadors and other public Ministers; he shall take Care that the Laws be faithfully executed, and shall Commission all the Officers of the United States.

Section 4. The President, Vice President and all civil Officers of the United States, shall be removed from Office on Impeachment for, and Conviction of, Treason, Bribery, or other high Crimes and Misdemeanors.

Article III

Section 1. The judicial Power of the United States, shall be vested in one supreme Court, and in such inferior Courts as the Congress may from time to time ordain and establish. The Judges, both of the supreme and inferior Courts, shall hold their Offices during good Behaviour, and shall, at stated Times, receive for their Services, a Compensation, which shall not be diminished during their Continuance in Office.

Section 2. The judicial Power shall extend to all Cases, in Law and Equity, arising under this Constitution, the Laws of the United States, and Treaties made, or which shall be made, under their Authority;—to all Cases affecting Ambassadors, other public Ministers and Consuls;—to all Cases of admiralty and maritime Jurisdiction;—to Controversies to which the United States shall be a Party;—to Controversies between two or more States;—between a State and Citizens of another State;—between Citizens of different States;—between Citizens of the same State claiming Lands under Grants of different States, and between a State, or the Citizens thereof, and foreign States, Citizens or Subjects.

In all Cases affecting Ambassadors, other public Ministers and Consuls, and those in which a State shall be Party, the supreme Court shall have original Jurisdiction. In all the other Cases before mentioned, the supreme Court shall have appellate Jurisdiction, both as to Law and Fact, with such Exceptions, and under such Regulations as the Congress shall make.

The Trial of all Crimes, except in Cases of Impeachment, shall be by Jury; and such Trial shall be held in the State where the said Crimes shall have been committed; but when not committed within any State, the Trial shall be at such Place or Places as the Congress may by Law have directed.

Section 3. Treason against the United States, shall consist only in levying War against them, or in adhering to their Enemies, giving them Aid and Comfort. No Person shall be convicted of Treason unless on the Testimony of two Witnesses to the same overt Act, or on Confession in open Court.

The Congress shall have Power to declare the Punishment of Treason, but no Attainder of Treason shall work Corruption of Blood, or Forfeiture except during the Life of the Person attainted.

Article IV

Section 1. Full Faith and Credit shall be given in each State to the public Acts, Records, and judicial Proceedings of every other State. And the Congress may by general Laws prescribe the Manner in which such Acts, Records, and Proceedings shall be proved, and the Effect thereof.

Section 2. The Citizens of each State shall be entitled to all Privileges and Immunities of Citizens in the several States.

A Person charged in any State with Treason, Felony, or other Crime, who shall flee from Justice, and be found in another State, shall on Demand of the executive Authority of the State from which he fled, be delivered up, to be removed to the State having Jurisdiction of the Crime.

No Person held to Service or Labour in one State, under the Laws thereof, escaping into another, shall, in Consequence of any Law or Regulation therein, be discharged from such Service or Labour, but shall be delivered up on Claim of the Party to whom such Service or Labour may be due.

Section 3. New States may be admitted by the Congress into this Union; but no new States shall be formed or erected within the Jurisdiction of any other State; nor any State be formed by the Junction of two or more States, or Parts of States, without the Consent of the Legislatures of the States concerned as well as of the Congress.

The Congress shall have Power to dispose of and make all needful Rules and Regulations respecting the Territory or other Property belonging to the United States; and nothing in this Constitution shall be so construed as to Prejudice any Claims of the United States, or of any particular State.

Section 4. The United States shall guarantee to every State in this Union a Republican Form of Government, and shall protect each of them against Invasion; and on Application of the Legislature, or of the Executive (when the Legislature cannot be convened) against domestic Violence.

Article V

The Congress, whenever two thirds of both Houses shall deem it necessary, shall propose Amendments to this Constitution, or, on the Application of the Legislatures of two thirds of the several States, shall call a Convention for proposing Amendments, which, in either Case, shall be valid to all Intents and Purposes, as Part of this Constitution, when ratified by the Legislatures of three fourths of the several States, or by Conventions in three fourths thereof, as the one or the other Mode of Ratification may be proposed by the Congress; Provided that no Amendment which may be made prior to the Year One thousand eight hundred and eight shall in any Manner affect the first and fourth Clauses in the Ninth Section of the first Article; and that no State, without its Consent, shall be deprived of its equal Suffrage in the Senate.

Article VI

All Debts contracted and Engagements entered into, before the Adoption of this

Constitution, shall be as valid against the United States under this Constitution, as under the Confederation.

This Constitution, and the Laws of the United States which shall be made in Pursuance thereof; and all Treaties made, or which shall be made, under the Authority of the United States, shall be the supreme Law of the Land; and the Judges in every State shall be bound thereby, any Thing in the Constitution or Laws of any State to the Contrary not withstanding.

The Senators and Representatives before mentioned, and the Members of the several State Legislatures, and all executive and judicial Officers, both of the United States and of the several States, shall be bound by Oath or Affirmation, to support this Constitution; but no religious Test shall ever be required as a Qualification to any Office or public Trust under the United States.

Article VII

The Ratification of the Conventions of nine States, shall be sufficient for the Establishment of this Constitution between the States so ratifying the Same.

Done in Convention by the Unanimous Consent of the States present the Seventeenth Day of September in the Year of our Lord one thousand seven hundred and Eighty seven and of the Independence of the United States of America the Twelfth

Appendix D

The Bill of Rights

Congress of the United States, begun and held at the City of New-York, on Wednesday the fourth of March, one thousand seven hundred and eighty nine.

THE Conventions of a number of the States, having at the time of their adopting the Constitution, expressed a desire, in order to prevent misconstruction or abuse of its powers, that further declaratory and restrictive clauses should be added: And as extending the ground of public confidence in the Government, will best ensure the beneficent ends of its institution.

RESOLVED by the Senate and House of Representatives of the United States of America, in Congress assembled, two thirds of both Houses concurring, that the following Articles be proposed to the Legislatures of the several States, as amendments to the Constitution of the United States, all, or any of which Articles, when ratified by three fourths of the said Legislatures, to be valid to all intents and purposes, as part of the said Constitution; viz.

ARTICLES in addition to, and Amendment of the Constitution of the United States of America, proposed by Congress, and ratified by the Legislatures of the several States, pursuant to the fifth Article of the original Constitution.

Note: The following text is a transcription of the first ten amendments to the Constitution in their original form. These amendments were ratified December 15, 1791, and form what is known as the "Bill of Rights."

Amendment I

Congress shall make no law respecting an establishment of religion, or prohibiting the free exercise thereof; or abridging the freedom of speech, or of the press; or the right of the people peaceably to assemble, and to petition the Government for a redress of grievances.

Amendment II

A well regulated Militia, being necessary to the security of a free State, the right of the people to keep and bear Arms, shall not be infringed.

Amendment III

No Soldier shall, in time of peace be quartered in any house, without the consent of the Owner, nor in time of war, but in a manner to be prescribed by law.

Amendment IV

The right of the people to be secure in their persons, houses, papers, and effects, against unreasonable searches and seizures, shall not be violated, and no Warrants shall issue, but upon probable cause, supported by Oath or affirmation, and particularly describing the place to be searched, and the persons or things to be seized.

Amendment V

No person shall be held to answer for a capital, or otherwise infamous crime, unless on a presentment or indictment of a Grand Jury, except in cases arising in the land or naval forces, or in the Militia, when in actual service in time of War or public danger; nor shall any person be subject for the same offence to be twice put in jeopardy of life or limb; nor shall be compelled in any criminal case to be a witness against himself, nor be deprived of life, liberty, or property, without due process of law; nor shall private property be taken for public use, without just compensation.

Amendment VI

In all criminal prosecutions, the accused shall enjoy the right to a speedy and public trial, by an impartial jury of the State and district wherein the crime shall have been committed, which district shall have been previously ascertained by law, and to be informed of the nature and cause of the accusation; to be confronted with the witnesses against him; to have compulsory process for obtaining witnesses in his favor, and to have the Assistance of Counsel for his defence.

Amendment VII

In Suits at common law, where the value in controversy shall exceed twenty dollars, the right of trial by jury shall be preserved, and no fact tried by a jury, shall be otherwise re-examined in any Court of the United States, than according to the rules of the common law.

Amendment VIII

Excessive bail shall not be required, nor excessive fines imposed, nor cruel and unusual punishments inflicted.

Amendment IX

The enumeration in the Constitution, of certain rights, shall not be construed to deny or disparage others retained by the people.

Amendment X

The powers not delegated to the United States by the Constitution, nor prohibited by it to the States, are reserved to the States respectively, or to the people.

The Constitution: Amendments 11-27

Constitutional Amendments 1-10 make up what is known as The Bill of Rights.Amendments 11-27 are listed below.

Amendment XI

Passed by Congress March 4, 1794. Ratified February 7, 1795.

Note: Article III, section 2, of the Constitution was modified by amendment 11.

The Judicial power of the United States shall not be construed to extend to any suit in law or equity, commenced or prosecuted against one of the United States by Citizens of another State, or by Citizens or Subjects of any Foreign State.

Amendment XII

Passed by Congress December 9, 1803. Ratified June 15, 1804.

Note: A portion of Article II, section 1 of the Constitution was superseded by the 12th amendment.

The Electors shall meet in their respective states and vote by ballot for President and Vice-President, one of whom, at least, shall not be an inhabitant of the same state with themselves; they shall name in their ballots the person voted for as President, and in distinct ballots the person voted for as Vice-President, and they shall make distinct lists of all persons voted for as President, and of all persons voted for as Vice-President, and of the number of votes for each, which lists they shall sign and certify, and transmit sealed to the seat of the government of the United States, directed to the President of the Senate; — the President of the Senate shall, in the presence of the Senate and House of Representatives, open all the certificates and the votes shall then be counted; — The person having the greatest number of votes for President, shall be the President, if such number be a majority of the whole number of Electors appointed; and if no person have such majority, then from the persons having the highest numbers not exceeding three on the list of those voted for as President, the House of Representatives shall choose immediately, by ballot, the President. But in choosing the President, the votes shall be taken by states, the representation from each state having one vote; a quorum for this purpose shall consist of a member or members from two-thirds of the states, and a majority of all the states shall be necessary to a choice. [And if the House of Representatives shall not choose a President whenever the right of choice shall devolve upon them, before the fourth day of March next following, then the Vice-President shall act as President, as in case of the death or other constitutional disability of the President. —]* The person having the greatest number of votes as Vice-President, shall be the Vice-President, if such number be a majority of the whole number of Electors appointed, and if no person have a majority, then from the two highest numbers on the list, the Senate shall choose the Vice-President; a quorum for the purpose shall consist of two-thirds of the whole number of Senators, and a majority of the whole number shall be necessary to a choice. But no person constitutionally ineligible to the office of President shall be eligible to that of Vice-President of the United States.

*Superseded by section 3 of the 20th amendment.

Amendment XIII

Passed by Congress January 31, 1865. Ratified December 6, 1865.

Note: A portion of Article IV, section 2, of the Constitution was superseded by the 13th amendment.

Section 1. Neither slavery nor involuntary servitude, except as a punishment for crime whereof the party shall have been duly convicted, shall exist within the United States, or any place subject to their jurisdiction.

Section 2. Congress shall have power to enforce this article by appropriate legislation.

Amendment XIV

Passed by Congress June 13, 1866. Ratified July 9, 1868.

Note: Article I, section 2, of the Constitution was modified by section 2 of the 14th amendment.

Section 1. All persons born or naturalized in the United States, and subject to the jurisdiction thereof, are citizens of the United States and of the State wherein they reside. No State shall make or enforce any law which shall abridge the privileges or immunities of citizens of the United States; nor shall any State deprive any person of life, liberty, or property, without due process of law; nor deny to any person within its jurisdiction the equal protection of the laws.

Section 2. Representatives shall be apportioned among the several States according to their respective numbers, counting the whole number of persons in each State, excluding Indians not taxed. But when the right to vote at any election for the choice of electors for President and Vice-President of the United States, Representatives in Congress, the Executive and Judicial officers of a State, or the members of the Legislature thereof, is denied to any of the male inhabitants of such State, being twenty-one years of age,* and citizens of the United States, or in any way abridged, except for participation in rebellion, or other crime, the basis of representation therein shall be reduced in the proportion which the number of such male citizens shall bear to the whole number of male citizens twenty-one years of age in such State.

Section 3. No person shall be a Senator or Representative in Congress, or elector of President and Vice-President, or hold any office, civil or military, under the United States, or under any State, who, having previously taken an oath, as a member of Congress, or as an officer of the United States, or as a member of any State legislature, or as an executive or judicial officer of any State, to support the Constitution of the United States, shall have engaged in insurrection or rebellion against the same, or given aid or comfort to the enemies thereof. But Congress may by a vote of two-thirds of each House, remove such disability.

Section 4. The validity of the public debt of the United States, authorized by law, including debts incurred for payment of pensions and bounties for services in suppressing insurrection or rebellion, shall not be questioned. But neither the United States nor any State shall assume or pay any debt or obligation incurred in aid of insurrection or rebellion against the United States, or any claim for the loss or emancipation of any slave; but all such debts, obligations and claims shall be held illegal and void.

Section 5. The Congress shall have the power to enforce, by appropriate legislation, the provisions of this article.

*Changed by section 1 of the 26th amendment.

Amendment XV

Passed by Congress February 26, 1869. Ratified February 3, 1870.

Section 1. The right of citizens of the United States to vote shall not be denied or abridged by the United States or by any State on account of race, color, or previous condition of servitude—

Section 2. The Congress shall have the power to enforce this article by appropriate legislation.

Amendment XVI

Passed by Congress July 2, 1909. Ratified February 3, 1913.

Note: Article I, section 9, of the Constitution was modified by amendment 16.

The Congress shall have power to lay and collect taxes on incomes, from whatever source derived, without apportionment among the several States, and without regard to any census or enumeration.

Amendment XVII

Passed by Congress May 13, 1912. Ratified April 8, 1913.

Note: Article I, section 3, of the Constitution was modified by the 17th amendment.

The Senate of the United States shall be composed of two Senators from each State, elected by the people thereof, for six years; and each Senator shall have one vote. The electors in each State shall have the qualifications requisite for electors of the most numerous branch of the State legislatures.

When vacancies happen in the representation of any State in the Senate, the executive authority of such State shall issue writs of election to fill such vacancies: Provided, That the legislature of any State may empower the executive thereof to make temporary appointments until the people fill the vacancies by election as the legislature may direct.

This amendment shall not be so construed as to affect the election or term of any Senator chosen before it becomes valid as part of the Constitution.

Amendment XVIII

Passed by Congress December 18, 1917. Ratified January 16, 1919. Repealed by amendment 21.

Section 1. After one year from the ratification of this article the manufacture, sale, or transportation of intoxicating liquors within, the importation thereof into, or the exportation thereof from the United States and all territory subject to the jurisdiction thereof for beverage purposes is hereby prohibited.

Section 2. The Congress and the several States shall have concurrent power to enforce this article by appropriate legislation.

Section 3. This article shall be inoperative unless it shall have been ratified as an amendment to the Constitution by the legislatures of the several States, as provided in the Constitution, within seven years from the date of the submission hereof to the States by the Congress.

Amendment XIX

Passed by Congress June 4, 1919. Ratified August 18, 1920.

The right of citizens of the United States to vote shall not be denied or abridged by the United States or by any State on account of sex.

Congress shall have power to enforce this article by appropriate legislation.

Amendment XX

Passed by Congress March 2, 1932. Ratified January 23, 1933.

Note: Article I, section 4, of the Constitution was modified by section 2 of this amendment. In addition, a portion of the 12th amendment was superseded by section 3.

Section 1. The terms of the President and the Vice President shall end at noon on the 20th day of January, and the terms of Senators and Representatives at noon on the 3d day of January, of the years in which such terms would have ended if this article had not been ratified; and the terms of their successors shall then begin.

Section 2. The Congress shall assemble at least once in every year, and such meeting shall begin at noon on the 3d day of January, unless they shall by law appoint a different day.

Section 3. If, at the time fixed for the beginning of the term of the President, the President elect shall have died, the Vice President elect shall become President. If a President shall not have been chosen before the time fixed for the beginning of his term, or if the President elect shall have failed to qualify, then the Vice President elect shall act as President until a President shall have qualified; and the Congress may by law provide for the case wherein neither a President elect nor a Vice President shall have qualified, declaring who shall then act as President, or the manner in which one who is to act shall be selected, and such person shall act accordingly until a President or Vice President shall have qualified.

Section 4 The Congress may by law provide for the case of the death of any of the persons from whom the House of Representatives may choose a President whenever the right of choice shall have devolved upon them, and for the case of the death of any of the persons from whom the Senate may choose a Vice President whenever the right of choice shall have devolved upon them.

Section 5. Sections 1 and 2 shall take effect on the 15th day of October following the ratification of this article.

Section 6. This article shall be inoperative unless it shall have been ratified as an amendment to the Constitution by the legislatures of three-fourths of the several States within seven years from the date of its submission.

Amendment XXI

Passed by Congress February 20, 1933. Ratified December 5, 1933.

Section 1. The eighteenth article of amendment to the Constitution of the United States is hereby repealed.

Section 2. The transportation or importation into any State, Territory, or Possession of the United States for delivery or use therein of intoxicating liquors, in violation of the laws thereof, is hereby prohibited.

Section 3 This article shall be inoperative unless it shall have been ratified as an amendment to the Constitution by conventions in the several States, as provided in the Constitution, within seven years from the date of the submission hereof to the States by the Congress.

Amendment XXII

Passed by Congress March 21, 1947. Ratified February 27, 1951.

Section 1. No person shall be elected to the office of the President more than twice, and no person who has held the office of President, or acted as President, for more than two years of a term to which some other person was elected President shall be elected to the office of President more than once. But this Article shall not apply to any person holding the office of President when this Article was proposed by Congress, and shall not prevent any person who may be holding the office of President, or acting as President, during the term within which this Article becomes operative from holding the office of President or acting as President during the remainder of such term.

Section 2. This article shall be inoperative unless it shall have been ratified as an amendment to the Constitution by the legislatures of three-fourths of the several States within seven years from the date of its submission to the States by the Congress.

Amendment XXIII

Passed by Congress June 16, 1960. Ratified March 29, 1961.

Section 1. The District constituting the seat of Government of the United States shall appoint in such manner as Congress may direct:

A number of electors of President and Vice President equal to the whole number of Senators and Representatives in Congress to which the District would be entitled if it were a State, but in no event more than the least populous State; they shall be in addition to those appointed by the States, but they shall be considered, for the purposes of the election of President and Vice President, to be electors appointed by a State; and they shall meet in the District and perform such duties as provided by the twelfth article of amendment.

Section 2. The Congress shall have power to enforce this article by appropriate legislation.

Amendment XXIV

Passed by Congress August 27, 1962. Ratified January 23, 1964.

Section 1. The right of citizens of the United States to vote in any primary or other election for President or Vice President, for electors for President or Vice President, or for Senator or Representative in Congress, shall not be denied or abridged by the United States or any State by reason of failure to pay poll tax or other tax.

Section 2. The Congress shall have power to enforce this article by appropriate legislation.

Amendment XXV

Passed by Congress July 6, 1965. Ratified February 10, 1967.

Note: Article II, section 1, of the Constitution was affected by the 25th amendment.

Section 1. In case of the removal of the President from office or of his death or resignation, the Vice President shall become President.

Section 2. Whenever there is a vacancy in the office of the Vice President, the President shall nominate a Vice President who shall take office upon confirmation by a majority vote of both Houses of Congress.

Section 3. Whenever the President transmits to the President pro tempore of the Senate and the Speaker of the House of Representatives his written declaration that he is unable to discharge the powers and duties of his office, and until he transmits to them a written declaration to the contrary, such powers and duties shall be discharged by the Vice President as Acting President.

Section 4. Whenever the Vice President and a majority of either the principal officers of the executive departments or of such other body as Congress may by law provide, transmit to the President pro tempore of the Senate and the Speaker of the House of Representatives their written declaration that the President is unable to discharge the powers and duties of his office, the Vice President shall immediately assume the powers and duties of the office as Acting President.

Thereafter, when the President transmits to the President pro tempore of the Senate and the Speaker of the House of Representatives his written declaration that no inability exists, he shall resume the powers and duties of his office unless the Vice President and a majority of either the principal officers of the executive department or of such other body as Congress may by law provide, transmit within four days to the President pro tempore of the Senate and the Speaker of the House of Representatives their written declaration that the President is unable to discharge the powers and duties of his office. Thereupon Congress shall decide the issue, assembling within forty-eight hours for that purpose if not in session. If the Congress, within twenty-one days after receipt of the latter written declaration, or, if Congress is not in session, within twenty-one days after Congress is required to assemble, determines by two-thirds vote of both Houses that the President is unable to discharge the powers and duties of his office, the Vice President shall continue to discharge the same as Acting President; otherwise, the President shall resume the powers and duties of his office.

Amendment XXVI

Passed by Congress March 23, 1971. Ratified July 1, 1971.

Note: Amendment 14, section 2, of the Constitution was modified by section 1 of the 26th amendment.

Section 1. The right of citizens of the United States, who are eighteen years of age or older, to vote shall not be denied or abridged by the United States or by any State on account of age.

Section 2. The Congress shall have power to enforce this article by appropriate legislation.

Amendment XXVII

Originally proposed Sept. 25, 1789. Ratified May 7, 1992.

No law, varying the compensation for the services of the Senators and Representatives, shall take effect, until an election of representatives shall have intervened.

Section. 2. The Congress shall have power to enforce this article by appropriate legislation.

LaVergne, TN USA
14 October 2010
200706LV00001B/2/P